Before the first shots were fired at Gettysburg – for many, the most significant engagement of the American Civil War – a private battle had been raging for weeks. As the Confederate Army marched into Union territory, the Federal Forces desperately sought to hunt them down before they struck at any of the great cities of the North. Whoever could secure accurate information on their opponent would have a decisive advantage once the fighting started. When the two armies finally met on the morning of 1 July 1863 their understanding of the prevailing situation could not have been more different. While the Rebel Third Corps was expecting to brush away a group of local militia guarding the town, the Federal I Corps was preparing itself for a major battle. For three brutal days, the Rebel Army smashed at the Union troops, without success. The illustrious Confederate General Robert E. Lee would lose a third of his army and the tide of the rebellion would begin its retreat. Robert Lee himself would begin the argument on the contribution of military intelligence to his defeat by seeking to blame his cavalry. Generations of historians would debate what factors played a decisive role, but no one has sought to explore the root of how the most able General of his era could have left himself so vulnerable at the climax of such a vital operation. *Much Embarrassed* investigates how the Confederate and Union military intelligence systems had been sculpted by the preceding events of the War and how this led to the final outcome of the Gettysburg campaign. While the success of the Confederate strategy nurtured a fundamental flaw in their appreciation of intelligence, recurrent defeat led the Federal Army to develop one of the most advanced intelligence structures in history. Lee was right to highlight the importance of military intelligence to his failure at Gettysburg, but he would never appreciate that the seeds of his defeat had been sown long before.

George Donne was born in Guildford, Surrey and was educated at the Royal Grammar School before completing a Batchelor of Arts in Classics at the University of Durham. Having started work in corporate finance, George became Executive Director of a small, public natural resources company. He is currently a Director of a number of renewable energy and mining ventures, focused on Latin America. A keen amateur historian, George earned a Master of Arts in Military History from the University of Buckingham in 2014. His thesis on the utility of military intelligence during the Gettysburg Campaign was awarded a distinction. *Much Embarrassed* is his first book. He currently lives in Surrey with his wife, Natalie.

"MUCH EMBARRASSED"

MUCH EMBARRASSED

Civil War Intelligence and the Gettysburg Campaign

Wolverhampton Military Studies No.23

George Donne

Helion & Company Limited

Helion & Company Limited
26 Willow Road
Solihull
West Midlands
B91 1UE
England
Tel. 0121 705 3393
Fax 0121 711 4075
Email: info@helion.co.uk
Website: www.helion.co.uk
Twitter: @helionbooks
Visit our blog http://blog.helion.co.uk/

Published by Helion & Company 2016
Designed and typeset by Mach 3 Solutions Ltd (www.mach3solutions.co.uk)
Cover designed by Paul Hewitt, Battlefield Design (www.battlefield-design.co.uk)
Printed by Lightning Source Limited, Milton Keynes, Buckinghamshire

Text © George Donne 2016
Images open source via author
Maps drawn by George Anderson © Helion & Company 2016

ISBN 978-1-910777-86-2

British Library Cataloguing-in-Publication Data.
A catalogue record for this book is available from the British Library.

For details of other military history titles published by Helion & Company Limited contact
the above address, or visit our website: http://www.helion.co.uk.

We always welcome receiving book proposals from prospective authors.

Contents

List of Illustrations

List of Maps

The Wolverhampton Military Studies Series
Series Editor's Preface

As series editor, it is my great pleasure to introduce the *Wolverhampton Military Studies Series* to you. Our intention is that in this series of books you will find military history that is new and innovative, and academically rigorous with a strong basis in fact and in analytical research, but also is the kind of military history that is for all readers, whatever their particular interests, or their level of interest in the subject. To paraphrase an old aphorism: a military history book is not less important just because it is popular, and it is not more scholarly just because it is dull. With every one of our publications we want to bring you the kind of military history that you will want to read simply because it is a good and well-written book, as well as bringing new light, new perspectives, and new factual evidence to its subject.

In devising the *Wolverhampton Military Studies Series*, we gave much thought to the series title: this is a *military* series. We take the view that history is everything except the things that have not happened yet, and even then a good book about the military aspects of the future would find its way into this series. We are not bound to any particular time period or cut-off date. Writing military history often divides quite sharply into eras, from the modern through the early modern to the mediaeval and ancient; and into regions or continents, with a division between western military history and the military history of other countries and cultures being particularly marked. Inevitably, we have had to start somewhere, and the first books of the series deal with British military topics and events of the twentieth century and later nineteenth century. But this series is open to any book that challenges received and accepted ideas about any aspect of military history, and does so in a way that encourages its readers to enjoy the discovery.

In the same way, this series is not limited to being about wars, or about grand strategy, or wider defence matters, or the sociology of armed forces as institutions, or civilian society and culture at war. None of these are specifically excluded, and in some cases they play an important part in the books that comprise our series. But there are already many books in existence, some of them of the highest scholarly standards, which cater to these particular approaches. The main theme of the *Wolverhampton Military Studies Series* is the military aspects of wars, the preparation for wars or their prevention, and their aftermath. This includes some books whose main theme is the technical details of how armed forces have worked, some books on wars and battles, and some books that re-examine the evidence about the existing stories, to show in a different light what everyone thought they already knew and understood.

As series editor, together with my fellow editorial board members, and our publisher Duncan Rogers of Helion, I have found that we have known immediately and almost by instinct the kind of books that fit within this series. They are very much the kind of well-written and challenging books that my students at the University of Wolverhampton would want to read. They are books which enhance knowledge, and offer new perspectives. Also, they are books for anyone with an interest in military history and events, from expert scholars to occasional readers. One of the great benefits of the study of military history is that it includes a large and often committed section of the wider population, who want to read the best military history that they can find; our aim for this series is to provide it.

Stephen Badsey
University of Wolverhampton

Acknowledgements

Tradition, story, history – all this will not efface the true grand epic of Gettysburg.[1]

This book would not have been possible without the help of the Military History Department of the University of Buckingham, particularly Dr. Spencer Jones and Professor Saul David for all their encouragement and advice. My publisher Duncan Rogers has been a huge help in guiding me through the process and I will be forever grateful to my wonderful wife Natalie, for her unceasing support and understanding.

1   Haskell, Frank, *The Battle of Gettysburg* (Wisconsin History Commission, 1908) p.185.

Prologue

The morning of 1 July 1863 began grey and cold, but with the promise that the drizzly rain of the previous evening would finally give way to sunshine. For Lieutenant Aaron B. Jerome of the U.S. Signal Corps, the gloomy but rain-free start to the day was a blessing as he climbed up to his position in the cupola of the small Lutheran Seminary in the little farming town of Gettysburg, Pennsylvania. Gettysburg was a modest community, but of strategic local importance as a junction of several thoroughfares connecting the state capital of Harrisburg to the north with Baltimore in the east and Washington to the south. Assigned to the 1st Cavalry division of the I Corps, led by John Buford, Jerome was part of an advance party of the mighty Federal Army of the Potomac, which had been ordered out to locate the 65,000 strong, Confederate Army of Northern Virginia led by its superlative commander, General Robert E. Lee. Although it numbered nearly 100,000 men, the Army of the Potomac had been repeatedly beaten in recent engagements by Lee and his men and now, fighting closer than ever to the major Northern cities of Baltimore and Washington, the upcoming battle could potentially deal a fatal blow to the Federal struggle to reunite the United States of America.

Without the soaking mists and low cloud, Jerome had a relatively clear view back towards the east, where the rest of the I Corps had rested a few miles away, but the signal officer's eyes were not looking backwards this morning. Only a few miles off to the west, between Gettysburg to Cashtown, was Lee's army and Buford and Jerome had little doubt that it would be marching towards them. Only a few hours after dawn, exactly as expected, the men of General Henry Heth's division of the Third Corps[1] of the Confederate Army of Northern Virginia marched at a steady pace down Cashtown Pike towards Gettysburg. The Rebel army had begun their march in Fredericksburg, on the southern bank of the Rappahannock River, and then had crossed the Potomac out of Confederate territory and into neutral Maryland and then Pennsylvania as part of the largest invasion into the North ever undertaken. Their intention was little more than to engage the Yankees in a major battle on their turf. For days, rumours had been swirling around camp that the Federal Army of the

---

1   The army corps of the Confederacy are denoted in letters, while those of the Union army are in Roman numerals.

Potomac was on its way to intercept them and drive them back into Virginia from where they had come. A victory now for the Rebellion could destroy all confidence in the restoration of the Union and critically undermine support in Washington for Abraham Lincoln's Republican government, in favour of a more moderate candidate, willing to parlay for peace. Defeat so far from home, on the other hand, could mean the end of the Army of Northern Virginia, the premier Rebel fighting force in the Eastern Theatre,[2] leaving the door to the Confederate capital in Richmond hanging open for the victorious Northern army. Confident as the Rebel soldiers were, the various corps of Lee's army had been operating in isolation from each other since leaving Fredericksburg and the orders to concentrate on Gettysburg had only been given three days before.[3] Until it could be reunited with the remainder of the Army of Northern Virginia, the Third Corps was vulnerable to being cut off by the Army of the Potomac and annihilated before Lee and his support could reach them. Less than a year earlier, the Rebel army had been caught by the Federals in a similar situation in Maryland, to the south of Gettysburg on the banks of the small river of Antietam, but following a day of horrific bloodshed, Lee and his army had survived.

For the men of the Army of Northern Virginia, the stakes had not been higher since they had forced the same Army of the Potomac away from the gates of the Confederate capital of Richmond a little over a year earlier, but where was the Federal army now? The previous day, Heth's division had exchanged fire with a hostile force some four miles west of the town, but high command was not concerned. The main Federal army was still reported to be 20 miles away and a previous Rebel incursion through the town by part of the Second Corps had swept through the feeble resistance of the Twenty-Sixth Pennsylvania Militia without fuss. Ambrose Hill had orders from his commander Robert Lee not to bring about a general engagement with the enemy whilst the three Rebel corps were unconsolidated and the exact whereabouts of the Federals was still unknown. To the north, the head of Richard Ewell's column was ten miles away, leading the Second Corps down from the Susquehanna River where they had been destroying bridges, railroads and generally terrorising the citizens of Harrisburg. From the south west approached Lee himself with General James "Old Pete" Longstreet's First Corps. Recent news of that the Army of the Potomac was on the march had forced Lee to bring the wings of his army together quicker than he would have liked and he did not want to trigger a battle with a larger force before he had sufficient numbers to bring to bear. But his men were hungry and short of provisions and there was the chance of good pickings in the farm town ahead. Despite

---

2   The Eastern Theatre was the region surrounding the Federal and Confederate capitals, sandwiched between the Appalachian Mountains and the Atlantic coast. The other major theatre, the Western, stretched from the Mississippi river to the western slopes of the Appalachian mountains and down to the Gulf of Mexico.

3   *The War of the Rebellion: a Compilation of the Official Records of the Union and Confederate Armies* in 128 volumes (Washington, Government Printing Office, 1880–1901) (hereinafter referred to as the 'O.R.') Series I, Vol. XXVII, Part III, p.943.

his commander's fears of what he had witnessed that day, Hill was resolute. Were there any reasons why they could not advance on Gettysburg tomorrow, he was asked; "None in the world," was his reply.[4]

None of this gave any comfort to General James J. Pettigrew, one of Heth's division commanders, who had overseen the advance towards Gettysburg the day before. The discipline and coordination of the hostile cavalry force he encountered was enough to make Pettigrew suspicious that this was no band of local ruffians, but Heth and his corps commander Ambrose Powell Hill were not interested in their junior's anxieties. Since the launch of the campaign almost a month earlier, the enemy had trailed in their wake and there was no news to suggest that they had caught up so quickly. If Pettigrew was still harbouring any fears of what might lie ahead in the sleepy farm town as the Third Corps set out for Gettysburg again that morning of the 1st, he would at least not have to suffer them long. Within about two and a half hours of starting out from camp at 5:00 a.m., his comrades were again taking fire with the same enemy cavalry straddled across Herr Ridge, the first of a series of small anticlines that ran north-south in parallel towards the town.

With the weight of the Third Corps behind them, Heth's divisions spread across Cashtown Pike to clear the enemy out of the way. The Rebels, however, were to be sadly disappointed as the cavalry on Herr Ridge gave way to infantry holding another elevated position of McPherson's Ridge closer to town. The defenders were stubborn, disciplined and supported by artillery. Time was passing, but little forward progress was being made. Rather than crumbling as expected, the opposition somehow seemed to be multiplying. By 10:00 a.m., enemy reinforcements were arriving and organising themselves to meet the oncoming invaders, who were by now struggling to hold their lines. Suddenly a ripple of shock thrilled through the Confederate ranks: men in unmistakable black hats were now bobbing into view to take their positions in the Federal front line. The Rebels had seen these men before, fighting with ferocity at almost every major battle in the East since South Mountain in 1862, where they had earned themselves the nickname of the "Iron Brigade."[5] This was the First Brigade of the First Division of the Federal I Corps, "There are those d———d black-hatted fellows again! 'Taint no militia. It's the Army of the Potomac." The Rebels had unknowingly stumbled right into the vanguard Federal army. While Hill had been trying to chew his way through their advanced cavalry, the commander of the I Corps, General John Reynolds, had arrived on the scene and sent the message out that, at last, the Rebel army had been found. Within hours, every soldier in the Army of Northern Virginia and the Army of the Potomac, together around 170,000 men would be converging on

---

4   *Southern Historical Society Papers*, 52 Volumes 1876 – 1959 (Southern Historical Society, Richmond)(hereinafter referred to as the "*SHSP*") Vol IV p.157.

5   Coddington, Edwin, *The Gettysburg Campaign: A Study in Command* (Dayton: Morningside House, 1979), p.262.

that quiet Pennsylvania town to join what would become the single bloodiest battle in American history and surely the most famous battle of the American Civil War.

For 150 years since the battle of Gettysburg was fought, protagonists and historians have puzzled over how General Lee's army allowed themselves to trigger one of the most significant engagements of the American Civil War without realising it. As the watery sun rose on the morning of 1 July, the Army of Northern Virginia had almost no positive intelligence on the position of the Army of the Potomac and no understanding of the prevailing situation. The Federals on the other hand appeared to know exactly what was coming, a pattern of small intelligence victories that would characterise the next three days of conflict and which would have a profound effect on their ultimate success. Those unfamiliar with the subject would be forgiven for wondering why, in a war that contained anything up to 10,000 military engagements and that has generated (it is thought) well in excess of 50,000 studies, Gettysburg remains for many the defining battle of the conflict.[6] Robert Lee, regarded by his peers as "in the first rank of generals of the English speaking race, with Marlborough and Wellington,"[7] would fight in many of the most significant engagements of the War, but none would lead to greater controversy or leave a greater impact on the Southern psyche than Gettysburg. Whether it is because of the later address given by President Abraham Lincoln to dedicate the new cemetery three months after the battle or the designation of a small clump of trees on Cemetery Ridge as the "High Water Mark of the Confederacy,"[8] the battle of Gettysburg has been the focal point of more passionate debate than any other.

In the search for answers, many followed the great general Lee's own opinion as to the failure. In his official report, submitted to the Confederate President Jefferson Davis at the end of July, Robert Lee was blunt in his assessment of the reasons for the defeat: "The movements of the army preceding the battle of Gettysburg had been much embarrassed by the absence of the cavalry,"[9] a specific reference to the failure of his main source of intelligence. With hindsight, Lee would become more sanguine in a private letter to Major William McDonald in 1868, explaining that "Its [Gettysburg's] loss was occasioned by a combination of circumstances. It was commenced in the absence of correct intelligence. It was continued in the effort to overcome the difficulties by which we were surrounded, and it would have been gained could one

---

6   McPherson, James, *Battle Cry of Freedom* (New York: Oxford University Press, 1988), p.ix.
7   Sorrell, G. Moxley, *Recollections of a Confederate Staff Officer* (New York: The Neale Publishing Company, 1905), p.123.
8   A phrase coined by one of the early authorities on the battle, John B. Bachelder referring to General Lewis Armistead's assault on Cemetery Ridge during Pickett's Charge on 3 July and immortalised with its own monument in 1892.
9   O.R., Series I, Vol. XXVII, Part II, p.321.

determined and united blow have been delivered by our whole line."[10] Although time had added some broader perspective, Lee's opinion on where the blame for the loss of Gettysburg lay was clear: he had been let down by those in charge of providing him with intelligence and, without good intelligence, his chances of winning the engagement had been fatally curtailed.

10   Lee, Robert, *Recollections and Letters of General Robert E. Lee* (New York: Garden City, 1904) p.102.

Introduction

In today's world of almost unlimited communications and real-time surveillance, it is easy to forget how challenging the exercise of even the basic fundamentals of military intelligence could be. Until the Civil War, many of the generals who would lead the armies of the Union and the Confederacy had scant experience or regard for the requirements of good intelligence operations. The most illustrious of all Union generals, Ulysses S. Grant, would succinctly describe war as "simple enough. Find out where your enemy is. Get at him as soon as you can. Strike him as hard as you can and as often as you can, and keep moving on."[1] Whilst Grant, a master in the art of reducing war to its lowest common dominator through both words and deeds, viewed warfare as easy, the first step of finding out where your enemy was amongst the thick forests, high mountains or deep valleys of the American east was not. During the War, military leaders would have to coordinate armies in excess of 100,000 men, having never before led forces greater than 10,000. Grant, who expressed these sentiments several years after the War, was himself an early beneficiary of a stout lesson on the consequences of poor intelligence planning, which nearly led to a premature end to his Civil War career. In the first significant battle in the West, Grant's Army of the Tennessee was nearly overrun in a surprise dawn raid by the Confederate forces under General Albert Sidney Johnston near Shiloh Church. Johnston's army had been encamped only two miles from Grant's lines without him ever being aware of their presence. When they attacked early on 6 April 1862, the Federal soldiers were still attending their cooking fires and boiling up their morning coffee. Only a strong rearguard action by General Benjamin Prentiss and the timely arrival of reinforcements from Don Carlos Buell saved Grant and won the battle for the Federals.

Intelligence, like every facet of warfare, was undergoing profound changes during the era of the American Civil War. The legacy of 19th Century still demanded the movement of large armies and their support based on the strategic and operational designs of leaders sometimes hundreds of miles away. The more information gained by a military planner on the location and composition of the enemy and the prevailing topography and environment, the greater the chances that he would have in leading a successful campaign. The depth of knowledge required on an enemy varied based

---

1   Brinton, John, *Personal Memories* (New York: The Neale Publishing Company, 1914) p.239.

on the level of command, from the state leaders of the warring nations down to the brigade commanders leading their men into action. Simply put, political leaders define the overall objectives for conduct of the war (strategy), senior military figures then determine how to execute the strategic plans within the various regions or theatres of war (operations), while the corps commanders and generals plan how each engagement or manoeuvre is undertaken (tactics).

In correlation to the number of decision-makers at the varying levels of command, so the level of intelligence detail required increases as one moves down the chain of command from strategy to tactics. Typically, the political leaders of the belligerent nation or group would develop their strategy based on the aims of the conflict, whether one of defence, invasion, occupation and so on, in conjunction with the military leaders, who would be tasked to execute that strategy. Strategic intelligence normally consists of supplying information to enable the war leaders to assess the quickest and least damaging way of achieving their aims, such as disabling their opponent's capacity to resist by force of arms, occupying or destroying its principal industrial and commercial centres or manipulating the will of its citizens to demand surrender. Good strategic intelligence will provide insights into the economic, military and political structure of an opposing state, with a particular focus on its vulnerabilities, as well as timely information on the changing domestic attitudes to the conflict. Operations are the broad military enactment of a stated strategy within a specific theatre of conflict. Once a strategic objective, such as the seizure of an enemy capital city, has been decided upon, military commanders develop the physical plan for achieving that objective. Normally, this plan will require the mobilisation of their armed forces with their support structures (food, ordnance, medical, communications and so on), into the target theatre as part of a coordinated movement or 'campaign'. Operational intelligence will be far more focused than that of strategic intelligence. When planning a campaign, a commander should develop a thorough knowledge of the environment in which he will be operating, as well as any threats to his forces or lines of communication and supply and the defensive capabilities of his opponent. Tactical planning demands the most detailed level of information since tactics are enactment of these military plans in direct or impending contact with the enemy. When approaching an armed engagement, the more intelligence that can be gathered about the size and composition of an opponent's forces (order of battle or 'ORBAT' information), his location, movements, operational objectives and the topography of the immediate environment, the better. If the opportunity arises, key advantages such as choosing the location of engagement, obtaining natural advantages (such as securing the army's flanks against natural obstacles like rivers or holding higher ground) can make a significant difference to chances of success in battle and the limitation of losses suffered to obtain success. Conversely, without good tactical information, an army can find itself subject to surprise attacks, flanking manoeuvres or even unknowingly launching attacks against much larger adversaries.

Intelligence begins with the acquisition of the raw information by specific agents or sources, transmitted through communications networks to the recipient for implementation into action. The acquisition of intelligence can be divided into two distinct sources. Intelligence gathered from human sources, such as spies or scouts, is referred to as Human Intelligence or 'HUMINT'. HUMINT was the lifeblood of 19th Century intelligence, as it had been for thousands of years. "When you asked me last evening how to obtain information of the enemy, I did not, perhaps, fulfill what you may think the requirements of your question," General French of the III Corps of the Army of the Potomac would write to his commander George Gordon Meade. "Good topographical maps, spies, prisoners, deserters, well-affected citizens, reconnoitering parties, and preparatory attacks – these are the means absolutely within our power."[2] During the War, however, there would be additional sources available to those able to grab them: those gathered from interception of signals or data transmissions as signal intelligence or 'SIGINT'. In modern military vocabulary, there is an important distinction to be made between 'information' and actual 'intelligence'. While information constitutes just the raw and unprocessed source data without any kind of critical analysis or verification, intelligence is the scrutinised output of various pieces of information into a distilled understanding of the prevailing situation that can be used by a commander in his planning. Interpretive services were usually the responsibility of a general's staff officers although it was common for many leaders to collect and interpret their own intelligence. Given that a centralised structure for interpretation of information did not exist at the time of the Civil War, it would be more correct to describe most generals as utilising military information rather than intelligence, although during the War a system would be developed to provide genuine intelligence for the first time, although it would ironically bare the name of the Bureau of Military Information.

While the art of war might have been simple for General Grant, the practice was much more complicated and the science was evolving significantly throughout the latter half of the 19th Century. The American Civil War is often characterised by its unique position as a major, albeit domestic, Western conflict between two great eras of warfare. The hard-learnt principles of Napoleonic massed armies, born from a period of relative scientific unsophistication, were mixing with the technological advances that would soon define the 'total' industrial wars of the 20th Century. Whether the Civil War is considered to be the last Napoleonic War or the first industrial war, there is no doubt that the paradigms were shifting and soldiers and generals would struggle to adapt. The development of increasingly accurate and powerful weaponry was one of the most obvious indications that the era of Napoleon was giving way to the new industrial age. According to Ulysses Grant's views, when the enemy used the traditional musket, "At the distance of a few hundred yards a man might fire at you all day without your finding it out."[3] The trusty muzzle-loading, smoothbore, flint-lock

---

2   O.R. Series I, Vol. XXVII, Part III p.667.
3   Grant, Ulysses, *Personal Memoirs of U. S. Grant, Volume I* (New York: Charles L. Webster & Company, 1885) p.38.

had an effective maximum range of around 250 yards, but since 1855 Acting Master Armourer of the Harper's Ferry arsenal, James Burton, had been working on the design to load Claude Etienne Minié's new conical 'minié ball'. Loaded into rifled muzzles, the bullet was spun, vastly improving range and accuracy. New Springfield and Enfield rifle-muskets would gradually phase out their flintlock predecessors within the first year of the War and be improved further still by later breech-loading carbine rifles. "Only seventeen hundred men? Pshaw!" scoffed Admiral David Dixon Porter to General Sherman, after his boys had been chewed up by the defenders of Chickasaw Bayou, "that is nothing... You'll lose seventeen thousand before the war is over, and will think nothing of it."[4]

The gulf between the previous experiences of Civil War leaders and the new paradigms of warfare that they were embracing can scarcely be exaggerated. The standing army at the beginning of 1861 was only 16,000 men, mostly scattered throughout the frontier territories. The last major war fought by the United States was the invasion of Mexico between 1846 and 1848, in which, at its height, the total American force barely numbered 14,000. A little over twenty years later, almost 200,000 men would slug out the fate of Richmond as Federal General George McClellan led a campaign to crack its defences along its eastern peninsula. "Our armies are necessarily very large in comparison with those we have heretofore had to manage," was Robert Lee's comment to Jefferson Davis in the spring of 1863. "Some of our divisions exceed the army Genl Scott entered the city of Mexico with, & our brigades are larger than his divisions."[5]

Even the professional soldiers had never been prepared for warfare on this scale and the massive blood-letting that it entailed. Many of the men donning the blue or grey would have had less than a year's training before they saw their first action and so much of the burden on their coordination and performance would fall on their superiors. Unlike Admiral Dixon, few commanders understood the reality of late 19th Century battle and while new weapons assisted the slaughter of more Americans than any other war, arguably their greatest damage was as a result of the failure of the generals to appreciate the dangers of operating at previously safe distances. Professional soldiers like General Robert S. Garnett, a former Commandant of the Corps of Cadets at West Point, while showing his men "a little example" of the ineffectiveness of Federal fire, was shot dead by a sharp shooter while walking slowly up and down in front of the enemy. Tragic as his death was, Confederate soldier and commentator Edward Porter Alexander would articulate the more fundamental loss

4   Arnold, James, *Grant Wins the War* (New York: John Wiley & Sons, Inc, 1997), p.38.
5   *Lee's Dispatches: Unpublished Letters of General Robert E. Lee 1862–1865*: Douglas Southall Freeman and Grady McWhiney (ed.)(New York: Putnam's, 1957), p.81.

felt by the Confederacy given Garnett's experience: "Had he lived, I am sure he would have been one of our great generals."[6]

Men of Garnett's experienced could not be replaced easily and their nations needed them to grasp quickly how innovations in technology would enforce changes in tactics and how the utility of military intelligence would be revolutionised by new innovations in surveillance and communications. The Mexican War was fought on foreign soil against an opponent adhering very much to Napoleonic principles. Now the two combatants would fight across an area of around 750,000 square miles, amongst a civil populace of common language and origin. The theatres were criss-crossed by natural and man-made logistical features, such as the mighty rivers of the Mississippi basin and the great railroads linking the eastern cities to western resources. The politicians designing their strategies and generals leading the operations would have to contend with both an astonishing paucity of some basic sources of available information, while evaluating the huge potential of new innovations. Even good local maps would be a luxury for many senior generals throughout the War, since the country was still growing faster than the science of cartography could cope with and even the older parts of America were still relatively unknown due to the difficulties of accurately covering the terrain. On taking command of the wide spaces of the Western Theatre, General Henry "Old Brains" Halleck[7] would be forced to buy maps of the region from a local book store. However, like arteries running through these new frontiers, railroads now provided the ability to move men and materiel hundreds of miles in a few days, while alongside ran miles of electric telegraph wiring, capable of carrying messages across vast distances in minutes.

The opportunities for HUMINT were nearly boundless as the armies marched across each other's territory and through the border states, but now they were complemented by potential for SIGINT as both side used new technologies to improve their communication. The question would be not whether intelligence could make a difference to military action, but who would be able to recognise and grasp the greatest value from the potential available. Halleck might have cursed the lack of independent data available on his theatre of operation, but soon his ire would be directed instead at General Grant, as a result of a communications failure. Halleck accused his commander of disobeying orders and acting independently only a matter of weeks after the Army of the Tennessee had won a significant early victory at Fort Donelson. After complaining to Washington, Halleck petitioned to have Grant relieved of command and imprisoned. Grant would later explain that he had never received any orders and would instead point the finger at the telegraph operator in Cairo. "This operator afterwards proved to be a rebel;" explained Grant, "he deserted his post after

6   Alexander, Edward Porter, *Military Memoirs of a Confederate* (New York: Charles Scribner's Sons, 1907) p.14.

7   Halleck earned his nickname through publishing his theory on military tactics, *Elements of Military Art and Science* in 1862.

a short time and went south taking his dispatches with him."[8] Just as Shiloh taught him the need for good HUMINT, so Grant would quickly learn the new potential danger and opportunity of SIGINT.

Rather than focus attention on the actual study of intelligence, the accusatory analysis started by General Lee and his disciples would instead search for those responsible for its abuse in order to solve the riddle of Gettysburg. The reasons for the absence of his cavalry in particular, and the leadership of Lee's key lieutenant, James Ewell Brown "Jeb" Stuart, would thereby become one of the major debating points of the campaign. But to seek answers in Confederate failure would only tell half the story. When asked his theories on the loss of Gettysburg, General George Pickett, one of the primary Rebel figures in the battle, simply answered, "I've always thought the Yankees had something to do with it."[9] The armies of the Union and the Confederacy were both formed from the root of the old Army of the United States and led by the men with the same training and experience. Similarly, in the field of intelligence, they had been trained in the same military principles and had access to largely the same technology and resources. However, the Rebels and Yankees would enjoy radically different intelligence positions at the opening of the battle of Gettysburg and this difference would only become more profound as the engagement continued.

Lee would point the finger at his cavalry, as his principal intelligence resource, and highlight the failure to coordinate later attacks, indicating poor communications amongst his staff and subordinates. What Lee either did not know or gave no credence to was that opposing him was one of the most sophisticated intelligence and communications systems of its age, which had been specifically designed not just to acquire information, but also to process and verify it into usable intelligence. This structure was itself supported by a system of communications developed during the War focused on assisting the armies in the field. As A.P. Hill sent his men marching down Cashtown pike, he was sure that the Federal army was miles from the town, based on the latest information provided by his commander, General Lee. The Federal cavalry waiting for him knew that he was coming and had acted accordingly in the knowledge that the rest of Army of the Potomac would soon be marching on the position. How could Lee, the foremost general of his era, have allowed himself to enter into one of the defining engagements of the war with such a shocking dearth of intelligence? How could the Federals, previously always one step behind the Rebels in military operations in the East, suddenly have manufactured an advantage in such a critical facet of the battle?

8   Grant, *Memoirs*, p.143.
9   McPherson, James, 'American Victory, American Defeat', in Boritt (ed.), Gabor, *Why the Confederacy Lost*, (New York: Oxford University Press, 1992) p.19.

1

We Should Assume the Aggressive

During the third week of May 1863, six weeks before the two armies would finally meet around that small Pennsylvania farming town, the President of the Confederate States of America, Jefferson Davis, held a series of meetings with his cabinet to discuss one of the most significant strategic decisions since secession from the Union. Present at the meetings, taking brief leave from his headquarters in Fredericksburg, was Davis's principal military advisor, Robert Lee.

The purpose of the meetings was to discuss the South's response to the aggressive Federal manoeuvres in the Western Theatre, which had finally succeeded in encircling the Mississippi stronghold of Vicksburg. Occupying a sharp S-bend in the river and protected by natural bluffs and concentrated artillery batteries, just reaching Vicksburg in sufficient numbers to mount a siege had taken Ulysses Grant over six months. Knowing that he needed results, Grant threw caution to the wind and took the bulk of his army on a circuitous march, across the swampland west of the city, to engage it from the south. Had he failed to link up with the Federal fleet, which had run the guns of Vicksburg to land below the city, and his remaining force and cavalry, which had kept the Rebels engaged from the north, he would have been cut off. But the gamble worked. Having pushed back the smaller Confederate army, commanded

Robert E. Lee, leader of the Confederate Army of Northern Virginia.

by Northern-born John C. Pemberton, from its positions east of the city, Grant pinned it against the river and isolated the great citadel town from resupply by land or water.

The fall of Vicksburg would all but secure the success of the Union strategy to assume control of the great rivers of the Mississippi basin. Grant had already swept west across the Tennessee River and then south down the Mississippi, overrunning the Rebel-held river forts and joining up with U.S. Navy coming up from Federal-occupied New Orleans. Vicksburg was the last, and most complicated, piece of the puzzle. Defeat here would leave the Confederacy all but completely encircled as the naval blockade of the Atlantic coast tightened. The loss of supplies from the breadbasket region west of the Mississippi would also devastate the strained Southern resources. "If Vicksburg falls, and the Valley be held by the enemy, then the Confederacy will be curtailed of half its dimensions," bemoaned J.B. Jones in May 1863. "What will remain of the Confederacy?"[1] The only hope for Pemberton was General Joseph E. Johnston, the commander of the Department of the West, but he was in Jackson and between him and Vicksburg stood Grant's army of 50,000 Yankees.

Never had the fledgling nation of the Confederate States of America faced such a critical choice than in the early summer of 1863. For the past two years, since the first states had declared independence from the Union, the Rebels had foiled all attempts to bring them to heel. On secession, there were no false apprehensions of the serious-ness of the task that lay ahead should they be required to secure independence by force; they were chronically out-manned and out-gunned by the North. The popula-tion of the eleven states that formed the Confederacy totalled around nine million (of whom roughly four million were slaves) in comparison to around 22 million still in the Union.[2] The North had all the advantages of numbers, a thriving industry and advancing technologies; what the South lacked in manpower and materiel, however, it made up for in spirit and leadership. President Davis was a graduate of the United States Military Academy at West Point, a veteran of the war with Mexico, where he had served with the 1st Mississippi Rifles, and a former U.S. Secretary of War. His opponent in Washington, President Abraham Lincoln, despite seeing some action during the Indian Wars, was not a military man, although this did not mean that he did not appreciate the need for military action. Lincoln had made it clear that reunifi-cation was his sole aim and so, with the North prepared to use force of arms, there was no chance of the Confederacy negotiating a peaceful recognition of their independent rights from Washington under Lincoln's Republican government.

Cognisant of the South's economic and military limitations, Davis understood that the key to success could still be found on the battlefield, by exploiting the divergent strategies of North and South. The Union alone bore the onus of achieving victory;

1   Jones, J.B., *A Rebel War Clerk's Diary at the Confederal States Capital* (Philadelphia: J.B. Lippincott & Co, 1866) p.328.
2   *The Library of Congress Civil War Desk Reference* (New York: Simon & Schuster, 2002) p.666-7.

if the Rebellion could ensure that the price in blood and treasure for military success was too high, their public (and thereby political will) would fail them. Despite the high emotion in the capitals, this was still civil war and families were being torn apart.[3] "Oh, my God, what a dreadful thing is a war like this," Lincoln would lament, "in which personal friends must slay each other and die like fiends!"[4] The president, perhaps even more that his generals, was keenly aware that as mothers lost sons to the battlefield, so the chorus of opposition to the War would grow. The War did not stop the democratic process and, throughout, the senate continued to meet and the people continued to vote. With this Federal political burden in mind, the military policy of the South would be one of aggressive defence. The Union could not hope to occupy the entirety of the Southern states and so would need to pick off strategic targets systematically, which would allow the Rebels to concentrate their forces to meet individual territorial incursions. The beauty of this strategy was that it could maximise one of the key advantages held by the defenders: the ability to use interior lines of transport and communication to coordinate and manoeuvre large forces quickly. In combination with this domestic policy of survival, the Confederacy would try and force recognition of sovereignty abroad. By leveraging their dominance of cotton production, the Rebels believed that an embargo of "King Cotton" would compel the European superpowers of Great Britain and France (already sympathetic to their cause) to confirm their independent status in return for resumption of supply. However, Lincoln's issuance of the Emancipation Proclamation in late September 1862 brought the tricky subject of the abolition of slavery to the fore as an objective of reunifying America and thus made the chances of foreign intervention almost impossible.

Having devised a formula for success, Davis threw his weight behind his military and was fortunate to have some of the most experienced generals of the former U.S. Army at his disposal. The backbone of this military force was a core of experienced generals such as Joseph Johnston, Pierre Beauregard, James Longstreet and of course Robert Lee. All had tasted martial victory in Mexico and were dedicated to protecting their homes and their way of life. With the break-up of the Union came the break-up of the army and, despite the inevitable advantages in men enjoyed by the Federals, the Rebels compensated with a far superior understanding of what was going to be required when the firing started. The General-in-Chief of the army at the outbreak of the Rebellion, Winfield "Old Fuss and Feathers" Scott, the hero of the Mexican War, decided that the regular Federal army units should be maintained in the belief that "this solid nucleus which would show them the way to perform their duty, and take the brunt of every

---

3   Men like John Pemberton, born and bred in loyalist Pennsylvania, would become fiercely devoted to the Rebel cause, while General John Gibbon of the Army of the Potomac would decline to join his two brothers in the Confederate army and donne the Yankee blue with distinction.

4   Macartney, Clarence Edward, *Lincoln and his Generals* (Philadelphia: Dorrance and Company, 1925), p.149.

encounter."[5] Such a strategy gave no thought to the possibility of a protracted conflict with high turnover of both soldiers and generals. In contrast, the Confederate government created entirely new regiments into which regular soldiers were scattered to help cushion the shock of battle on the new civilian volunteers. "They had no standing army and, consequently, these trained soldiers had to find employment with the troops from their own States," was Ulysses Grant's appraisal. "In this way what there was of military education and training was distributed throughout their whole army." Knowledge of warfare and tactics was therefore disseminated across the new Confederate armies, as was a factor not appreciated by the Union until after the first significant engagement, experience under fire. In a conflict of amateur soldiers, the compound benefit of seeing the man next to you stand his ground in the face of a round of musket fire or bayonet charge could not be understated. In Grant's words: "The whole loaf was leavened."[6]

With their early embrace of the reality of the conflict and imbued with the perceived righteousness of their cause, the Rebel self-defence strategy worked well during the early stages of the War. An unexpected victory against a larger Federal army at the First Battle of Bull Run[7] established the Rebel occupation of a blocking position on the overland route between Washington and Richmond. Progress from initial victories in the Eastern Theatre during 1861 was interrupted, however, the following year by a major invasion by the Army of the Potomac, led by Union military darling General George Brinton "Little Mac" McClellan.

McClellan's army was dropped by ship on the Atlantic coast of the Virginian peninsula between the James and Pamunky rivers, east of Richmond, and marched directly on the Confederate capital. When the danger was as its greatest, however, providence intervened. While leading the first defensive action at the Battle of Fair Oaks, Joseph Johnston, (who would later assume command of the Western Theatre), was hit by artillery shrapnel and would be obliged to hand command of the armed forces around the city over to Robert Lee. Lee quickly established his credentials as the greatest Confederate general by driving McClellan back from the gates of Richmond in a week-long series of battles, which finally saw Little Mac watching the final engagement from the safety of his barge on the James. These consecutive tactical victories during the summer of 1862, collectively named the Seven Days Battle, which brought about the end of McClellan's Peninsula campaign, had showed that Johnnie Reb was every bit the match of Billy Yank, while the superior leadership of Lee and

5   *Battles and Leaders of the Civil War*, Robert Underwood Johnson and Clarence Clough Buel eds. (New York: Century, 1887 – 1888)(hereinafter referred to as *Battles and Leaders*) *Vol I*. p.94.
6   Grant, *Memoirs*, p.124.
7   The Battle of Bull Run was named after the small river which ran between the two armies, as opposed to Manassas, the nearest town. Like their armies, the North usually named battles after the rivers, while the Confederates named them after towns. In this book, the Federal title will be used.

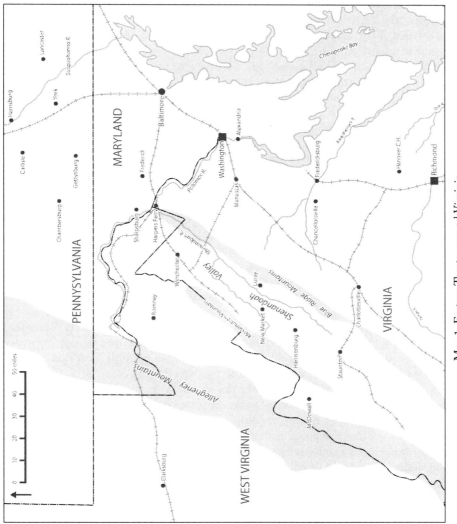

Map 1 Eastern Theatre around Virginia.

his subordinates (like Longstreet, A.P. Hill and Thomas "Stonewall" Jackson), made a mockery of their inferiority in men and metal.

Meanwhile, the loss began a merry-go-round of Federal leadership in the East and command was passed around between a series of generals, as each of them tasted defeat at the hands of Lee's Army of Northern Virginia. After failure on the Peninsula, McClellan gave way to John Pope, only to re-assume command again after Pope's defeat at the Second Battle of Bull Run (the second time that the Union had lost in that part of Virginia) before being stripped once more after the bloodbath of Antietam, Maryland. For all his failings in battle, McClellan had at least ensured that Lee abandon his aggressive campaign into Maryland and retreat back into Virginia. Little Mac's successor as commander of the Army of the Potomac, the hapless Ambrose Burnside, twice failed to pry Lee's army out of its stronghold at Fredericksburg until finally, in January 1863, command was given to Joseph "Fighting Joe" Hooker.[8] Like his predecessors, Hooker was not short of bluster and arrogance, but he was an effective administrator with no shortage of battlefield experience. Sadly, as the spring of 1863 gave way to summer, Lee again achieved another extraordinary tactical success by reversing a surprise attack by the Army of the Potomac at Chancellorsville, only a few miles west of Fredericksburg.

Astonishingly successful as the Army of Northern Virginia had been in enacting Davis's strategy of aggressive defence, after two years of brutal fighting, several uncomfortable realities were becoming evident. Firstly, the War was not only being waged in the East and, while Lee was merrily dispatching leaders of the Army of the Potomac, in the West, the Union strategy of seizing control the Mississippi was drawing ever closer to success. Although Lee would try and trivialise Grant's progress, he too knew that the fate of Vicksburg would be a devastating blow to the Rebellion. Secondly, for all the suffering so far, Abraham Lincoln was no closer to softening his stance on total reunification at all costs. Lee's failure to secure a definitive victory from his campaign into Maryland had given Lincoln the political breathing space to issue the Emancipation Proclamation, bringing slavery to the centre of the Rebellion debate abroad and thus relieving the fear of foreign intervention. Meanwhile, at home, unpopular as the War had become in some quarters, patriotism (sweetened by financial incentives) continued to ensure a steady flow of men donning the Federal army blue. While the bloody slugging match had yet to sap Northern morale materially, it was quickly draining Southern human resources.

The Rebellion had blocked multiple operations by the Federals to march on Richmond from both the east and west of the city, but these tactical victories had come at a terrible cost. In the twelve months prior to the start of Lee's march to Gettysburg, the Army of Northern Virginia had been involved in three of the bloodiest battles of

---

8   The nickname of "Fighting Joe" was bestowed on Hooker by an accident of journalism after the Battle of Malvern Hill. Hooker himself never took to the name: "People will think I am a highwayman or a bandit," *Battles and Leaders, Vol III*, p.217.

the entire War: the Seven Days, Antietam and Chancellorsville. These battles alone accounted for an estimated 45,000 Rebel casualties and an unfortunate theme of each was the greater proportional losses suffered by the Confederates.

Chancellorsville was a crushing blow to the confidence of Hooker and Lincoln, but, like previous engagements at Bull Run and Fredericksburg, it had again fallen short of the magnitude of defeat required to force Washington to consider peace. Instead, Confederate casualties at Chancellorsville alone totalled almost 13,000 representing over 28 percent of his effective force. "Such was the terrible sacrifice," remarked James Longstreet, "that half a dozen such victories would have ruined us."[9] With Pemberton suffering in the West, another punishing defensive engagement in the East could all but cripple the Confederate ability to keep the Yankees out of Richmond.

One solution to the problem of the increasing pressure in the West, advocated by Confederate Secretary of War James A. Seddon, was to send additional troops from the East to bolster General Braxton Bragg's Rebel Army of Tennessee. If a suitable threat could be raised against General William S. Rosecrans's Federal force in East Tennessee, there would be calls from Washington for Grant to leave Vicksburg and come to his aid or find himself suddenly isolated. However, with all other forces engaged, the only troops that could be easily spared would have to come from around Richmond, more specifically, the Army of Northern Virginia. Lee's army was the largest in the Confederacy and with the repeated failures of the North to mount a signifi-cant challenge in the Eastern Theatre, it seemed realistic that troops could be spared while the Army of the Potomac still reeled from yet another defeat. This plan did have strategic merit and was backed by even Lee's "Old War Horse", James Longstreet. Most of Longstreet's First Corps had been absent during the Battle of Chancellorsville, while

General James Longstreet, leader of Lee's First Corps and one of his most trusted subordinates.

9   *The Annals of the War Written by Leading Participants North and South*, McClure, Alexander Kelly (ed.) (Philadelphia: Times Publishing 1879) (hereinafter referred to as the *Annals*) p.457.

resupplying around Suffolk, south-east of Richmond. Now on his way back to join Lee at Fredericksburg, Old Pete stopped in at the capital and added his voice to Seddon's plan to divert his troops to support Johnston and Bragg in the West since, "the only prospect of relieving Vicksburg that occurred to me was to send General Johnston ... to reinforce General Bragg's army; at the same time the two divisions of my command ... to the same point."[10]

Lee, however, had other ideas, which had been in formulation well before Grant had unpicked the lock of the Yazoo Delta and squelched his way to the gates of Vicksburg. Unlike Davis, Lee was a career soldier and as such saw the battlefield as a place of martial victory, not political survival. Lee had served with distinction as a military engineer during the Mexican War under the revered Winfield Scott, during which Lee was made a brevetted colonel for heroism. After the war, Scott had personally singled Lee out for greatness remarking,

> If I were on my deathbed tomorrow, and the President of the United States should tell me that a great battle was to be fought for the liberty or slavery of the country, and he asked my judgment as to the ability of a commander, I would say with my dying breath, 'Let it be Robert E. Lee.'[11]

Scott had recognised that war ran through Robert Lee's veins, having been born into one of few military families in America. Lee was the son of Lieutenant Colonel Henry "Light Horse Harry" Lee, who led the 2nd Partisan Corps of George Washington's Continental Army in the War of Independence. Induction into the military academy of West Point was a foregone conclusion. West Point, the sole such academy in America, with a syllabus firmly rooted in the Napoleonic rigours of military engineering and mathematics as defined by Baron Antoine-Henri Jomini, taught successive generations of American officers the value of geometry and fortification, but precious little in the art of good collection and implementation of information. After graduating second in the class of 1829, the young Lee followed his training was recruited into the newly-formed U.S. Corps of Engineers. The Corps of Engineers had been established to improve logistics and intelligence for the army, but their approach was steeped in the backward traditionalism of West Point.

Robert Lee had run the same calculation on the merit of eastern and western operations as his president, but reached a slightly different answer. Rather than waiting for the Federals to blunt their axe, Lee articulated his alternative strategy for the Confederate army in early January, stating that "The lives of our soldiers are too precious to be sacrificed in the attainment of successes that inflict no loss upon the

---

10   Longstreet, James, *From Manassas to Appomattox: Memoirs of the Civil War in America* (Philadelphia: Lippincott, 1896) p.327.

11   Macartney, *Lincoln and his Generals*, p.23.

enemy beyond the actual loss in battle."[12] Simply put, the Rebels could not continue to suffer losses purely in the pursuit of defence. Only a significant defeat on their home soil could turn the tide decisively against the North and so, if they wished to claim independence, the Confederates must be prepared to seize the opportunities to attack. Lee may have participated in the bloodiest engagements of the War so far, but he believed that this was justified if the outcome had a decisive effect. Shoring up Bragg's army was a purely defensive measure, which could never be expected to lead to a greater result than momentary relief for Pemberton.

Instead, a repeat of his truncated 1862 invasion of Maryland would combine the benefits of meeting the pressing need to find new forage for his troops and horses, ending the stalemate across the Rappahannock by drawing Hooker out of his defences to meet the threat to the major Union cities and further encouraging the peace advocates in the North. Despite the lost opportunity to weaken Lincoln's support in the previous year's mid-terms, the Northern Democrats advocating peace, (nicknamed "copperheads" after the venomous North American snake or "locofocos" in Maryland since "they are the meanest, dirtiest snakes that ever crawled")[13] were again finding their voice in Washington. Thanks to the regularity of the American democratic process, even so soon after their victory, the Republicans could not feel secure in government with presidential elections less than 18 months away. "If successful this year" Lee confided to his wife April, "next fall there will be a great change in public opinion at the North. The Republicans will be destroyed & I think the friends of peace will become so strong as that the next administration will go in on that basis."[14]

The time was right to act, as Lee could feel the balance of power shifting under the Federals' feet. The summer of 1863 would see the Army of the Potomac undergoing another significant structural upheaval that would undermine their strength. Between May and July, around 40,000 two-year and nine-month volunteers would be mustered out of the Yankee army, to be replaced by temporary militia and green recruits.[15] Thanks to the Federal approach of non-integration of new troops into veteran units, it would take several months for these new volunteers to become battle-ready. To Davis, this plan was of no surprise since Lee had already apprised him of it in April,

> we should assume the aggressive ... when we may expect Genl Hooker's army to be weakened by the expiration of the term of service of many of his regiments, and before new recruits can be received. If we could be placed in a condition to

---

12   O.R. Series I, Vol. XXI, p1086.

13   Brooks, Noah, *Washington in Lincoln's Time* (New York: The Century Co, 1896) p.85. The copperheads duly embraced their nickname and began to wear the head of Liberty cut from copper pennies on their lapels.

14   Dowdey, Clifford, *The Wartime Papers of R. E. Lee* (Boston: Little, Brown & Company, 1961) p.438.

15   *Report of Joint Committee on the Conduct of the War* (Washington: Government Printing Office, 1865)(hereinafter referred to as the *Report of the Joint Committee*) Part I, p.XLII.

make a vigorous advance at that time I think the [Shenandoah] Valley could be swept of Milroy and the army opposite me be thrown north of the Potomac I believe greater relief would in this way be afforded to the armies in middle Tennessee and on the Carolina coast than by any other method.[16]

Sound as his military logic was, an invasion of the North would have a secondary purpose for Lee, one much more personal to the old general than he would care to admit publicly. On the assumption of hostilities, the ageing Winfield Scott invited Lee to take command of the U.S. Army in the swift suppression of the Confederate States. Wrenching as the decision was, Lee was forced to reject the offer and resign from the army to lead the defence of his own home state of Virginia, which joined the Rebellion two days after Scott's invitation. His allegiance to Old Dominion outweighed his loyalty to the Union army and "Save in defense of my native State, I have no desire ever again to draw my sword."[17] Since then, the majority of significant conflicts in the Eastern Theatre had taken place in Virginia and the state had been so ravaged by war that it had prompted Longstreet's journey east to find forage. Successful as Longstreet had been, better supplies could be found in the untouched farmlands of Maryland and Pennsylvania. Losing part of his force to the West would leave his army as little more than a blocking force to protect Richmond and so Virginia could expect another long summer of hardship at the hands of the Army of the Potomac. It was too much for Lee to stand and the general was convinced that just as a march north could relieve Virginia as much as Vicksburg, a defeat on their home soil could force the North to capitulate, no matter what Grant might be up to on the Mississippi.

In September of 1862, Lee had written to President Davis espousing the potential benefits of an offensive into Maryland in order to divert attention in the Eastern Theatre away from Richmond.[18] In addition to keeping the Union army on the back foot, following their disastrous defeat for the second time around the area of Bull Run, the biting effect of the cotton embargo in Europe was provoking increased calls for intervention in London and Paris. Already holding a position at Manassas, by seizing the initiative and delivering a resounding defeat to the Federals near their own soil could precipitate foreign recognition of sovereignty and potentially force Lincoln to the negotiating table. With his president's sanction, Lee launched his campaign into Maryland, the furthest north any Rebel army had ever been. Having fixed his initial operational objective as the Federal garrison of Harper's Ferry, on the banks of the Potomac, Lee divided his army into three to encircle the town, but he would be undone by the sudden speed of the Federal pursuit. Benefitting from an extraordinary piece of intelligence fortune, McClellan cornered Lee (with only part of his army) close to the small creek of Antietam near Sharpsburg.

16   Dowdey, *The Wartime Papers*, p.435.
17   Dowdey, *The Wartime Papers*, p.10.
18   Dowdey, *The Wartime Papers*, p.292.

On 15 September, across the Antietam, Lee's 19,000 men faced the oncoming 70,000 of the Army of the Potomac, but McClellan did not attack. For an entire day, the Rebels held their breath as Little Mac considered his options. By the time he launched his assault on the morning of the 17th, the Rebel force had been reinforced to around 35,000, with A.P. Hill's column still on the march. The fighting at Antietam was shocking, but the Americans were getting used to the new standards of bloodshed. McClellan hurled his men forward, first Fighting Joe and Edwin 'Bull' Sumner ploughed into the Rebel left and then Ambrose Burnside ignored potentially easier crossing routes of the creek to concentrate on getting his IX Corps over a small bridge directly in front of Longstreet's guns. While the advance on the left was bloodily repulsed

Federal General George Brinton McClellan.

by Stonewall Jackson and General D. H. Hill, weight of numbers drove Burnside's march inexorably onwards. Then, at the crucial moment "as if summoned by the lamp of Aladdin,"[19] Ambrose Hill's division of 11,000 arrived from Harper's Ferry to smash into the IX Corps and throw them back in an attack "as terrible as any ever delivered by the Old Guard, with Ney for a leader."[20] As dawn broke on the morning of 18 September, McClellan still had a significant numerical advantage over Lee and would receive around 13,000 additional men as the day wore on, but the fight had left him. Later that night, the Army of Northern Virginia was allowed to limp away having lost around a quarter of their numbers.

Lee had bluffed his way out of total defeat while Little Mac would be left incensed by the lack of congratulation from Washington for stopping the Rebel invasion of Maryland. Writing to his wife after the battle, McClellan confessed that "I feel some little pride in having with a beaten and demoralized army defeated Lee so utterly, & saved the North so completely."[21] Lincoln did not agree and McClellan was replaced by Burnside as commander of the Army of the Potomac. Over 25,000 casualties were suffered by both sides as Lee's Maryland campaign came to an abrupt end in the

19   *Annals*, p.701.
20   *Annals*, p.702.
21   McPherson, *Crossroads of Freedom*, p.131.

The dead lie after the battle of Antietam.

single greatest day of bloodshed in American military history. Although the battle was a tactical victory for Lee, the defeat of his operation and retreat back into Virginia silenced Republican critics long enough to allow Lincoln to secure an ongoing mandate in government a few months later. Furthermore, it emboldened the Federal president to issue his Emancipation Proclamation, outlawing slavery in all Rebel states and thereby effectively isolating the Confederacy from foreign support.

He may have fallen short of his objective of a significant victory, but Lee had succeeded in creating panic in Washington and had demonstrated that a defensive strategy did not mean that the Rebels had to remain purely reactive to Northern operations. Although the chance for foreign intervention had essentially gone, Lee had dealt a serious blow to the Federal army with only a portion of his own force available. He still saw the blueprint for winning the whole war in inflicting a punishing defeat on the Yankees in their own territory and thereby weakening Lincoln's support base in Washington and destroying the Union war effort from the inside. Polite and mild-mannered though Robert Lee was, the archetype of a Southern gentleman, he was also an unusually aggressive soldier for his time and an unrepentant risk-taker. Time and again he had defied the odds against the larger Federal armies, even subdividing his smaller force in the face of the enemy, and still come out on top. Much of the reasoning behind Lee's pursuit of such an aggressive strategy, in the face of such disproportionate disadvantages in men and materiel, was rooted in his firm belief in the superior fighting capability of his army. Since the early victory at First Bull Run, the South had enjoyed most of the major spoils in the Eastern Theatre and the lacklustre performance of the Federals seems to have given credence to Lee belief that the Army of Northern Virginia would be "invincible if it could be properly organized and officered."[22] By 1863, this belief had evolved into a near total disregard for his opponents with Lee frequently referring to the Yankee soldiers as simply "those people."[23] Lee had already seen "Mr F.J. Hooker"[24] wilt under the pressure of battle at Chancellorsville and now, playing for the highest stakes of all where defeat could leave both Federal and Confederate capital cities open, the gambler believed that he had seen his mark.

Unsurprisingly, when Robert Lee arrived in Richmond to plead his case on 14 May, he headed straight into private discussions with Davis and Seddon before the cabinet met the following day. It was only two weeks since Hooker had scurried back across the Rappahannock, but across in the West, Grant's men were on the east bank of the Mississippi and shaping up for a fierce confrontation at Champion's Hill, which would throw Pemberton back into Vicksburg and finally cut him off. Over two days, the great men of the Confederacy debated the merits of East and West with the cause of the relief of Vicksburg championed by Postmaster General John Henninger Reagan, a Texan and so blessed with some awareness of circumstances west of the Mississippi. Having pushed the debate into a second day, the Confederate leaders agreed to Lee's plan and proposals for a relief mission to the West were abandoned. What Lee had proposed to Seddon and Davis was to draw all eyes to the Eastern Theatre with another provocative move north, but this time he would not stop at Harper's Ferry; he would be heading for Pennsylvania. Two months earlier, Stonewall Jackson had called his senior topographical engineer Jedediah Hotchkiss to his headquarters at Miss Stover's house at Narrow Passage Creek in the Shenandoah Valley to give him a simple task: "I want you to make me a map of the [Shenandoah] Valley, from Harper's Ferry to Lexington, showing all the points of offence and defence in those places."[25] From this, Lee would sketch out his operation to leave Fredericksburg and drive north, up the "Great Highway of Invasion"[26] or Shenandoah Valley as it was more conventionally known.[27] Shielded from Federal view by the Blue Ridge Mountains to the

22   Hood, John B., *Advance and Retreat: Personal Experiences in the United States and Confederate Armies* (New Orleans, 1880) p.53.
23   Taylor, Walter, *Four Years with General Lee* (New York: D. Appleton and Company 1878) p.95; Captain Robert Bright of General Pickett's staff would report that he only once heard Lee refer to the Federals as the "enemy", immediately following the repulse of Pickett's Charge, *SHSP Vol XXXI*, p.234.
24   Dowdey, *The Wartime Papers*, p.408.
25   Sharpe, Hal, *Shenandoah County in the Civil War* (Charleston: The History Press, 2012), p.65.
26   Doubleday, Abner, *Chancellorsville and Gettysburg* (New York: Scribner's, 1882), p.53.
27   The Shenandoah Valley stretches north-east up the western edge of Virginia, between the Blue Ridge and Allegheny Mountain chains, all the way to the Potomac River.

east, his army could cross the Potomac River and march directly through Maryland and into Pennsylvania. Once there, he would be in a position to threaten multiple points at once: the bridges over the Susquehanna could be destroyed, ruining the Union transport links between east and west; not just Washington, but Baltimore and Philadelphia would all be at his mercy.

In order to protect his supply lines after leaving Fredericksburg, an advanced party of the Army of Northern Virginia would be required to sweep the Shenandoah clear of Union troops, while his cavalry would protect the eastern side of the mountain passes and scout for Federal movements in pursuit. In typical fashion, Lee devised a complex operational plan to divide his army into three corps in order to ensure that he could advance into safe territory without exposing either his rear or Richmond to an opportunistic attack. One corps would advance up the Valley and neutralise the Federal base at Winchester, and if necessary Harper's Ferry, before crossing the Potomac and sweeping into Maryland and Pennsylvania, to give the Yankees a taste of the suffering so generously meted out to Virginia for the last two years. A second would remain for a period in Fredericksburg to disguise the main movement and prevent any march against him by Hooker, still doubtless stationed at his headquarters at Falmouth, on the northern side of the Rappahannock. The final corps would trail the first and make an early move into the contested ground east of the Blue Ridge Mountains before crossing over one of the major passes into the Valley and disappearing out of Hooker's view. By the time the Federal army had realised what was happening, Lee would be on Northern soil and preparing for a Napoleonic battle that could break the Union army spirit completely and send Lincoln and the Republicans into panic.

As a gambler, Lee knew that much of his Gettysburg campaign relied on bluff. It would only be a matter of time before Hooker was compelled to come after him and then Lee could not avoid the fact that, once again, he would likely be outnumbered. Therefore, he had to provide a contingency plan to break up the Federal counter and also increase his own numbers. An integral part of Lee's operational strategy, therefore, was the synchronised movement of a second body of Rebel troops to a strategic position straddling the Orange and Alexandra railroad around Culpeper Court House. Such a force would compel Hooker to check his pursuit, lest this second Rebel army launch an attack on Washington.[28] By playing on Federal paranoia, Lee would gain sufficient time to achieve his first operational objective of getting far enough north to threaten Harrisburg and perhaps even cause a split in the pursuing Army of the Potomac. Whatever the final operational target chosen, Hooker would have to move away from his defensive positions around Falmouth and engage Lee in the field of the Rebels' choosing. The pressure on Fighting Joe both to protect Washington and Baltimore and to attack the Confederate force was no secret to the Rebels, thanks to their strategic intelligence resources seeded in the Federal capital. Once it was clear that Lee's designs were not on Washington, Hooker would come looking for him.

28 O.R. Series I, Vol. XXVII, Part III, p.931.

Just like McClellan before him, the hesitant Hooker would have to rush to track him down, except that this time the Army of Northern Virginia would be waiting.

Such an exaggerated movement north could not be disguised for long and Davis had no greater desire to expose Richmond than Lincoln did Washington. As a result, Lee did not get exactly everything he wanted. Distrustful of the whims of the War Department, Lee chose not to reveal his idea of a secondary army until the campaign was well underway and (he believed) Richmond was too invested in his success to deny him. This would prove to be a decision that he would later regret. In fact, Lee even suggested that the force that he would eventually request, that of General Beauregard, (sunning himself on the Atlantic coast of the Carolinas), would be more profitably used if sent west to join Johnston in Tennessee.[29] Instead, rather than reveal his full plan, Lee repeatedly petitioned General D.H. Hill to send him additional troops from his position east of Richmond, which he felt would be under no threat from a Federal attack during the summer. Hill, however, had no desire to hand his men over to the Army of Northern Virginia and so the exasperated Lee would request that Hill be left to look after his own affairs and put in charge of the area between the James and Cape Fear. The great general was still subject to his Commander-in-Chief and so would not be permitted to exercise control over all the troops he felt he needed; little did he know it, but he had more in common with Mr F.J. Hooker than he would have liked to admit.

The Gettysburg campaign would be the most ambitious undertaking of Lee's entire career and probably the biggest gamble of the Rebellion. While they stayed within their own borders, the Rebels held a considerable intelligence advantage since the geography of the Confederate states was so poorly understood that local knowledge was critical in tactical planning. As well as the obvious problems of having to create and hold external lines of communication between commander and corps, a lack of local maps and popular support had played no small role in the failure of all previous Union operations into the South. To march into Maryland and Pennsylvania would reverse the usual advantage of local knowledge and internal lines of communication and logistics and cede them to the Yankees. If the Gettysburg campaign would essentially be an invasion, Lee's intelligence services would need to be tailored to provide information that could contribute to operational and tactical success. These would need to be able to function autonomously as he moved away from his supply and communications base at Fredericksburg. Lee's earlier Maryland campaign had been conducted in a neutral state, which still contained many Confederate sympathisers, albeit he had received little actual assistance. The curtailment of his progress by McClellan's rapid concentration at Antietam, however, meant that the Rebels never reached much further north than Boonsborough, Maryland. As a result, they never over-stretched their key lines of logistics or communications. To move as far north as Pennsylvania would present a whole new set of intelligence challenges, unprecedented for Lee or his army.

29   Dowdey, *The Wartime Papers*, p.503.

2

A Country Full of Spies

As the Confederate cabinet met to endorse Robert Lee's proposal, none were under any false impressions as to the risks that their senior commander was asking them to take. They were agreeing to send away the largest army in the Confederacy, currently the only force large enough to block Hooker from the path to the Rebel capital. Lee's march would take him on a circuitous route into enemy states with the deliberate intention of bringing on a Federal attack. As well as the logistical challenge of marching so many thousands of men hundreds of miles away from their support base, Lee would have to be entirely self-sufficient in the collection of his intelligence prior to the inevitable battle, assuming that Hooker did not try and attack him or Richmond before he even left Virginia. Lee's army would be divided, occasionally separated by several days march, and despite his indecision a few weeks before, there was no guarantee that Hooker would be as wasteful as McClellan if he cornered one of Lee's corps on the road to Pennsylvania.

Despite these serious challenges, Robert Lee had managed to persuade the Confederate cabinet and in particular President Davis, of the merits of his plan. His success in convincing Davis to take such an enormous gamble reveals not only the trust between the Confederate president and his senior military adviser, but also a fatal flaw in the Rebel intelligence system, which had generated from Davis's election as Commander-in-Chief. With his pedigree as both a former soldier and a secretary of war, Jefferson Davis was an ideal candidate to lead a nation born in the crucible of conflict, as the Confederate States had been. Similarly, although the breakaway nation managed to retain much of its military infrastructure, it also had the advantage of being able to shed some of the bureaucracy and politics that had become attached to the U.S. Army. The Confederate government was built for war and Davis was a capable and experienced leader with a clear strategy for bleeding the Union until it could stand no more. However, his formulation and oversight of strategic policy extended into personal interference in his generals' operations and his high-handed manner led to friction with several of his senior commanders. It was no accident that the highly experienced Joseph Johnston had found himself thrown down from the defence of Richmond to command one of the furthest departments away from the Rebel capital.

Although often an unwanted distraction during times of crisis, Davis's personal behaviour was less of a critical issue than the strategy he imposed. Whilst an aggressive defence strategy maximised the Confederate strength of interior lines, it also required a centralised system of coordination to ensure that an adequate proportion of the South's limited resources were dedicated to meet the offensive movements of the Union as they occurred. Coupled with Davis's proclivities for micromanagement, Richmond had soon consolidated almost all control over operations in every theatre. The meetings of early May illustrated exactly the key problem, which had permeated into the fabric of the Rebel war machine and which would have a profound effect on its exercise of military intelligence. The Rebel strategy required an efficient marshalling of the South's limited resources with a complementary understanding of Northern operational plans and morale. The Federal offensives in both the Eastern and Western theatres were already forcing Davis and his War Department to choose how the armies would be deployed to respond, but, despite the multiple threats, Davis insisted in orchestrating the Rebel defence from Richmond and held personal sway over the strategic objectives and planning.

Confederate President
Jefferson Davis.

This overwhelming bias of command towards policy-makers rather than battle leaders (since Davis considered himself one and the same), meant that the creation of the Rebel intelligence services would be dedicated almost entirely towards the acquisition of strategic information for the benefit of the government, rather than operational and tactical information to win battles. In order to be able to gauge the effectiveness of its strategy, Jefferson Davis and the War Department were less concerned with body-counts than they were with ballots. The spectre of the venomous Democratic peace party loomed large over Lincoln and the Republicans at all times. Two of their most important victories in the War were significant for the Federals, not for their tactical value, but for their timing immediately before the North went to the vote: McClellan's push of Lee out of Maryland in September 1862 and William Sherman's seizure of Atlanta in September 1864. To measure the success of their strategy, therefore, Davis needed to put his fingers on the pulse of the Northern people and Capitol Hill and so he instituted a system of information collection that favoured high-level decision making rather than battle planning.

Since Richmond was not primarily interested in data from the front lines, therefore, the sources of the information that it required would also not come from soldiers or generals. Unlike the grand European wars of Napoleon, which still filled the text-books of West Point, the Civil War would be fought entirely within a single country where language was common and, depending on the situation, there may be no shortage of people willing to share information. "The country is full of spies, and our plans are immediately carried to the enemy,"[1] complained Lee before embarking on his Maryland campaign and few countries had a richer history of such activity than America. When the Confederate States launched their bid for independence, many on the eastern side of the Atlantic believed that their success was a foregone conclusion. Not only was the South seen to wield far too much global power in its cotton production, but there was already a precedent for an American force achieving sovereignty against a larger oppressor. Soon there were comparisons between America's struggle for independence and that of the Confederacy and Richmond was quick to emulate the lessons of their founding fathers in warfare and particularly intelligence.

Nearly 100 years beforehand, General George Washington devised a strategy of employing a guerrilla-style of combat to negate the British strength in set-piece battle. By concentrating his limited force at small and isolated pockets of the enemy and by collaborating with foreign nations, keen to recognise an independent America, Washington managed to extract a victory out of the British without ever having to assault high risk areas such as New York. Such a strategy required a high level of knowledge on enemy position and composition so that engagements could be carefully chosen and Washington displayed a keen awareness of the power of good intelligence as a 'force multiplier'. From the very first incidents, which would later be carved into legend, the American War of Independence was an excellent blue-print

1   O.R. Series I, Vol. XI, Part III, p.602.

for the Confederacy of how good intelligence, with espionage as a prominent feature, could be used by an astute leadership to counteract a numerically superior force. Right from the start, legends were created in the field of intelligence: Paul Revere, a citizen spy from Boston, part of a partisan group observing British operations for the Massachusetts Provincial Congress, coordinated the transmission of intelligence on the British march on Lexington and Concord on the night of 18 April 1775. When the British arrived at Lexington the following day, the Minutemen were waiting and the War began.

Under General Washington, the Americans had the perfect leader to coordinate a complex strategy based on extracting the greatest possible value from the various forms of HUMINT information available, both tactical and strategic. A veteran of the Seven Years War fighting alongside the British, Washington learnt the arts of good soldering and leadership, as well as the lessons of how good intelligence could be part of used to improve planning. He had helped spy on the French forces in Pennsylvania and acted as aide-de-camp to General Braddock on his disastrous attempt to capture Fort Duquesne in 1755. Braddock's failure both to hide his advance on Fort Duquesne and adequately scout ahead to reprise himself of the enemy situation around the fort led to an unexpected meeting engagement where his force succumbed to a combined French and Native American army of around half the size of his. A canny military mind like Washington could not fail to have been impressed by the influence that advanced knowledge of enemy manoeuvres coupled with good understanding of the local terrain could have on a battle, even against a larger army of professional soldiers.

Now in command of the American Continental Army, Washington understood exactly the strategy that must be employed to overcome his better trained and equipped British adversaries. Vital to the success of this strategy would be the acquisition of accurate information on the enemy composition and deployment, as well as a thorough knowledge of the geography of the chosen fields of battle. Observation of the enemy by professional or amateur scouts coupled with effective reconnaissance from his specially developed cavalry units (of whom Light Horse Harry was a flamboyant member) would need to be complemented by espionage activities in the major enemy-held cities. Washington recognised that, by having an ear to British strategy, he could greatly enhance his opportunities for pre-empting their operations and even preventing major campaigns through counterintelligence. To facilitate a centralised system of espionage in one of the centres of the enemy command, New York, Major Benjamin Tallmadge was engaged to run a group citizen spies. Tallmadge recruited Abraham Woodhull and Robert Townsend to acquire information from inside the city and transmit it to him in Long Island. The pair was named the "Culper Spy Ring" after their aliases Samuel Culper and Samuel Culper Jr. From their positions in the heart of the enemy-held city, the Culper Spies fed Tallmadge information on British strategy and operations. Tallmadge then passed this raw data directly to his commander. One of the most famous examples of the success of the Culper Spy Ring was the stoppage of a pre-emptive British strike on the French force of the Comte de

Rochambeau at Rhode Island in July 1780. Alerted to the plan to hit the French as they landed, Washington used his spies to spread counterintelligence rumours of an American plan to attack New York. Fearing this phantom attack, the British cancelled their intended offensive against Rhode Island and prepared for defence of their own, more strategically significant, city.

While the Rhode Island incident provides a good example of how non-military HUMINT sources could harvest good intelligence for a commander, such sources were defined by the quality of the agents used and their access to information. The Culper Spy Ring was effective at acquiring information for Tallmadge, but they were typically reliant on hearsay and would not necessarily always be able to appreciate fully the significance of the information that they collected. Such spying activity was undoubtedly successful on occasion, but perhaps it is telling that probably the most famous example of Revolutionary War espionage was the failure of Nathan Hale, who had volunteered to spy on the British in New York and was promptly captured and executed. His mission might have been ill-fated, but he would still win immortality by his final words: "I only regret, that I have but one life to lose for my country."[2] Although Hale might be remembered for the wrong reasons, he is still a fine example of Washington's appreciation of the need to diversify his sources of intelligence and his recognition of the potential opportunities afforded to him for improving the quality of his intelligence. The divisive nature of the Rebellion and the limited number of British troops dedicated to suppressing it, had created a need for American volunteers to fill the loyalist ranks. Just as he had seeded occupied cities with volunteer spies, he also sent infiltrators into the enemy ranks. Daniel Bissell faked desertion from the Continental Army and joined Benedict Arnold's Loyalist American Legion in August 1781 and remained undercover for over a year.

The use of espionage would quickly become a central plank of the Confederate intelligence effort and the citizen spies themselves, mostly concentrated in Washington, would gain considerable fame during and after the War. The Federals likewise would quickly realise the potential danger of such an easily mobilised fifth column in their seat of power. The first major engagement of the War at Bull Run River in July 1861 would make a previously obscure Washington socialite a household name. Living within "easy rifle-range" of the White House was Rose O'Neal Greenhow, who, although born in Maryland, had married a Virginian gentleman and became a staunch supporter of the Southern cause.

Her connections into Northern high society quickly attracted the attention of Colonel Thomas Jordan, a former U.S. Army officer and now adjutant-general for General Beauregard's Army of the Potomac.[3] Under instruction from Richmond and in emulation of George Washington's model, Jordan established a spy ring in the Federal capital to procure military and political information, before leaving to join the

---

2   Quoted in Crocker, H.W., *Don't Tread on Me* (New York: Crown Publishing, 2006) p.57.
3   Not to be confused with the Federal army later raised by General McClellan.

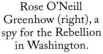

Rose O'Neill
Greenhow (right), a
spy for the Rebellion
in Washington.

Rebel army. He would keep up communications with his informants such as Greenhow through his pseudonym "Thomas John Rayford".[4] As the first conflict was brewing, so Ms Greenhow was wining and dining the Federal elite and subtly pumping them for information. Twice before the battle began, Greenhow sent messages to Beauregard warning that the order had been given to Federal General Irvin McDowell to march on the Rebel army and, according to his own testimony, Beauregard alerted his troops to be watchful for the Federal attack based on this information.[5] Whether Greenhow's messages truly made a difference to the battle is a moot point, but the information provided by her, Jordan and other notable Washington-based spies was of great importance to President Davis.

Espionage in the latter half of the 19th Century had not varied too much from the days of the War of Independence and just as Washington had found the need to vary his acquisition resources, so too would the Confederate look to exploit other available opportunities. In particular, one source favoured by the Culper Spies had spread throughout the nation since the time of independence from Britain. In order to get British tongues wagging, Robert Townsend posed as a journalist with the *Royal Gazette*, a newspaper set up in New York by James Rivington as a loyalist publication,

4   O.R. Series II, Vol. II p.564.
5   *Battles and Leaders, Vol. I*, p.199-200.

but in fact loyal only to the Revolution. With the proliferation of the press throughout America in the subsequent century, such subterfuge would not be required to acquire such gossip. Now, a voracious and politically-driven media would trawl for any information worth publishing, whether in the national interest or not. Local newspapers had been established in nearly every major city in the North and South for a number of years and all sent their correspondents along with the armies as they marched. For the first time, reportage could be delivered from the front line within a matter of hours and generals would have to contend with potentially valuable intelligence leaking from their own side. So accurate were some of the reports that enemy newspapers were highly prized and generals would despair that "the newspapers say much more than we have ever learned from any other source."[6] Not only could they give away sensitive operational information, but they were also a window into the political and social conditions.

The problem that faced military strategists during the Civil War, with regard to the ubiquity of journalists following and commenting on the actions of both sides, served as a further example of how the conflict was to represent a sign of things to come. Future generations would learn the importance of working with the media to help control the flow of information, both to their own people and the enemy, but such a situation was not fully appreciated in 1861 and control would prove to be nearly impossible. It goes without saying that the Civil War generals did not appreciate the near-constant presence of these "sneaking croaking scoundrels"[7] and General Hooker made a policy of targeting the newspaper men as soon as he assumed command of the Army of the Potomac. Within two months, he had tried to have Edwin Denyse of the *New York Herald* jailed for publishing a letter reporting the army's imminent operations. Although the man was ultimately only banished, the vendetta forged between the *Herald* and Hooker would even see an order from the commander to have all copies of the paper burned.[8] His initial successes was short-lived, however, and on the eve of the launch of his Chancellorsville offensive, the *Washington Morning Chronicle* would publish accurate ORBAT estimates for his entire army, inadvertently provided to them by a major in the Surgeon General's office. Fortunately for the Federals, Lee did not pick up the information until after the ensuing battle.[9]

Local media obviously did not intentionally seek to undermine the war effort, but the will of the 'free press' to report whatever it felt would win them greater readership was coupled with the powerful influence of the political factions in Washington. Throughout the War, the generals did not just do their fighting in the field and as it dragged on, so the mud-slinging and back-biting behind the scenes became chronic. The press was

6   O.R. Series I, Vol. XXVII, Part III, p.218.
7   Arnold, *Grant Wins the War*, p.96.
8   Sparks, David (ed.), *Inside Lincoln's Army, The Diary of Marsena Rudolph Patrick, Provost Marshal General, Amy of the Potomac*, (Thomas Yoseloff: New York, 1964), p.247-8.
9   Dowdey, *The Wartime Papers*, p.482.

A party of journalists from the *New York Herald Tribune* travelling with the army.

more than a willing tool for such intrigues, at the right price. "There are those who think nothing was gained or done well in this battle," observed Frank Haskell, General John Gibbon's aide-de-camp, after Gettysburg "because some other general did not have command. Military men do not claim or expect this, but the McClellan destroyers do, the doughty knights of purchaseable newspaper quills; the formidable warriors from the brothels of politics."[10] Even Hooker would eventually have to call a truce and try and strike a bargain with the journalists embedded in his camps. In return for ceasing to publish information on troop numbers and movements and generals' official reports, "every facility possible will be given to reporters and newspapers in this army, including the license to abuse or criticise me to their hearts content."[11]

Having developed the network to acquire strategic information from Washington, therefore, Richmond required a dedicated communications system to ensure its safe delivery. Although the Rebel capital was situated only a hundred or so miles from Washington, the Potomac River provided a considerable barrier to the safe conduct of Southern personnel. It was for that reason it would be the Rebels who first formalised a dedicated communications system into their new military structure. The Confederate

10   Haskell, *The Battle of Gettysburg*, p.145-6.
11   O.R. Series I, Vol. XXVII, Part III, p.192.

Signal Bureau (the "C.S.B.") was formed in April 1862 and approved under General Order 40 a month later to bring signal communications under control of the War Department.[12] Its chief was Major William Norris, who made his name by establishing a line of signals, based on naval signalling methods, across the James River to assist General "Prince" John Bankhead Magruder, a colourful Rebel leader, who would teach General McClellan a lesson in the art of subterfuge during the early stages of his Peninsula campaign.[13]

Head of the Confederate Signal Bureau, Major William Norris.

Norris, a former lawyer who had developed a strong grounding in signalling and communications, was an able candidate to run the C.S.B., but the manner of his selection gave a clue as to why the tactical communications service of the Confederacy would never match that of its opponent. Also in contention to lead the bureau was a young professional soldier named Edward Porter Alexander. Alexander had been part of the original team under the leadership of the godfather of American signalling, Albert J. Myer, who had been conducting experiments into a new system of mobile signals for use by the army for several years before the outbreak of the War. Having parted conpany with Myer to join the Confederacy, Alexander displayed his credentials by being the first to demonstrate the potential effectiveness of signals during the First Battle of Bull Run.[14] After the battle, however, Alexander would refuse a colonelship in the newly formed "Department of Signals,"[15] to become a lieutenant-colonel in the artillery of the Army of Northern Virginia. Although the Confederacy had established a signal corps first, their refusal to recognise the value its officers played to the military effort, and thereby encourage quality volunteers into the C.S.B., would prevent its organic evolution as a tactical weapon. Instead, the bureau became an effective, but limited, earpiece for Davis into Washington, with Norris acting as little more than his personal information assistant.

---

12   O.R. Series IV, Vol. I, p.1131-32.
13   Magruder made his small force of around 11,000 troops parade across the same clearing in sight of the Federal army to convincing McClellan to besiege Yorktown rather than ignore it.
14   Alexander, *Military Memoirs* p.30.
15   Alexander, *Military Memoirs* p 52.

By September 1862, the C.S.B. had grown to over 60 officers responsible for signal communications and encryption, as well as basic observation and scouting, supported by anything up to 1,500 men during the course of the War.[16] Every division of infantry and brigade of cavalry was assigned a three-to-five man squad with flags and torches for mobile tactical signalling, but this would not become the primary role of the C.S.B. Instead, under direction from Richmond, the C.S.B. would prioritise the coordination of the transmission of intelligence and personnel from the North to the South, rather than facilitation of the acquisition of the information itself. This bifurcation of responsibilities of the main intelligence organ of the Confederacy was highlighted in Norris's own "missions and functions" statement for the C.S.B., which included:

- management and supplying of secret lines of communication on the Potomac
- provide transportation across the Potomac for agents, scouts and others passing from and to Baltimore and Washington
- procuring files of the latest Northern newspapers for the Executive Department
- obtaining books, "small packages," etc. for heads of bureaus[17]

To cover these additional covert activities, a secondary department was established within the C.S.B., that of the Confederate Secret Service Bureau (the "C.S.S.B."). The C.S.S.B., also under Norris, ran spies from Richmond into the Union territories and operated the "Secret Line" of communications across the Potomac. In his fascinating account of his travels among the Rebels during the summer of 1863, *Three Months in the Southern States*,[18] Lieutenant-Colonel Arthur James Fremantle of the Coldstream Guards (and later Governor of Malta) describes his time spent with Norris being shepherded across the Potomac under the noses of the Federals, eventually arriving at Gettysburg on the eve of the battle. Norris is described as "the chief of the secret intelligence bureau at Richmond"[19] and, at its peak, the C.S.S.B. was delivering newspapers to the Confederate government from Washington and Baltimore the day after publication and from New York the day after that.[20]

While Lee was often critical of the quality of the Confederate espionage network in Washington,[21] he was a devoted believer in the Northern press for providing both

---

16   Gaddy, David, *William Norris and the Confederate Signal and Secret Service* (Maryland Historical Magazine Volume 70, Number 2 Baltimore: Maryland Historical Society 1975) p.172-3.
17   Gaddy, *William Norris*, p.173.
18   Fremantle, Arthur, *Three Months in the Southern States* (New York, John Bradburn, 1864).
19   Fremantle, *Three Months in the Southern States*, p.198.
20   Taylor, Charles, *The Signal and Secret Service of the Confederate States* (North Carolina Booklet Vol II, Hamlet, North Carolina, March 1903) p.22.
21   O.R. Series I, Vol. XXV, Part II, p.832-3.

strategic and tactical information.[22] Lee knew that the real power of his army lay in the damage that it could do to Northern morale and perception abroad. As such, he was an avid follower of the exploits of the Copperheads at home and the statements of foreign governments, but that is not to say that the journalists were not also willing providers of potentially critical operational or ORBAT intelligence. However, the effectiveness of the Rebel system was undermined by a fundamental failure to include any kind of interpretive capacity in the functions of the C.S.B. or C.S.S.B. While obtaining information material at source might be relatively straightforward, sifting useful information and verifying its accuracy was not. The sheer weight of

Lieutenant-Colonel Arthur James Fremantle, who toured the Eastern Theatre with the Rebels during the Gettysburg campaign.

information, both accurate and inaccurate, sourced by the Signal and Secret Service Bureaus required considerable resources to process useful material, which Richmond never correctly incentivised.

One needs look no further than the build-up to Hooker's Chancellorsville campaign to witness the weakness of interpretative function in the Confederate intelligence machine. By mid-April, General Lee was in no doubt that the new fighting season was upon him again and that if he did not move then the Federals surely would. "The grass is springing", he mused to his wife, "I suppose I shall soon hear from Genl Hooker."[23] If the commander of the Army of Northern Virginia was confident of Hooker's intentions, the same could not be said of his understanding of his opponent's strength. On 16 April, Lee wrote to his Adjutant General Samuel Cooper of his thoughts on the Federal threats in the different theatres and was forced to guess at the effective size of the Army of the Potomac from reports of the number of rations drawn.[24] The day after Lee wrote this message, the letter from Surgeon Letterman to Hooker was published in the *Washington Morning Chronicle* detailing the number of sick in his army and their ratio to each 1,000 soldiers in each corps. To Hooker's mind, the information disclosed "Its [the Army of the Potomac's] complete organization … and in the case of two corps the number of regiments. The chief of my secret service department would have willingly paid $1,000 for such information in regard to the

22   O.R. Series I, Vol. XXV, Part II, p.752.
23   Dowdey, *The Wartime Papers*, p.433.
24   O.R. Series I, Vol. XXV, Part II, p.725-6.

enemy at the commencement of his operations."[25] Indeed, Lee would have paid a high price to discover such detailed ORBAT intelligence on his enemy at such a time, but the he would not learn of the information until well after the battle was fought. The failure to pick up this piece of highly valuable intelligence, so close to a major engagement, was shocking and exemplifies the lost opportunities that would haunt Rebel military operations. Not only could the information have been of vital importance to Lee's tactical preparations, but it also represented first-hand verifiable information, which could also have been used to improve further the accuracy of other acquired information.

The intrusion of the media also served as a clear example of how all information sources had to be constantly monitored and cross-checked in order to improve intelligence quality. With such a large number of publications competing to get the greater scoops on the progress of the War, erroneous reports could quickly proliferate. Much of this inaccurate reporting was as a result of dubious source-work, but definitely not all. Since it was no secret that both combatants read each other's news, so the deliberate planting of fake reports of upcoming operations would also become commonplace. Just as George Washington had skilfully used counterintelligence to foil the British at Rhode Island, so the more savvy Civil War generals also engaged in the art of deception. Such a piece of accurate information as the *Chronicle's* article could have provided a factual baseline for all further ORBAT intelligence collected during the rest of the operations against the Army of the Potomac that summer. An integrated system of both acquisition and interpretation would have greatly aided the Confederacy in combating the threat of counterintelligence, but it had not been designed with such sophistication in mind.

Despite the Confederacy stretching from Virginia to Texas, the centralised intelligence system developed by President Davis focused almost exclusively operations around the Potomac (i.e. between Washington and Richmond). Similarly, espionage activities and the transmission of information through enemy lines became its primary goal, at the expense of utility for the generals. This diversification of duties for the C.S.B., from being a tactical to a strategic intelligence support service, reveals the fatal flaw in the Confederate system: the Confederate strategy to win the War was based on success in the field; its intelligence service was built with barely any thought to providing a platform to secure the best quality intelligence to the generals at the front. Due to President Davis's intention to run the War entirely out of Richmond, from where he would have oversight of all theatres of operations, the Rebel government developed an intelligence apparatus grounded in the capital and dedicated to the acquisition of information solely for the use of high command. As a result, this attempted centralisation led to the diminished effectiveness of the service on the battlefield.

25   O.R. Series I, Vol. XXV, Part II, p.239.

If this was not enough to neuter the possible effectiveness of the C.S.B. as an intelligence weapon, it was not even allowed to monopolise its own operations in Virginia. In fact, Norris, who had ostensibly been appointed head of the Rebel intelligence service through his capacity as both head of the Signal Bureau and leader of the Secret Service, was not even permitted a monopoly over signalling duties. An alternative service, the aptly named Independent Signal Corps, under the charge of James F. Milligan, ran communications in the area between the Appomattox and James rivers, immediately south of Richmond, instead of Norris.[26] Milligan, a former midshipman in the U.S. Navy and veteran of the Mexican War, had been made a signal officer to the Department of Norfolk on the Peninsula due to his experience of naval signalling. The Independent Signal Corps reported separately to Davis and jealously regarded Norris and his higher-esteemed service. Needless to say, the existence of rival corps was not conducive to effective operations and further exemplified of the lack of coherent understanding and coordination of the intelligence services by the Confederacy.

26   Gaddy, *William Norris*, p.174; O.R. Series I, Vol. XXVII, Part III, p.964-5.

3

I Leave the Matter to God

Supremely confident as he was, one would have thought that Robert Lee must have contemplated long and hard as to how he could maximise his intelligence operations and communications before he set out on the greatest gamble of his career. Beyond the basic logistical challenges, the coordination of three separated corps operating in enemy territory, whilst keeping in touch with his commander-in-chief in Richmond would be a fearsome challenge. His army would eventually be strung out from the middle of the Shenandoah all the way up to the Susquehanna River and his movement would take him around 200 miles from President Davis and the headquarters of the Confederate Signal Bureau. As he moved into the Northern states, communication by courier would become increasingly slow and perilous and Lee's plans demanded that information on Hooker's army be obtained without giving away the intentions of his own. Now undertaking an invasion, the normal character of Confederate operations, built around a structure of exploiting defensive positions and interior lines, would be inverted and Lee's intelligence resources would be shorn of many of his usual sources of acquisition. As the foremost military leader of his age prepared to lead his army into the territory of the enemy, with the express purpose of meeting them in a potentially decisive confrontation, he did so again with no centralised structure for acquiring, interpreting and applying information.

Despite the obvious risks to his lines of communication, however, Lee took no additional precautions in advance of his march. Throughout the operational stages of the campaign, as Lee moved up through the naturally protected Shenandoah Valley, he would still largely be relying on his courier communications with the Confederate capital (via Winchester and Fredericksburg) for news on the Federals that he could not acquire himself. Without good communications to transmit their information, any intelligence acquired would be increasingly out-of-date by the time of receipt by Lee's headquarters and increasingly at risk of interception once the Army of Northern Virginia crossed the Potomac. Although personnel from the C.S.B. were assigned to each of the infantry corps, no chief signal officer was attached to Lee's base to coordinate their operation. Ironically, although any strategic information acquired in the North through the War Department in Richmond could do little to assist the general in measuring the strength or intention of Hooker's army, it was espionage that would prove the key to revealing the whereabouts of the on-rushing Army of the Potomac. The critical information, however, was obtained independently of the C.S.S.B. and not through the Secret Line.

Should Robert Lee have wished for a clearer warning as to the importance of good intelligence operations during a campaign of invasion, he needed only to cast his mind back to the events of the previous summer. Having seized the initiative to march into neutral Maryland after his victory over John Pope at the Second Battle of Bull Run in early September, Lee divided his army of 55,000 men into three arms to surround the Union garrison at Harper's Ferry. As expected, George McClellan's pursuit was cautious, since he lacked the intelligence function within his army to track his prey. Then, on the afternoon of 13 September, First Sergeant John M. Bloss and Private Barton W. Mitchell of Company F of the 27th Indiana Volunteers approached their colonel with a curious discovery. Found in a field just outside Frederick, where Company F were resting, and wrapped around three cigars was Special Order 191 addressed to General D.H. Hill and purportedly signed by Lee's chief of staff Robert H. Chilton.[1] The "Lost Order", intended for Hill had been issued on 9 September and called for a concentration of the separate parts of the Rebel army on Harper's Ferry. For the first time, the Federals had clear evidence that Lee had split his forces, which now could be crushed individually if McClellan could isolate them before they reconsolidated. It was an intelligence coup of almost unprecedented proportions. On seeing the paper, Little Mac famously promised John Gibbon: "Here is a paper with which if I cannot whip Bobbie Lee, I will be willing to go home."[2]

The small problem for McClellan was that, by the time this spectacular piece of SIGINT was discovered, it was already four days old and the divided Rebel corps had deviated significantly from Lee's original instruction. Although

Robert Chilton, Lee's chief-of-staff.

1   *Battles and Leaders, Vol II*, p.603.
2   Gibbon, John, *Personal Recollections of the Civil War* (New York: G.P. Putnam's Sons, 1928) p.73.

McClellan had learnt a vital piece of information about his opponent, in fact, it did not give him any additional accurate details on the location of Lee's scattered army. Learning of the existence of the Lost Order and that the Federals were marching on him, Lee managed to delay successfully their crossing of South Mountain[3] in order to gift himself some time to gather some of his forces together before he faced McClellan at Antietam. One of the undeniable truths of intelligence is that even the best information cannot guarantee the right result, since its utility and effectiveness is ultimately determined by the recipient. Even when provided with one of the intelligence finds of the War, the capture of the Lost Order still did not conquer McClellan's natural caution and persuade him to attack when he had the Army of Northern Virginia at his mercy.

The Battle of Antietam should have been a chastening experience for the Rebellion and should have revealed to its premier commander the importance of enhancing and protecting his intelligence and communications. However, this underlying weakness in the Confederate intelligence apparatus was not of concern to Lee nor Davis nor had it yet been revealed in the operations of the Eastern Theatre. As Davis's chief military adviser, Lee was an avid reader of the Northern press as a committed believer in the Confederate strategy of enforcing peace through popular or foreign intercession. As a commander, however, he had little interest in anything other than getting his army into a tactically beneficial position to engage the enemy. Although much of his acclaim would be rightly based on his willingness to tear up the rule-book of prevailing American military teaching, he was thoroughly orthodox and indeed conservative in his practice and utilisation of military intelligence. The U.S. Army, like any force that had developed to tackle threats against foreign nations or engagements far away from its political centre, had evolved a structure whereby a commanding officer would seek the acquisition of tactical information from specific sources in order to determine his next decision. Typically, the information would be received raw and the only assistance available would be from staff officers, for whom the processing of military information would be one of a large number of duties as part of running the army. The demands of coordinating armies of nearly a hundred thousand men meant that, without a dedicated intelligence function, Lee's small staff of less than 15 men (which included numerous specialist positions such as chief of ordnance and artillery colonel) would never be able to process the vast quantity of raw information into usable intelligence while also satisfying their other duties.[4] During the summer of 1863, these few officers processed over 4,000 documents on behalf of the Army of Northern Virginia and, in reality, only selected staff officers such as Charles Marshall, Walter Taylor and Charles Venables provided assistance in the collection of information reports. The intelligence work undertaken by these officers,

---

3   South Mountain is the name given to the extension of the Blue Ridge Mountains north of the Potomac River, where the Shenandoah Valley gives way to the Cumberland Valley.
4   Tidewell, William, *Come Retribution* (Jackson and London: University Press of Mississippi, 1988) p.108.

however, was predominantly administrative rather than analytical. With no form of intelligence structure providing interpretation services for him and no staff officer dedicated to intelligence duties within the Army of Northern Virginia, Lee served as his own intelligence analyst, a role in which he was content and in which history had suggested that he excelled at. In all likelihood, even if the Confederacy had instituted a centralised service dedicated to intelligence operations in support of its generals, Lee probably would not have used it.

Robert Lee's myopic view on the utility of intelligence very much reflected his laissez-faire style of command. Unlike many contemporaries, he was not concerned about retaining complete control over his generals during proceedings, but was happy to issue orders at the start of the day and let his commanders execute them as they saw fit. Lee disliked interfering in the actions of his lieutenants and described his role as head of the army as merely to deliver his troops to the appropriate location for battle and then "I leave the matter to God and the subordinate officers."[5] Such a style of command was aligned to Lee's views of the traditional methodologies of warfare. Contrary to the formulaic mechanics of battle taught at West Point, Lee was ultimately an aggressive pragmatist. Any attempt to coordinate the attacks on the field personally would be logistically impossible and would, at least, result in unhealthily slow troop movements. Instead, a heavy responsibility was placed on his corps commanders to enact his orders and Lee was lucky to have some of the most experienced and effective generals, such as Stonewall Jackson and James Longstreet, at his disposal.

Cognisant of the need to make execution of his tactics and operations more efficient following the narrow scrape at Antietam, rather than perfecting a system that would facilitate information flow quickly and securely to and from his commanders, Lee viewed the challenge in a different manner. The issue was already weighing heavily as he contemplated execution of his summer campaign in 1863,

> I have for the past year felt that the corps of this army were too large for one commander ... Each corps contains when in fighting condition about 30,000 men. These are more than one man can properly handle & keep under his eye in battle in the country that we have to operate in. They are always beyond the range of his vision, & frequently beyond his reach.[6]

This seemingly progressive stance towards the changing face of command was only enhanced by the loss of one of his most senior and trusted generals, Stonewall Jackson. During the battle of Chancellorsville, Jackson had been shot by friendly fire from one of his own pickets as he returned from a personal reconnaissance of the Federal lines during the gloom of early evening. He would die a little over a week later and Lee

---

5   Cited in J. Luvaas, 'Lee and the Operational Art: The Right Place, The Right Time' (U.S. Army War College, 1992) p.2.
6   O.R. Series I, Vol. XXV, Part II p.810.

and the Confederacy would be left reeling from the loss of one of its most effective commanders.

So instead of embracing modern intelligence practices as a method of rising above his orthodox peers, Lee's utility of intelligence remained firmly rooted in the past. His experience had been forged as one of the U.S. Army Corps of Engineers in the deserts of Mexico, a war of professional armies and set-piece engagements, utilising permanent or ad hoc fortifications wherever possible. As a war of conquest with a well-defined strategic objective, (that of marching from the designated landing point of Veracruz inland to seize the capital of Mexico City and enforce a negoti-ated peace), the Corps of Engineers were given clear responsibilities for both logistics and formulating plans to overcome the imposing Mexican fortifications. While oper-ating increasingly far from American soil, any army would have to be self-sufficient in intelligence gathering. The primary available sources were HUMINT related, since the landscape of southern Texas, future New Mexico and northern Mexico allowed plenty of potential for good observation by both scouts and pickets, while cavalry were free to operate unrestricted. This is not to say, however, that certain opportunities for espionage did not exist despite the lack of a common language. Initially estab-lished as a method for protecting communications, the "Mexican Spy Company" was incubated between General Ethan Allen Hitchcock of Scott's staff and local bandit Manuel Dominguez. Lubricated by American dollars, the Spy Company would grow to over 100 men providing security for couriers and personnel, tactical observation and strategic intelligence through infiltration of enemy cities, often with great success. At the end of the war, Dominguez was so despised at home that Hitchcock arranged for him to be relocated to New Orleans and appealed to the state senator for him to be provided formal protection. The senator for Mississippi at the time, having just returned from the war himself, was Jefferson Davis.[7]

Despite the assistance of the Spy Company, the lifeblood of tactical intelligence operations throughout the Mexican War were the engineers. Lee had been one of Old Fuss and Feathers' senior staff and so an agent of intelligence – and a particularly good one. The future general would personally play a significant role in the successful actions against the heavily fortified positions such as city of Monterrey, guarded by its imposing Black Fort citadel, scouting the enemy positions and deciding the most effective placements for artillery. Mexico City would fall only 16 months from the outbreak of war and the traditional methods of information acquisition had proven themselves sufficiently effective. The traditionalist view on the scope of information acquisition and the utility of intelligence would, therefore, be allowed to permeate through the armies of the Civil War, as Robert Lee and his engineering peers repre-sented an extraordinary number of senior generals on both sides. In fact, were it not for the Mexican weakness in heavy guns, one particular incident could have changed

---

7   Ethan Allen Hitchcock and the Mexican War Spy Company, Fort Huachuca Museum online, http://huachuca.army.mil/files/History_MHITCH.PDF, p.4.

the entire course of Civil War history. In order to reconnoitre the beach in front of
Veracruz in March 1847, Scott took a party of engineering officers with him in a
small boat, which duly drew fire from the gun emplacements of the Fort of San Juan
de Ulúa.[8] Aboard with Scott were Lee, George Meade, Joseph Johnston and Pierre
Beauregard; a single well-aimed Mexican shell could have robbed the Confederacy
and the Union of some of their most prominent future generals.

If Lee was unprepared to accept new intelligence methods, few amongst his government
were willing to argue against his astonishing success whilst in command of the Army
of Northern Virginia. Ignoring the scalps of Federal generals made redundant by Lee
and his commanders, however, experience should have taught Lee that his complex
operational plans were often beyond the capabilities of his army. His commanders were
scarcely able to keep up with his programme of manoeuvres even when operating on
their own soil, let alone in enemy territory. The Seven Days Battle had proved a spectacular success as the huge Federal force was stopped and thrown backwards through the
swamplands east of Richmond over a week of hard fighting. The attacks on McClellan's
forces required the coordination of his various corps to strike different sections of the
enemy in synchronous movements. In truth, however, the plans were actually poorly
executed and understandably so given the inexperience of Lee's commanders in handling
such large bodies of men and the tiny infrastructure in place to support them. The
desperate fighting of those defending their homeland and McClellan's inept handling of
his own army contributed as much to Lee's success as his complex tactics.

   While his commanders struggled to execute his plans, Lee's preference for retaining
a small staff and issuing verbal orders to them, to then communicate to his subordinates, had the potential to bare extremely bitter fruit. The attack on Malvern Hill, the
final act of the Seven Days, was a risky proposition at the best of times, with success
resting on a coordinated infantry strike following an intense artillery barrage to soften
up the Federal emplacements. Judging the success of the guns and the timing of the
attack, however, would be left up to brigade commander Lewis Armistead, thanks to
Lee's chief of staff Robert Chilton. Chilton translated the battle plans into a succinct
order: "Batteries have been established to act upon the enemy's line. If it is broken
as is probable, Armistead, who can witness the effect of the fire, has been ordered to
charge with a yell."[9] Armistead could hardly be expected not to attack with the whole
Army of Northern Virginia waiting for him and subsequent confusing orders to Lee's
other lieutenants, particularly John Magruder, resulted in the attack degenerating
into a piecemeal charge into the path of the Federal guns, which had most certainly
not been broken. Malvern Hill became the only outright defeat for Lee in the entire
operation and one that was entirely avoidable. The Rebels would lose more than 5,500
men on 1 July 1862, almost double the Federal total. "As each brigade emerged from

8   Eisenhower, John: *So Far From God* (New York: Anchor Books, 1989), p.258.
9   Sears, Stephen, *To the Gates of Richmond* (New York: Ticknor & Fields, 1992) p.317.

The battle of Malvern Hill, the final engagement of the Seven Days Battle.

the woods," wrote D.H. Hill, "from fifty to one hundred guns opened upon it, tearing great gaps in its ranks ... It was not war – it was murder."[10] It would also not be the last time that verbal orders passed by Lee through his staff officers would have potentially disastrous consequences.

However, the stunning victory of Chancellorsville and the relative ease of the earlier repulse of Burnside's attack on Fredericksburg had put the memories of Malvern Hill and Antietam far back in the Rebel consciousness and served to reinforce the lessons of Mexico and West Point. These were the lessons that Lee would draw upon when defining his military intelligence system. HUMINT acquisition south of the border had been limited to the personal observation of enemy positions and forces by professional soldiers and engineers. Such surveillance and reconnaissance operations could still be done by one's own troops (in the form of pickets, posted on the very periphery of the army as look-outs and guards), the cavalry or by guides attached to the army. Scouts and guides could either be professionals, employed for their abilities in covert observation, or civilians recruited for their specific understanding of the local conditions and terrain. Depending on the sophistication and experience of the scout, his efforts may be limited just to advising on the best pathway through difficult ground or evading enemy pickets and look-outs. Although certain talented, non-military scouts could provide greatly enhanced surveillance, many Civil War generals had far more primitive views on their duties and treated them as little more than educated guides, rather than potential intelligence resources. A legacy of the U.S. Corps of Engineers, tactical intelligence was often confined to providing corps commanders with the necessary understanding of how to get their armies moving and where to move them to, rather than gaining a better understanding of enemy characteristics. A knowledge of the local thoroughfares and their suitability for carrying men and arms was seen as satisfactory for success during the Mexican War and so, particularly in the early days of the Rebellion, few generals asked for anything more. This is not, however, to say that such basic information on local geography could not be hugely influential.

No incident better illustrates the power of local knowledge than Lee's startling victory at Chancellorsville. Joseph Hooker's astonishing covert manoeuvre, at the end of April 1863, threatened the Army of Northern Virginia with attack from both sides, but his hesitation in the impenetrable thickets of the Virginia 'Wilderness' gave Lee the opportunity to seize the initiative. With the enemy camped only a few miles away, during the evening of 1 May, James Power Smith of Thomas Jackson's corp stumbled across two men, sat on cracker boxes warming themselves over a fire; "I had but to rub my eyes and collect my wits to recognize the figures of Robert E. Lee and Stonewall Jackson."[11] The two greatest commanders of the Confederacy were concocting a daring plan for Jackson's Second Corps to march round Hooker's left flank, occupied by General Oliver Otis Howard's men of the XI Corps. The crucial question, however, would be how Jackson could navigate the thick underbrush without alerting the Federals of his passage. A former professor in the Virginia Military Institute and a staunchly religious man with an unusual habit of continually sucking on lemons, Jackson would no doubt have attributed the decisive intervention of a local guide down to Divine Providence.

As it happened, Jackson's chaplain, Beverly Tucker Lacy, had previously lived in the area of Chancellorsville and so was able to direct them to Charles Wellford, who revealed a little-known path around the Yankee pickets and right up to Howard's unwary troops.[12] It should be noted that Wellford was not a member of the Rebel military personnel, but a local community member and

General Thomas "Stonewall" Jackson, the fearsome Confederate leader of the Army of the Shenandoah.

11   *Battles and Leaders, Vol III*, p.205.
12   Sears, Stephen, *Chancellorsville* (Boston: Houghton Mifflin, 1996), p.234.

proud Virginian, therefore similarly dedicated to the cause. Being able to draw on the knowledge and casual observation of the local populace would be a form of intelligence denied to the Federal army for much of the War, since they would typically be the invading force. The absence of such supportive local citizens as a potential source of intelligence should have been of material concern for the Rebels, as Lee planned to lead them into Unionist Pennsylvania a year later.

To be truly valuable, any information gained on tactical position of the enemy and his environment would need to be augmented by intelligence on his composition, since an understanding of one's comparative strength prior to battle would have a meaningful effect on tactics, including whether the fight should be joined at all. A regular theme of the official reports of Civil War generals was the comparative numerical advantages that their adversaries seemed to hold over them before engagement. It could be viewed that these comments were judiciously added in attempt to pre-empt any blame for later failures, but in certain cases, most notably that of McClellan, poor ORBAT intelligence created total tactical paralysis. While scouts and amateur citizen spies could be excellent sources of information on the whereabouts and movements of an army, good ORBAT information acquisition would be limited to those individuals with appropriate experience to allow them to identify accurately the constitution of military forces. With the best will in the world, an amateur guide would probably not understand what makes a road suitable for an army, its artillery pieces and supply train, let alone be expected to count and identify regiments of thousands of men. Both of the senior generals during the Pennsylvania campaign were well aware of the dangers of using non-military sources to gather information for their armies. Lee would warn Secretary Seddon that "Information should be obtained by our own scouts ... not liable to excitement or exaggeration."[13] Hooker was a little more forthright with his intelligence staff: "employ only such persons as can look upon a body of armed men without being frightened out of their senses. Tell me whether it is infantry, cavalry, or artillery they have seen."[14]

Like Daniel Bissell during the Revolution, professional spies with military training were capable of extraordinary feats of surveillance if they were able to infiltrate an enemy. Such a task might sound extremely perilous, but could be accomplished safely by taking advantage of the rather loose nature of poorly trained volunteer regiments, since keeping a clear and reliable account of personnel was almost impossible. This would lead to a blurring of the lines between normal military surveillance and espionage, which would greatly increase the risk for those involved, given the severe punishments meted out for the latter. Socialite or working class spies living off the tittle-tattle of loose-lipped politicians or soldiers was one thing; spies in your own ranks was quite another and generals were far more sensitive to the loss of accurate tactical information than that of strategic. The Union would eventually formalise the

13   Dowdey, *The Wartime Papers*, p.387.
14   O.R. Series I, Vol. XXVII, Part III, p.225.

distinction between authentic scouts undertaking surveillance and spies through the prism of the level of deception being practiced. A scout would naturally be dressed in his regular uniform or normal civilian clothing (if not a soldier); a spy would be dressed mendaciously in enemy clothing in order to conceal his true identity.[15] The punishment for spying was execution and several men on both sides would fall foul of this distinction, such as Timothy Webster, a Union spy hanged in April 1862 after being implicated by Federal counterintelligence agents captured in Richmond.[16]

With Confederate spies flourishing throughout both the loyalist and rebellious states, the utility of professional spies was widespread and Lee was keen to exploit them as much as possible. Men like E. Pliny Bryan, Charles Cawood, Benjamin Franklin Stringfellow, Thomas Nelson Conrad and Henry Harrison would find considerable fame for their daring espionage activities during the War and proved often to be extremely effective in providing both strategic and tactical intelligence.[17] Brave and resourceful as these men were, however, the C.S.S.B. had not been designed to run multiple spies for the army. As a result, they were not formally integrated into any part of the military structure, but rather run as independent agents of specific commanders. Stringfellow became one of the most trusted agents of Jeb Stuart and towards the end of the War used the cover of a dental assistant in Alexandria on the south bank of the Potomac, opposite Washington. Before

Henry Harrison, Longstreet's spy.

the launch of the Gettysburg campaign, Jeb sent him into the Federal capital as part of a mission to harvest information on the Federal response, but not content with just one spy in the Federal capital, Stuart also sent Thomas Nelson Conrad to "report condition of things to these headquarters as soon as possible."[18] James Longstreet, meanwhile, also had a trusted agent and before he marched out of Fredericksburg in June, he had dispatched Henry Thomas Harrison on an identical assignment to that of Stringfellow and Conrad.

15   Jones, *A Rebel War Clerk's Diary*, p.325.
16   Jones, *A Rebel War Clerk's Diary*, p.119.
17   Many of the spies would publish tales of their daring to thrill audiences and enhance their own reputations, such as Thomas Nelson Conrad's *The Rebel Scout*.
18   Conrad, Thomas Nelson, *The Rebel Scout* (Washington: The National Publishing Company, 1904), p.81.

Longstreet first met Harrison earlier that year when he had been sent to Old Pete by Secretary Seddon. By the end of May he was "my scout Harrison" and sent to the Union capital "with secret orders, telling him that I did not care to see him till he could bring information of importance."[19]

While there would always be value in retaining independence between agents during espionage operations, the disaggregated structure practiced by the Confederate generals bred disorganisation and confusion. Harrison had previously been in the employ of Beauregard before being requisitioned by Longstreet and while this would prove a positive for the Rebel operations in Pennsylvania, General Lee would suffer the opposite effect. In the spring of 1863, Lee sent his personal favourite, E. Pliny Bryan of the C.S.B., across the Potomac to make observations on the Federal side of the river, only for him to be then dispatched by the War Department to Charleston to help General Beauregard. Bryan had been trained by Edward Porter Alexander, during his early foray into Confederate signalling, and then sent to Washington to gather information and transmit it back to Richmond.[20] This work later developed into the Secret Line, but it also meant that Bryan's services were in high demand. "Some of my best scouts are absent," Lee complained to Seddon "and Captain [E. P.] Bryan, of the signal corps, whom I had sent into Maryland to watch the river on that side, was, without my knowledge ... ordered to report to General Beauregard."[21] In contrast, the spy network run by the Federal Bureau of Military Information, which drew from its own agents such as well as the work of external spy networks (such as the Pennsylvanian citizen spies reporting to the Department of the Susquehanna in Harrisburg), was centralised to ensure that all information of substance would eventually find its way to the senior commander, General Hooker.

For all its potential effectiveness in gathering first-hand information, the abilities of scouts, guides and citizens to provide close observation of the enemy were constrained by the time and space he allowed you. During operations, armies would be in fluid motion and so difficulties in the tracking and observation of an enemy would be increased by the time taken to find and report back to one's own side. Throughout the Civil War, therefore, generals placed a great reliance on the quickest traditional method of scouting and reconnaissance: the cavalry. For Robert Lee, no better intelligence resource existed. For more than 50 years, since the Napoleonic Wars, the role of cavalry had been changing on the battlefield, from one of a potentially decisive offensive weapon to that of a skirmisher and protector of an army's flanks. The Crimean War had demonstrated the folly of charging against modern massed guns and, in truth, America had no tradition of utility of the cavalry charge as part of its martial strategy. Little of the terrain in the East was suitable for the tactical deployment of

---

19   Longstreet, *From Manassas to Appomattox*, p.333.
20   O.R. Series I, Vol. LI, Part II, p.341.
21   O.R. Series I, Vol. XXV, Part II, p.691.

troopers in sufficient numbers to be decisive in the field. Even by 1860, much of the mountainous and heavily wooded country between the Appalachians and the Atlantic was still uncultivated, making maintaining large numbers of horses logistically and economically prohibitive. Instead, the most effective use of cavalry was in destructive hit-and-run raids behind enemy lines, targeting their communication and supply, and as agents of both positive and counterintelligence.

Arguably the master of Confederate offensive cavalry tactics was Nathan Bedford Forrest, who terrorised the Union armies in the West right up to the point of Confederate surrender. Forrest fought with unbridled aggression at most of the major engagements in the West including Shiloh, Chickamauga and the siege of Fort Donelson, where, disgusted with plans to surrender, he fought his way out rather than capitulate to the hated Yankees. However, his understanding of the potential of the horse to provide mobility and elusiveness, coupled with the wider open spaces of the West, meant that he was most effective when launching daring raids against key Federal logistical targets. His attacks against Grant's supply bases and communications during December 1862, while the Federal General grappled with the conundrum of how to reach Vicksburg, put an end to any thought of an offensive that winter. Forrest inflicted around 2,000 Union casualties, while also destroying telegraph and rail lines, leaving Grant temporarily marooned in enemy territory. Ironically, however, after Forrest's attacks and the destruction of the Union supply base at Holly Springs, Grant was forced to resupply himself from the surrounding countryside and came to the realisation that it was possible for his army to become completely self-sufficient. "I was amazed at the quantity of supplies the country afforded," reflected Grant years later. "It showed that we could have subsisted off the country for two months instead of two weeks without going beyond the limits designated … Our loss of supplies was great at Holly Springs, but it was more than compensated for by those taken from the country and by the lesson taught."[22]

Although Forrest's attacks had considerable military benefit, the role of the cavalry in fact, played a far more important hand in the acquisition of critical operational and tactical HUMINT intelligence. "An army without cavalry in a strange and hostile country is as a man deprived of his eyesight and beset by enemies; he may be ever so brave and strong, but he cannot intelligently administer a single effective blow."[23] Cavalry superiority in the Civil War could be likened to air superiority today, where to control the neutral tactical space between the two military forces could accomplish both aggressive and defensive roles. As well as being able to strike quickly and gather information, troopers could play a role in counterintelligence by preventing the enemy getting close enough to perform his own scouting. With pickets protecting the front, the cavalry would often be positioned as guards on the flanks and to be on the watch for opportunities to plunge through gaps in the opposition. While the army was in

22   Grant, *Memoirs*, p.193.
23   *Annals*, p.307.

motion, and therefore vulnerable to attack from the side, cavalry units would create a mobile barrier between the two forces to prevent both attacks and enemy reconnaissance. Effective cavalry screening could allow an enemy separated only by a few miles to be left completely unaware of the movement of thousands of men for several days and certain members of the Confederacy, in particular, would master the art. This was particularly prevalent in the Eastern Theatre, where topographical features such as the Blue Ridge Mountains or the densely-forested Wilderness region of Virginia could provide their own natural protection from prying eyes.

A well-trained cavalry unit would be able to cover large distances and get much closer to the enemy with a greater chance of successfully returning to his own lines than any foot-soldier. This is, however, not to say that additional speed meant that cavalry surveillance was necessarily safer. Improvements in accuracy and range of infantry rifles were no less effective against a mounted solider than one on foot and generals were particularly susceptible. Two of the finest generals never to have the chance of making a substantial contribution to the Battle of Gettysburg were shot on horseback whilst making tactical observations in close contact with the enemy. While Stonewall Jackson would not live to see the start of the Gettysburg campaign, after being shot off his horse in the dusk of the first day of Chancellorsville, General John Reynolds of the I Corps was shot and killed on arrival at the battlefield on the morning of 1 July.

Universally respected and liked within the Army of the Potomac, Reynolds would pass over the chance to lead it into battle, but would still play a critical role in the preceding days that would help shape the result. A Rebel sharpshooter, however, would ensure that his involvement would be limited to only a few hours and leave the Federal force scrambling for leadership during those crucial opening phases. With

Leader of the Federal I Corps, General John Reynolds is shot by a Rebel sharp-shooter at the beginning of the battle of Gettysburg.

the commanding general yet to take the field, Reynolds' death meant that control of the Federal army on the field passed between no fewer than seven generals during the opening phase of the battle.

The undisputed champion of the Rebel cavalry in the Eastern Theatre was James Ewell Brown Stuart, a young and ebullient trooper, who became the chief cavalry officer for the Army of Northern Virginia. Arthur Fremantle, who met most of the senior generals of Lee's army after he joined them in Pennsylvania, recounted that, unlike the unashamedly aggressive Forrest, Jeb's cavalry corps was less inclined to fight than others. His preference for horsemanship than gun-play, however, in no way protracted from his abilities and even Stuart's opponents such as General John Sedgwick credited him as "the best cavalryman ever foaled in North America."[24] So effective was Jeb at acquiring and interpreting vital pieces of intelligence for Lee that he was the closest Lee ever had to an intelligence analyst. Dashing and courageous, his undoubted military skill was matched with a natural daring and sense of flamboyancy and Jeb would burst upon the Civil War stage with an extraordinary piece of reconnaissance improvisation during McClellan's Peninsula campaign.

As it happened, Lee and Stuart's path to Civil War collaboration had been set in motion even before cessation, when U.S. Army Colonel Lee directed the young lieutenant of the First Regiment of Cavalry to parlay a peace with firebrand abolitionist John Brown, whose seizure of the arsenal at Harper's Ferry catalysed the North/South divisions over slavery.[25] Perhaps ironically, Jeb, like many of his countrymen, was initially less than enthusiastic about Lee replacing Joe Johnston, believing him to be too conservative.[26] Stuart had little taste for the legacy of Robert Lee's West Point education, which led the defender

General James "Jeb" Stuart, Lee's most trusted cavalry officer.

24   *Annals*, p.665.
25   *Annals*, p.666.
26   Beckett, Ian, *The War Correspondents: The American Civil War* (Dover: Alan Sutton, 1993), p.59.

of Richmond to reach for the pick and the shovel rather than for the musket and sabre. The prioritisation of proper trenches and fortifications around the Confederate capital brought catcalls of "Granny Lee" and the "King of Spades" from the media, but these would quickly fade as McClellan's massive army hove into view. It did not take long, however, for both Stuart and Lee to realise each other's quality and it would not take the Federals much longer.

On assuming command of the Army of Northern Virginia, Lee immediately sought to assume the initiative against the ponderous McClellan and sent Jeb out to scout the Federal right flank, believing it to be 'in the air' (unprotected by a natural obstacle). Stuart executed Lee's orders with his usual efficiency, assisted by a young cavalry officer named John Singleton Mosby, and quickly identified that Fitz-John Porter's First Division of the III Corps was separated from the rest of the Army of the Potomac by the Chickahominy river. This left the door open for Stonewall Jackson, returning from the Shenandoah Valley, to march down on Porter from the northwest. This intelligence precipitated the engagements at Mechanicsville and Gaines Mill, the first in the string of contests which became the Seven Days Battle, but Jeb would not be satisfied with a simple reconnaissance. Having provided the critical tactical intelligence with which Lee could formulate his plan, Stuart then faced the dilemma of whether to turn back and end his ride or continue and risk being isolated by the Union army. Barely pausing for thought, he struck out on a rapid circuitous gallop around the entire Army of the Potomac, purely for the glory of it. Such daring arrogance instantly won him the love of the Southern people and the trust of Robert Lee. This partnership, forged on the Peninsula, would become arguably the most effective tactical intelligence force in the Confederacy and their relationship would evolve into a near personal dependence. "He was the eyes and ears and strong right arm of the commander"[27] wrote G. Moxley Sorrell and, on learning of his death in May 1864, the usually reserved Lee could scarcely hide his emotion, claiming, "I can scarcely think of him without weeping."[28]

It would be wrong, however, to believe that Jeb was the sole cavalry intelligence resource available to the Rebels as he was aided in the Eastern Theatre by the "Gray Ghost" John Mosby. Mosby had joined the 1st Virginia Cavalry before being appointed to Stuart's personal staff. Having won Jeb's trust during his scouting of the Federal positions on the Peninsula, Mosby persuaded Stuart to allow him to form a small band of men for scouting and raiding operations in northern and central Virginia. "Mosby's Partisan Rangers", (latterly formally adopted into the Army of Northern Virginia as the 43rd Battalion Virginia Cavalry)[29] proved to be a constant menace to all Federal activities, providing not only good information on their activities, but

---

27   Sorrell, *Recollections*, p.163.
28   *Annals*, p.665.
29   O.R. Series I, Vol. XXV, Part II, p.857; Stuart dubbed the men "Mosby's Regulars" since he deemed the term Partisan Ranger to be "in bad repute".

also participating in numerous raids. So effective were Mosby's operations that, by mid-1864, he officially declared his own 'Confederacy' in the region between Aldie and the Blue Ridge Mountains. During the start of the Gettysburg campaign, Hooker and his cavalry commander Alfred Pleasanton were so concerned by Mosby's potential threat that they even tried to bribe him to turn against his Southern comrades. "Do not hesitate as to the matter of money" was the instruction to Pleasonton.[30] Sadly their plan was foiled by being unable to catch him, but the Gray Ghost's dedication to the Rebel cavalry would continue beyond the War and Mosby would become one of the most impassioned defenders of Stuart and his actions during the Gettysburg campaign.

John Singleton Mosby, the "Gray Ghost" and leader of the Partisan Rangers.

A good cavalry, however, was a precision instrument and, as the Federals in particular would learn, constituted far more than just soldiers on horses. If Stuart was the lynchpin of information collection for the Confederate generals, unfortunately very few of his Federal counterparts in the East could also claim to be such an effective asset. Although certainly not lacking in skill, the Federal cavalry was widely mismanaged by the army and poorly led by their corps commanders for much of the early part of the War. Heavy criticism was levelled at the Federal cavalry for their performance during the period between 1862 and 1863 (and it is hard to deny their deficiencies), but it must also be noted that they were often used more as an offensive, rather than intelligence force. No one would learn this lesson harder than John Pope, who displayed for all to see how the cavalry could be turned from your greatest strength into your greatest weakness. Pope, the hero of Island Number 10 on the Mississippi, had been called over to the East in mid-1862 to link his Army of Virginia with McClellan's Army of the Potomac, now extracted from the Peninsula. Sensing that the opportunity was greater than the threat, Lee pulled his army out of Richmond and sent an advanced Rebel

30 O.R. Series I, Vol. XXVII, Part III, p.72.

column under Stonewall Jackson to harry Pope and stop him from joining McClellan. A second column under James Longstreet was then launched to crush him in a pincer. Relentless cavalry reconnaissance ensured that Pope was wise to the danger and made aware that, if he could avoid the closing jaws of the two wings of Lee's army, he had the opportunity to beat each independently. Sadly for Pope, he was facing a tactical master, this time it was Thomas Jackson in his element.

Stonewall had gained a reputation for eccentricity, stern devoutness and astonishing aggression in equal measure. "Throughout this war it has been the practice of General Jackson to throw himself, disregarding his own inferiority of numbers upon large bodies of his enemy," opined British journalist Francis Lawley reporting in November 1862. With no little prescience, Lawley continued, "the day is ordinarily half-won by the suddenness and desperation of the attack."[31] A few months earlier, Jackson had given a masterclass in guerrilla warfare to the hapless Federal generals Nathaniel P. Banks and John C. Frémont in the Shenandoah Valley. Using his detailed knowledge of the terrain, as a born and bred Valley-man, and by utilising a fearsome combination of stealth and extreme speed[32] his 17,000 strong 'Army of the Shenandoah' tied up no fewer than 60,000 Federal troops. With repeated 'peek-a-boo' strikes against his larger opponents, Jackson prevented these additional troops from marching against Richmond from the west as McClellan's launched his Peninsula campaign from the east.

Now it was poor General Pope's turn. Desperate to locate Jackson's men, the Yankee general ran his horsemen to the point of exhaustion. When Jackson finally presented himself for battle in late August, at almost the exact spot of the first Rebel victory on the banks of the Bull Run creek, Pope's horses were shattered from days of galloping around Centreville looking for him. He had lost his principal tactical intelligence resource and was unaware of Lee's reinforcements arriving from the south. Despite the brevity of his tenure of command in the East, Pope had at least showed an awareness of the value of acquiring good tactical intelligence, but his reliance on the cavalry would be his downfall. Having already destroyed most of his popular support with provocatively boasting speeches about his success in the West, few in the East would weep as he was sent back.[33] Meanwhile, less than a day's march away, George McClellan held back his army in spite of pleas from Washington to hasten to Pope's aid. "Again I have been called upon to save the country,"[34] he would write to his wife; command of the Federal forces in the East was Little Mac's once more, just as the Army of Northern Virginia was shaping to pounce on Maryland. It would not be until the arrival of General Joe Hooker that the cavalry was finally organised into its own

---

31   Beckett, *The War Correspondents*, p.78.
32   So hard did Jackson march his men that they won the nickname "foot cavalry".
33   Beckett, *The War Correspondents*, p.62: "Drunkards, when sober, do not relish the spectacle of another man's intoxication, and a blustering public, does not look with complacency upon a blustering General".
34   Sears, Stephen, *George B. McClellan, The Young Napoleon* (New York: Ticknor & Fields, 1988), p.263.

division, rather than being an extension of the infantry. Even Fighting Joe, however, would first have to be reprised of the deficiencies of the Federal cavalry before he achieved any progress. His senior cavalry officer, General George Stoneman, gave a masterclass in how to mismanage his tactical duties and a fundamental component to the Chancellorsville campaign would utterly fail under his watch.

So as Robert Lee prepared to lead his army from the relative safety of Fredericksburg to pick a fight with a bigger opponent on his home turf, his narrow and traditionalist view of the purpose and utility of military intelligence would limit his acquisition strategy to the reconnaissance work of Jeb, a handful of professional spies and a steady flow of Northern news from Richmond. During the early days of the Gettysburg campaign, until his cavalry could be unleashed into the neutral spaces of Virginia to monitor the Federal pursuit, Lee was more concerned with counterintelligence than positive intelligence. His operational plan was predicated on getting ahead of the Army of the Potomac until he could get his men into the protection of the Shenandoah Valley. Thus, he would need to withdraw from Fredericksburg and the watching eyes of General Hooker gradually, so as not to arouse suspicion. If Hooker got wind of the withdrawal of the Army of Northern Virginia westward and away from its base, he could strike either at Lee's rear or directly against Richmond. The division of his army and the retention of A.P. Hill at Fredericksburg, while his two other corps moved north, served the dual purpose of protecting his rear and disguising his movements. He could expect little help from Richmond as he began his operations, since the inherent intelligence system was not structured to acquire the form of intelligence he required. Furthermore, as the distances between him and his War Department increased, so the relevance and value of the information they provided decreased. In spite of these challenges, his confidence in the ability of his army, born of his recent victories, gave him few causes for concern. Lee had proven time and again that, by seizing the initiative, he could overcome any discrepancies in numbers and tactics. In leading a campaign north, Lee could secure the advantage of getting ahead of the Yankees and choosing the location where the final engagement would take place. By spring 1863, so great was his self-assurance that later, with typically insightful hindsight, the new Federal Union cavalry commander, Alfred Pleasonton, would judge that Lee had broken one of the underlying principles of war: never hold your enemy in contempt.[35]

35 *Annals*, p.457.

4

To Punish Any Force of the Enemy

To undertake such an ambitious plan with such extraordinary risks less than a year after the failure of a similar operation might seem needlessly foolhardy, but Lee was no fool. What he may have lacked in appreciation in the advantages of modern military intelligence, he compensated for in aggressive war-craft and an ability to see into the psyche of his opponent. His inability to adapt to the abounding innovations might leave Lee potentially vulnerable to a more open-minded enemy, but fortunately most of his peers were no better at identifying the potentially revolutionary opportunities of intelligence acquisition and interpretation being developed. By the summer of 1863, Lee still did not believe that there was a Federal general capable of beating him on the battlefield. Perhaps more significantly, he was keenly aware of the strategic burden that Washington placed on its military and he knew how to exploit it.

By the start of the year, the Army of the Potomac was approaching its nadir. General Ambrose Burnside had had the greatness of command thrust upon him, having previously refused it on John Pope's demise. Having been thwarted in his attempts to stop Lee digging in around the town of Fredericksburg, Burnside was obliged to undertake punishing attempts to cross the Rappahannock and to overwhelm or outflank the entrenched Rebel soldiers with his Grand Divisions. Having launched himself across the river in mid-December, Burnside made two coordinated attacks on the Rebel flanks. While some success was found on the Confederate right, where Burnside had unfortunately chosen not to commit fully, the left side (commanded by Bull Sumner and Fighting Joe) turned into a killing field as the Federal soldiers charged over a dozen times against the raking artillery fire positioned on the ridge of Marye's Heights. The Union suffered around 12,500 casualties while the Confederacy lost less than half that number. The bravery and savage handling of the Yankee charges drew both admiration and disgust: "It is well that war is so terrible," Lee would confide to James Longstreet, "we should grow too fond of it!"[1] Few others could share his military purist's point of view. "There, in every altitude of death, lying so close to each

---

1   Douglas Southall Freeman, *R.E. Lee: A Biography, 4 vols* (New York, 1934-35, II pg 463).

The battle of Fredericksburg, a severe defeat for General Ambrose Burnside's Army
of the Potomac.

other that you might step from body to body, lay acres of the Federal dead" reported
Francis Lawley. "By universal consent of those who have seen all the great battles of
this war, nothing like it has ever been seen before."[2]

In the cold and mud of the winter of 1862, the morale of the Army of the Potomac
sank. Burnside barely complained when he was stripped of leadership of the Army of
the Potomac and packaged off to run the Department of the Ohio in Cincinnati, until
he learnt that his replacement was Joe Hooker. For the fourth time in barely two years,
Lincoln was looking for a new leader and with limited options for a replacement, the
president made the personally uncomfortable step of turning to Fighting Joe. Hooker
had been scheming against the McClellanite Burnside even before his second attempt to
march on Fredericksburg in January literally got stuck in the mud. Once again, the president would rise above the petty squabbling of his generals and made the decision for the
greater good. Just as Burnside was bringing charges against Hooker for "having been
guilty of unjust and unnecessary criticism of the actions of his superior officers ... having
... endeavored to create distrust in the minds of officers who have associated with him,

2   Beckett, *The War Correspondents*, p.83.

and for habitually speaking in disparaging terms of other officers,"[3] Lincoln was enacting the change of command. Hooker's machinations, however, had not gone unnoticed in Washington and the president was quick to mark his card, "I think that during General Burnside's command of the army you have taken counsel of your ambition," concluded Lincoln to Hooker, "and thwarted him as much as you could."[4]

Unlike President Davis, the Federal commander-in-chief and former lawyer, Abraham Lincoln had little formal military training. Having inherited an existing structure of army and government, he delegated martial responsibility largely to his War Department. Understandably, therefore, Lincoln had much less interaction with operational

General Ambrose Burnside.

and tactical military affairs, but held the reins over a strategic policy on which he was steadfast: restoration of the Union at all costs. While he was willing to stay out of the preparation of operational plans, the ruthlessness with which he adhered to and enforced his strategy upon his generals was extraordinary. In the Eastern Theatre alone McDowell, McClellan (twice), Pope and now Burnside had all succumbed to Lincoln's relentless demands for progress, fuelled itself by his own precarious position as the democratically elected sponsor of an increasingly unpopular war.

The brilliant, but ageing, Winfield Scott had provided a strategy for victory, based on a suffocation of the nascent Confederacy by surrounding her by land and sea. He believed that this strategy would end the War "in two or three years, by a young and able general – a Wolfe, a Dessaix, or a Hoche – with three hundred thousand disciplined men (kept up to that number)."[5] Three years from April 1861, however, would require success in one mid-term election and give him little contingency for delays before the next presidential election. Such an attritional strategy over an extended period was too great a risk for a leader whose power rested on the goodwill of his people and so he needed results quickly. Lincoln understood that this was not a fight to overcome another nation; this was a fight for unity and that there could be no half-measures. Since the South was not yet an independent nation, but rather a collection

3   Macartney, *Lincoln and his Generals*, p.135.
4   O.R. Series I, Vol. XXV, Part II, p.4.
5   Macartney, *Lincoln and his Generals*, p.18-19.

of like-minded states, it had no historical centre of power and so only the destruction of its ability to resist (specifically its army), not its cities was the quickest way to victory. Ultimately, the death knell for the Confederacy would not be the seizure of Richmond in April 1865, but the surrender of the Army of Northern Virginia at Appomattox a week later when "the structure of the Confederacy, losing its key-stone, fell with a resounding crash."[6] Infusing that strategy into the operational objectives of the generals, however, was a constant struggle for the War Department. "In all our interview I have urged that our first objective was not Richmond," bemoaned the new General-in-Chief, Henry Halleck, to the departing Ambrose Burnside, "but the defeat or scattering of Lee's army."[7] While his generals would be free to select their own method of bringing about the end of Southern resistance, Lincoln and the War Department in Washington watched their every move and the president himself would often be found prowling the offices of the US Military Telegraph Service to read first hand dispatches from the field.

Hooker, like his predecessors, would be allowed extraordinary latitude not only in preparing his army and executing his operations, but also in his conduct towards his superiors. Throughout the war, Lincoln would have to stomach some extraordinary arrogance from his generals, none more so than from George McClellan. Little Mac's diaries and letters would later revealed the true depths of his conceit, referring to Lincoln as a baboon and a gorilla, but his behaviour left little doubt as to his character. In one infamous incident, before the general had even started to prove his value on the battlefield, the President of the United States paid him a visit at his house in Washington to discuss events. Not only would Little Mac keep his commander-in-chief waiting over an hour, but, on returning to his house, he walked right past Lincoln and retired to bed without a word. Few would begrudge Honest Abe if he had sacked McClellan right then and there, but with the self-effacing pragmatism that would make him such a powerful figure in American history, Lincoln ignored the personal sleight. "Never mind," was his phlegmatic response, "I will hold McClellan's horse if he will only bring us success." In light of these difficulties, it is little wonder that the straight-talking General Grant would find such an avid supporter in Washington.

Although, certainly not as invasive as Davis, Lincoln as commander-in-chief did make some political demands of the army, specifically in the appointment of certain generals. His Republican majority government was finely balanced between staunch abolitionists within his own party and Southern-friendly Democrats. With his term of office still to run just four years, he was forced to play the political game throughout the War, including the appointment of civilian politicians to senior command positions in order to curry favour with certain states. Much would be made of the wisdom of allowing men like Daniel Sickles (appointed to command of the III Corps of the

6   Swinton, William, *Campaigns of the Army of the Potomac* (New York: Charles Scribner's Sons, 1892), p.622.
7   O.R. Series I, Vol. XXV, Part II, p.13.

Army of the Potomac) to lead men into battle, although it would not be correct to believe that such political influence on the army was purely negative. None other than Ulysses Grant would attribute his own reinstatement to the U.S. Army to Governor Robert Yates of his home state of Illinois, after he had unsuccessfully appealed to the Adjutant-General, (and his promotion to brigadier-general was also subsequently elicited by Illinois politicians in Washington).[8] History may have been very different if politics had not helped the most successful Federal general of the War to be accepted back.

Political pressures would see the president forced to deal in a currency of favour and privilege with his

Federal President Abraham Lincoln.

peers, but it was the ever fluctuating public opinion that would be at the forefront of his mind and would have the greatest influence on his relationship with his generals. With an army of volunteers and the front line sometimes little more than 25 miles from the capital, operations in the East pivoted between the desire for annihilation of Southern independence and the requirement for protection of the great cities of the North, especially Washington. Unlike the Confederacy, the loss of the seat of American government would almost certainly see the intervention of a foreign power and a capitulation to the copperheads. Tactical losses in the field could be damaging and would take an inevitable toll on the will of his people to continue the struggle; the loss of a major city would be unthinkable. On taking over command of the army, Hooker's instruction contained two central planks that defined Federal strategy in the Eastern Theatre:

> In regard to the operations of your own army, you can best judge when and where it can move to the greatest advantage, keeping in view always the importance of covering Washington and Harper's Ferry, either directly or by so operating as to be able to punish any force of the enemy sent against them.[9]

8   Grant, *Memoirs*, p.105-6,111.
9   *Report of the Joint Committee*) Part I, p.XLII.

This 'Lincolnian dichotomy' of both offensive and defensive responsibilities served to detach strategic objectives from operational planning. The dual objectives were not mutually compatible and Washington would seek to dictate which had priority at any given moment. As such, Hooker would have to coordinate his operational plans with Lincoln's strategic views. Satisfying these "Herculean tasks"[10] had already proved too much for George McClellan, who had placed the blame squarely on the president for the failure of the Peninsula campaign. After Lincoln blocked the release of an additional 50,000 troops from their duties guarding the western flank of Washington, to augment his already bloated army in front of Richmond, Little Mac vented: "If I save this army now, I tell you plainly that I owe no thanks to you or to any other persons in Washington. You have done your best to sacrifice this army."[11] McClellan's petulance was an early sign of the difficulties to come for any future leader of the Army of the Potomac and Hooker was no exception. These combined responsibilities also meant that Hooker's intelligence, unlike Lee's, would need to be able to adapt to work on both strategic and tactical levels at very short notice.

Despite this fracture in their strategic visions, however, the partnership of Lincoln and Hooker breathed new life into the army. Even General Darius Couch, a man who had resigned from the army in protest at Hooker's bungling of Chancellorsville, admitted that "I have never known men to change from a condition of the lowest depression to that of a healthy fighting."[12] General Lee, however, was not impressed by Mr F.J. Hooker's administrative skill nor did he put much stock in the ability of the Army of the Potomac. In full knowledge of the burden Hooker's Lincolnian dichotomy, which would compel the Federal general to assume the defensive upon learning of any aggressive move from Fredericksburg, Lee was assured to have the initiative as he started his march north. Not until the War Department was sure that Washington was not the primary objective would they release the Army of the Potomac to go in search of the Rebels. By then, Lee was confident that he would have had sufficient time to prepare a suitable welcome for Fighting Joe. Provided that his tactical intelligence operations were successfully monitoring the approaching Federal army, Lee felt no need to maintain communications with Richmond in advance of any battle.

If Lee and his generals could be accused of failing to appreciate the opportunities for military intelligence strategy provided by the advance of technology, then their opponents in the North were doubly culpable. For all their pioneering spirit that had carried them down the path of industrialisation and away from the traditional culture still ingrained in the South, the Yankees dismally failed to encourage the deployment

---

10   *Battles and Leaders, Vol II*, p.161.
11   *Battles and Leaders, Vol. II*, p.438; When McClellan's message actually reached the telegraph office in Washington, the supervisor was so shocked by the final statement that he deleted it before it reached Stanton or Lincoln.
12   *Battles and Leaders, Vol III*, p.119.

of new intelligence methods. With the legacy of the ante-bellum U.S. Army, the various military intelligence initiatives already in incubation and the greater proliferation of communications advances, such as the telegraph system and railroad, it would be natural to assume that the North would be quicker to break the mould of traditional doctrine. Unfortunately, the humiliation of the first major battle would shape the development of the Federal intelligence effort and revert it towards entrenched traditional methods.

When the army of the Federal Department of Northeastern Virginia, under Irvin McDowell, confronted General Pierre Gustave Toutant Beauregard's Army of the Potomac in July 1861, Washington and the Northern people expected a swift thrashing would sweep the Rebel army out of northern Virginia, open up the overland route to Richmond and put an end to the ridiculous claims for independence. Both were veterans of the Mexican War, but McDowell had five divisions totalling around 35,000 men while the Rebel army only had around 20,000. Cognisant of their deficiencies, the Rebels looked to exploit anything that might give them an advantage against the greater Yankee numbers, including their interior lines and innovative applications of military intelligence. Beauregard had occupied the crucial railway junction at Manassas, which joined the Manassas Gap Railroad, which ran west across the Blue Ridge Mountains, with the Orange and Alexandria Railroad, which ran north to Washington. Between his army and Joseph Johnston's 11,000 strong Army of the Shenandoah, stationed south of Winchester sixty miles west, they held the 'Alexandria Line', blocking the overland route to Richmond. Beauregard's and Johnston's armies, therefore, were joined by rail and telegraph between both each other and the Confederate capital, thereby giving them a distinct tactical communications advantage. This tactical advantage was enhanced by Edward Porter Alexander's fledgling signalling operation and complemented by a flow of strategic information from Thomas Jordan's network of espionage agents in Washington via Richmond's evolving Secret Line.

McDowell's tactical plan was straightforward: to hit Beauregard from the north across the Bull Run by making a sweeping movement around Sudley Church and turning the Rebel left, which would be held in place by demonstrations at the Stone Bridge, in the centre of the line. The intelligence effort which preceded the formulation of these tactics was equally simple and McDowell only ordered basic reconnaissance by his engineers on the enemy positions around Manassas to assess their weaknesses.[13] As McDowell himself reflected in his official report after the battle, the objective of the movement was to interpose himself between Beauregard and Johnston and cut the Alexandria Line. The principal risk, obviously, would be Johnston moving across from the West along the very rail line that he was trying to sever and combining with Beauregard to draw up "certainly much more than we

13 O.R. Series I, Vol. II, p.307-8.

[McDowell's army] attacked them with."[14] Johnston was currently held in check by General Robert Patterson and his 18,000 men stationed north, between the Army of the Shenandoah and Harper's Ferry. Despite being aware of "rumors" that Johnston had joined Beauregard,[15] McDowell undertook no coordinated intelligence effort to improve his understanding of the operational situation and plan accordingly. Instead, he relied on his engineers' reports on the Rebel position and the assumption that the Patterson threat was enough to hold Johnston in place.

The Confederates were not leaving anything up to assumption. After it was clear that McDowell was planning to make his move, Beauregard, Johnston and Davis set the telegraph lines buzzing. Left to decide whether to order Beauregard to withdraw from Manassas or allow him to strike at the Federals (as the sparky Creole general desired), Jefferson Davis ordered Johnston east, an action made with rightful disregard for the threat of Patterson. Johnston had been monitoring the enemy movements throughout June and early July using his scouts, pickets and cavalry and judged that, even with Patterson in pursuit, his proximity to the Manassas Gap Railroad would give him the speed necessary to reach Beauregard before Patterson could stop him.[16] For a veteran solider, who had been given instructions to hold Johnston in position, Patterson's conduct during the days before First Bull Run was woeful. On 18 July, the day Johnston marched to Manassas, Patterson telegraphed Scott to assure him that "The enemy has stolen no march on me. I have kept him actively employed, and by threats and reconnaissance in force caused him to be reinforced."[17] On the eve of the battle, he would be obliged to report that "With a portion of his force Johnston left Winchester by the road to Millwood on the afternoon of the 18th. His whole force was about thirty-five thousand two hundred."[18] How could such a highly-experienced officer have allowed a significant opposing force to disappear from under his very nose? The key to Patterson's ignorance was the effective screening work of an up-and-coming Confederate cavalry officer, Colonel James E. B. Stuart, who had been assigned to support Thomas Jackson. Stuart had been scouting the terrain around Harper's Ferry and Winchester efficiently in the build-up to the battle, but his real triumph came in the shielding of Johnston's movement away from Patterson and thereby allowing the Rebels to match McDowell's surprise attack with close to equal numbers.

Johnston's march to reinforce the Army of the Potomac would be decisive in settling the result of the battle, but credit for the timely decision would be attached to someone neither in northern Virginia or Richmond. Whether Rose Greenhow's tip-offs of 12 and 16 July made a significant difference when battle was finally joined on

---

14   O.R. Series I, Vol. II, p.325.
15   O.R. Series I, Vol. II, p.308.
16   O.R. Series I, Vol. II, p.172.
17   O.R. Series I, Vol. II, p.168.
18   O.R. Series I, Vol. II, p.172.

the 21st is less certain. General Order 17 putting his army in motion was indeed given by McDowell on 16 July,[19] the day of Greenhow's final warning to Beauregard, but the plan of attack had been approved by Scott a week earlier. Furthermore, Beauregard had already acquired a significant intelligence asset, a captured clerk in McDowell's adjutant-general's office, who freely imparted his invaluable ORBAT and operational information. What was missing from Ms Greenhow's information and any of the military intelligence in Rebel possession on the night of 20 July was McDowell's actual tactical plan for flanking Beauregard's left and, with Johnston's army still arriving during the day of the battle, it was a different source of intelligence that would prevent disaster.

Sat on the a small hill next to Mr Wilcoxen's farm in the far eastern flank of Beauregard's army on the morning of 21 July, watching the summer sun push away the shadows from the Virginia fields stretched out before him, was Captain Edward Porter Alexander. In light of his work with Albert Myer, Alexander had been ordered to report to Beauregard in order to establish signal stations overlooking the Bull Run area and he had wasted no time in setting up three stations spanning the width of the Confederate line. With the rising sun behind him, Alexander spotted the glimmer of metal amongst the fields beyond their left side and, quickly deducing that this was a major force of the enemy, he signalled directly to Colonel Evans at the Stone Bridge, "Look out for your left; you are turned."[20] Demonstrations against various points in the Rebel line had been ongoing since just after 5:00 a.m., but with the aid of this additional piece of information Evans (and later Johnston), was convinced that this was the main Union thrust. He therefore promptly abandoned his duel with the Federal 1st Division over the Stone Bridge, who had been ordered to keep Evans busy, and turned to meet the oncoming McDowell. Evans was soon joined by the vanguard of Johnston's force, the brigades of General Bernard Bee and Thomas Jackson, who had been sent to reinforce the Rebel left after also being signalled by Alexander.[21] While Evans resisted the onslaught from McDowell as well as could be expected, it was the additional numbers of Bee and Jackson that proved the difference and ultimately converted near defeat into stirring victory for the South. Whilst the battle of First Bull Run would become forever synonymous with one name, Thomas "Stonewall" Jackson,[22] in intelligence circles it would be Rose Greenhow and not Edward Porter Alexander who would have her name carved into the legend of that particular battle. Greenhow would become probably the most celebrated spy of the War and a global

---

19   O.R. Series I, Vol. II, p.303.
20   Alexander, *Military Memoirs*, p.30.
21   O.R. Series I, Vol. II, p.474.
22   Jackson was supposedly christened by General Bee's rallying cry of "See Jackson standing like a stone wall," as he established a defensive line at Henry House Hill and stopped the Rebel rout. Alexander also noted that the same description would later be given by Joseph Johnston to Colonel James Preston, but there would be no Stonewall Preston (Alexander, *Military Memoirs*, p.36).

celebrity, while Alexander would decline an offer to lead the Confederate signal corps in favour of a position in the artillery.

As a consequence of the shambolic defeat of their army at Bull Run, the existing paranoia in Washington concerning Rebel spies was enflamed. Rather than turning their attention towards the tactical military intelligence failures of the battle, the Union would focus their attention on counterespionage. With the shock of that first defeat, the Federal Secret Service was created to correct the supposed mismatch in intelligence shown during the battle. It was no great surprise, therefore, that the first military intelligence operations would be undertaken by the most efficient counterespionage agent in the Union, Alan Pinkerton. A Scot whose National Detective Agency in Chicago ran well into the 20th Century, Pinkerton had worked for the Federal government in

Edward Porter Alexander, a colleague of Albert Myer and James Longstreet's senior artillery officer at the battle of Gettysburg.

investigating rumours of an assassination plot against the newly elected Abraham Lincoln as he travelled from Springfield, Illinois, to the capital. Pinkerton's work led to Lincoln being sneaked into Washington under cover of darkness a day before his inauguration and he would soon be tasked with counterintelligence operations in and around Washington. It would be "Mr E.J. Allen" (Pinkerton's *nom de guerre*) who would eventually expose and arrest Rose Greenhow. George McClellan, during his time as chief engineer of the Illinois Central Railroad, had worked closely with Pinkerton's Agency, which provided "various operations affecting their [Central Railroad's] interests." Again, it would be to Pinkerton that the new commander of Federal forces in the East turned in order to service his intelligence requirements "in the organization of a secret service for his department."[23]

Just as the operational freedoms that Lincoln granted his generals would be exploited by Hooker to create an enviable intelligence apparatus, it had the opposite effect in the hands of a less sophisticated commander like George McClellan. Pinkerton's

---

23   O.R. Series II, Vol. II, p.569; Pinkerton, Allan, *The Spy of the Rebellion Being a True History of the Spy System of the United States Army during the Late Rebellion* (New York: Dillingham 1883), p.459-460, 139.

appointment as "Chief of the Federal Secret Service" (a seemingly self-appointed title) came in tandem with the rise to prominence of Little Mac from the ashes of the First Battle of Bull Run, as he commandeered the Agency to supply him with intelligence. A product of the private investigations system, the Federal Secret Service relied almost entirely on non-military information acquisition methods, primarily developed from counterespionage, and employed no current or former soldiers. Evolved from a system designed to acquire information for an existing interpretive justice system, Pinkerton's new Secret Service had little analytical capability of its own. As such, it was simply neither capable of providing a centralised structure able to adapt to the fluid demands of operations and tactics nor interpreting acquired information into usable intelligence. The results were vastly inflated ORBAT estimates of the Rebel forces, which instilled in his commanding officer paranoia of being constantly outnumbered. The Rebels would be estimated to have sometimes hundreds of thousands of men, even though the largest army ever assembled by the Confederacy was the 90,000 strong force collected together under Johnston and then Lee in the defence of Richmond in 1862. Unfortunate instances of Pinkerton's dreadful work litter the historical record of the Civil War, despite attempts afterwards to justify it in the face of overwhelming contrary evidence. Even when it was known that the opposing force had been subdivided, the Federal Secret Service would still inadvertently cook the books. Commenting on the battle of Antietam, Pinkerton would defiantly state "My own judgement is, that at no time during the fight was the Confederate army ever confronted with a force outnumbering its own."[24] Although he would attempt to justify this view by pointing out that McClellan only used four of his six corps, Pinkerton's shocking ORBAT still failed to account for the fact that A.P. Hill would not arrive until midway through the following day.

When judging the work of the Federal Secret Service, however, it should not be forgotten that Pinkerton's was a tactical intelligence role. He reported directly to McClellan and so it would be wrong to focus too much blame away from the commanding general responsible for overseeing the collection and implementation of his intelligence. In truth, McClellan did not need the spectre of inflated enemy numbers to paralyse his operations, since he was more than capable of doing that himself. Having assumed command of the Army of the Potomac in August 1861, it would take months of goading by Lincoln and the War Department to force Little Mac to stop drilling his new army and march it out into the field. His first act as leader of the premier Federal offensive force in the Eastern Theatre was to stall for weeks in front of the fortified position occupied by Johnston after Bull Run. When he finally summoned the will to storm the works, he found them empty and the rows of canon that had held him in check to be "quaker guns" (wooden logs painted black). Even when in possession of definitive evidence of the fragmentation of Lee's army and having pinned the great general down at Antietam, McClellan would still prevaricate

---

24   Pinkerton, The Spy of the Rebellion, p.568.

The head of the Federal Secret Service, Alan Pinkerton (seated bottom right).
Standing behind him is John Babcock.

for 24 precious hours while the Army of Northern Virginia hurried to concentrate on Lee's position. Experienced and competent as he was as an administrator, one of the few American generals who would experience European warfare,[25] Little Mac was simply not a battle leader. Rather than construct an intelligence system that would make his job easier, the Federal Secret Service merely dumped volumes of raw information, complied largely from shaky testimony and questionable arithmetic, upon him and thus only added greatly to his workload. Much was wrong with the work of Chief of the Federal Secret Service, but he certainly was not responsible for turning a great general into a poor one.

With the McClellan – Pinkerton partnership dominating Federal intelligence in the Eastern Theatre for the opening years of the War and with Pope and Burnside never established in the role long enough to institute change, it would not be until January 1863 that the Union army found a leader who fully appreciated the value of military intelligence and understood how its utility needed to adapt to the changing nature of warfare. That man was Joseph Hooker, an astute and brave soldier, who had seen some of the fiercest fighting at both Antietam and Fredericksburg, but whose pugnacity on the battlefield was matched by his ambition off it.

25   McClellan had been invited as an observer during the Crimean War.

As an abolitionist, who doubted McClellan's conviction to put down the Rebellion rather than make peace with it,[26] Fighting Joe was equally dismissive of Little Mac's followers, such as Ambrose Burnside. Irrespective of his politics, his willingness to undermine his superior to further his own career started his relationship with Lincoln off on completely the wrong foot. His lifestyle of drinking and womanising was very much not to the president's abstemious tastes and his early insistence for more autonomy in administration of the army could not have endeared him less to the War Department. Hooker was intent on unpicking the traditional multi-corps structure of the Army of the Potomac, after Burnside's restructuring into his Grand Divisions, including giving the cavalry its own command. In addition, Fighting Joe saw the need to wrest certain key functions – specifically intelligence – away from Washington. Luckily for Hooker, Lincoln displayed his usual extraordinary pragmatism by swallowing his pride once again, provided that it would get his results.

General Joseph "Fighting Joe" Hooker, who assumed command of the Army of the Potomac in January 1863.

I have heard, in such way as to believe it, of your recently saying that both the army and the Government needed a Dictator. Of course it was not for this, but in spite of it, that I have given you the command. Only those generals who gain successes can set up dictators. What I now ask of you is military success, and I will risk the dictatorship.[27]

Luckily for Lincoln, although Hooker's managerial style was not to his taste, he was an excellent administrator. His reinvigoration of the Army of the Potomac was

26 McClellan was a devoted democrat who would run against Lincoln in the 1864 election, where his failure to rule out the possibility of a negotiated peace with the Confederacy would constantly undermine his campaign.
27 O.R. Series I, Vol. XXV, Part II, p.4.

astonishing and "a day-spring came with the appointment of General Hooker to the chief command."[28]

Not only did Hooker instil some much-needed fibre and discipline into his beleaguered troops after a succession of bloody defeats by the Army of Northern Virginia, but more than any other general in the War he understood the need for good military intelligence and the advantages that it could bestow. Having seen more than his fair share of blood already, Hooker was fully aware of the shocking neglect shown by the Federal command in developing any form of intelligence system that could support him, a situation evolved from the War Department's disinterested in the generation of strategic or tactical intelligence and McClellan's allegiance to Pinkerton. As Daniel Butterfield, one of a new general staff that Hooker appointed upon taking command, would described:

Daniel Butterfield, Joseph Hooker's chief-of-staff.

> when General Hooker assumed command of the army, there was not a record or document of any kind at headquarters of the army that gave any information at all in regard to the enemy. There was no, means, no organization, and no apparent effort to obtain such information. And we were almost as ignorant of the enemy in our immediate front as if they had been in China. An efficient organization for that purpose was instituted, by which we were soon enabled to get correct and proper information of the enemy, their strength and their movements.[29]

The new commander of the Army of the Potomac was consumed by the need to level the playing field and to exploit any advantage at his disposal. To realise this goal, he was not afraid to embrace new intelligence technology and break away from narrow traditionalist thinking. Immediately on taking control, Hooker placed a priority on gathering and interpreting good operational and tactical information and processing

28   Swinton, *Campaigns*, p.267.
29   O.R. Series I, Vol. XXV, Part II, p.6.

The men of the B.M.I. George Sharpe is seated far left, next to John Babcock.
John McEntee is seated far right.

it in a new and revolutionary centralised structure that was finally fit for purpose. This was the foundation of the most advanced military intelligence agency of its age, an intelligence revolution for which Joseph Hooker would receive almost no credit during the War or after it. The Bureau of Military Information ("B.M.I.") was established in February 1863 by Provost Marshal Marsena Patrick and led by Colonel George Sharpe, a former lawyer who had enlisted with the 120th New York regiment. The only survivor from the Federal Secret Service was Sharpe's assistant John C. Babcock, a trained architect, who had served Pinkerton and then Burnside as a topographical engineer.

Other than the skill and capability of its staff, the strength of the B.M.I. lay in its structure as the first "all-source" interpretive intelligence service. Mistakes and missed opportunities were inevitable unless the intelligence apparatus possessed the means to verify data through collation and cross-checking against all available information. The B.M.I. would not only be running their own scouts and spies, but they would accept and process other sources, for instance testimony from captured prisoners, freed black slaves, citizens and deserters. Before any acquired data would be accepted as intelligence, Sharpe would assess it against his existing information to verify its accuracy and provide a composite intelligence picture for Butterfield to pass on to Hooker. This system allowed the B.M.I. to maintain the same utility irrespective of the changing operational or tactical conditions and the more information it was fed, the more accurate it would become. By taking the onus of intelligence interpretation away from the commander, it allowed him to focus on coordination his army and the distilled intelligence he received was tailored exactly to his operational demands. Unlike the C.S.B. and the C.S.S.B., the B.M.I. was designed by and for the commanding general and so not reliant on service from Washington. As it was attached to the army, rather than government, it was also focused away from strategy and so could be adapted to support the changing demands of the campaign, specifically as the troops began their pursuit of Lee and priorities changed from defensive to offensive. Once the structure had been established, all it needed was to be plugged into the existing Federal information and communications network.

Although the institution of the B.M.I. as an interpretive intelligence service would be a revolution, the methods of information acquisition employed by the Federals would largely be consistent with those of their rebellious opponents. Having created a platform for the coordination of all possible sources of acquisition, Hooker encouraged as many different sources as possible. These ranged from traditional HUMINT, to new forms of SIGINT, provided by a developing communications service that would also greatly enhance Hooker's intelligence system. Given the typically invasive nature of their campaigns, it was widely assumed that information from local citizens would be a luxury to Union generals and so increasing pressure would be put on professional scouts and the cavalry to provide information, but there were alternative sources of real-time observation available. If the object of tactical intelligence gathering was to find information on the circumstances of an enemy, the best potential secondary source of information would be representatives of that very enemy, assuming that their testimony could be corroborated. Whilst the armies were in close proximity, it would become increasingly possible to capture enemy soldiers or deserters, while intercepted orders or instructions could provide details of manoeuvres, conditions of the army and accurate ORBAT intelligence.

With the majority of orders and communications being transported by hand, the opportunities to acquire information from captured couriers were plentiful. These may be on foot or horseback depending on the distance from source to recipient and the dangers associated with this means of communication are obvious. James Watters, a member of Harry Gilmor's command of the Army of the Northern Virginia during the Gettysburg campaign, described being sent by Lee to deliver a message to Jeb Stuart to rejoin the army: "Each man of the squad received sealed orders, addressed to General Stuart, with the injunction to scatter and find Stuart at the earliest moment possible, and if there was danger of capture, destroy the dispatches".[30] At the time, Jeb was operating behind enemy lines and so the chances of Watters or his colleagues ending up in enemy hands by getting lost or captured was high and it was not unheard of for couriers to lose their messages entirely. Sergeant Bacon of Company A, Third Virginia Cavalry, was not as fortunate as Watters when delivering a message from Jeb to Lee before the Battle of Chancellorsville, but at least "He was smart enough to swallow the dispatch and keep mum."[31] While the perils of carrying sensitive information in close proximity to the enemy were obvious, it should not be forgotten that probably the most famous piece of SIGINT captured in the entire war, the Lost Order, was in fact the result of pure absent-mindedness.

A supply of enemy soldiers willing and able to pass on sensitive information might be sparse in situations of professional armies invading foreign territories, but the Civil War was fought between volunteers whose allegiance was often based more on economics than principles. As the War moved into its third year, both sides could assume that they had already attracted all of those citizens moved by pure patriotism and so soldiers had either been conscripted or induced by bounties for service. As the War dragged on and the hardships and brutality of army life and fighting took their toll on the common soldiers, belief in the cause became an increasingly less powerful force binding the troops together. As such, a supply of enemy captives was never a rare commodity. Whether voluntarily crossing the lines or swept up as they tried to make it home, captives and deserters abounded and instead the principal challenge was to verify any information they provided. Particularly when seeking information on enemy tactics, rumour and hearsay were rife around the camps and so defining genuine intelligence was a complicated process requiring detailed cross-examination. Conscious of the problem of losses of personnel during operations, both sides recognised the opportunity to spread both direct and indirect counterintelligence and the spread disinformation could be very effective. Here, not only did the advanced interpretation services of the B.M.I. allow for detailed cross-referencing of prisoner testimony, but Sharpe and his colleagues became experienced and skilled interrogators, probably in no little part due to their legal training. The legal profession donated many senior intelligence personnel to both sides during the war, including both Norris and Sharpe, but it would be the B.M.I. who mastered the art of complex interrogation both to extract and verify information from prisoners and deserters.

This is not to say, however, that Sharpe and his men were impervious to Rebel counterintelligence measures and occasionally it seems that their opponents knew how to manipulate them. On the eve of the Battle of Chancellorsville, the B.M.I. had focused their efforts on establishing accurate ORBAT intelligence for General Hooker to determine not just what was in front of him, but (now that it was known that the enemy had spotted his advance) on what the Rebel response might be. During the day of 1 May, two deserters from New York came into the Hooker's camp and were duly interrogated. The information extracted indicated that the divisions of Generals John Bell Hood and George Pickett, both attached to Longstreet's First Corps, who had

---

31 *SHSP Vol. VIII*, p.253.

moved to east Virginia, were on the march and "would be here in time for the fight."[32] In truth, both Pickett and Hood were still feeding their horses on the other side of Richmond, but perhaps this dubious testimony had been approved by Sharpe due to his innate trust of men from his own home state. It would not be until 5 May, when the battle was over, that Babcock would finally lay Sharpe's erroneous belief to rest.[33]

Although the Union would normally be operating in hostile Southern territory, there was a particular source of sympathetic local support that could be relied upon, if it could be obtained. Unique to the Union was the potential to illicit information from freed black servants and slaves or "contraband"[34] as they became known. These men, particularly escapees from the service of senior military personnel, could have almost unlimited access to extraordinarily sensitive information and were particularly welcome to the Federal intelligence effort. Information from a black freedman, William H. Ringgold, became one of the most prominent sources of intelligence for General McClellan during the early part of his push to Richmond, providing the only detailed description of the Rebel defences on the Yorktown Peninsula.[35] A year later, captured contrabands had become pivotal to guiding soldiers around the region surrounding Fredericksburg, as both sides became entrenched after the autumn of 1862.[36]

Just as with prisoners or deserters, however, the dangers of the proliferation of misinformation from such sources were acute. Whether provided in error due to their own misunderstanding of the situation or as a result of deliberate counterintelligence efforts, creditable misinformation could be extremely harmful. Although acquisition of intelligence from these HUMINT sources would often be easier, slowly the generals would come to realise the dangers of relying on such raw and unverified information. Just as he had recognised the potential power of planting deserters with false information, General Lee also quickly learnt that contraband were also being used to extract information on his movements. Before embarking on the Gettysburg campaign, Lee warned Colonel Critcher of the 15th Virginia Cavalry that "The chief source of information to the enemy is through our negroes. They are easily deceived by proper caution."[37] Just weeks before the armies met at Gettysburg, the dangers of relying on data from contrabands were highlighted when Alfred Pleasonton was nearly thrown off the scent by captured black servants (and Southern newspapers),

32   O.R. Series I, Vol. XXV, Part II, p.332.
33   O.R. Series I, Vol. XXV, Part II, p.421.
34   General Benjamin Butler christened them "contraband of war" in 1861 when furnished with information on the Rebel defences around Fort Monroe by a runaway slave named George Scott; since Scott and other runaways were still technically property of the Confederacy, they were referred to in material terms.
35   O.R. Series I, Vol. XI, Part I, p.266-7.
36   O.R. Series I, Vol. XXV, Part II, p.366.
37   O.R. Series I, Vol. XXV, Part II, p.826.

who reported that Lee was returning to Virginia in order to refocus on the relief of Vicksburg.[38]

While these traditional close-quarter HUMINT sources had provided the backbone of operational and tactical intelligence for centuries, and would remain fundamental throughout the Civil War, the North in particular would eventually begin to accept the incorporation of new technologies. The previous decades had seen huge advances in long-range communications both for civil and military purposes and the integration of these, along with the potential new long-distance surveillance, could provide new opportunities not just to improve the quality of acquired intelligence by speeding its transmission, but also for SIGINT acquisition. While the Confederate generals lacked the desire and resources to invest heavily into new methods of intelligence acquisition and transmission, their more industrially-minded (and increasingly desperate) opponents grew an appetite for exploring innovation and the enhanced interpretive system designed by Hooker would permit the institution of these new technologies. That is not to say, however, that this process would be a smooth or entirely successful one and even an innovator like Hooker would not be entirely receptive to all new forms of intelligence acquisition.

Possibly the best example of the opportunities and problems provided by such scientific advances was the Balloon Corps, established initially under the Corps of Topographical Engineers before being transferred to the office of the Quartermaster. Hot air balloons had first been used in the French Revolutionary Wars, most notably during the battle of Fleurus in 1794 when the reconnaissance balloon "l'Entreprenant" reported the movement of the Austrian forces to General Jean-Baptiste Jourdan.[39] When utilised correctly, the balloon as a method of observation of enemy emplacements and movements could be a powerful intelligence weapon and its potential was not lost on either side.

The most famous of the army aeronauts was the (self-entitled) "Chief Aeronaut of the U.S. Army Balloon Corps," Professor Thaddeus Sobieski Constantine Lowe. A dedicated proponent of the benefits of the balloon for topographical reconnaissance, Lowe succeeded on having his balloon trialled by General Tyler around Falls Church in June 1861. Lowe's second ascent into the skies on the western outskirts of Washington revealed the perils of the Civil War aeronaut, when his course took him over enemy lines and back again. Unable to prove himself a Yankee, Lowe was promptly fired upon by his own troops and was forced to land between the lines and run the gauntlet of a walk back to Washington. The Rebels also used the balloon in the early part of the War, with similar teething problems.[40] Captain John Randolph Bryan accidentally sailed straight out of Rebel controlled-land while making an ascent above Yorktown in April 1862, only to fly straight over the enemy and back again,

---

38   O.R. Series I, Vol. XXVII, Part I, p.908.
39   O.R. Series III, Vol. III, p.253.
40   O.R. Series III, Vol. III, p.255-8.

narrowly avoiding ditching in the James River.[41] Ultimately, however, its logistical difficulties and a crippling lack of material, principally silk, put an end to the Rebel balloon experiment; sadly for the South, there were some things that King Cotton could not replace.

The effectiveness of his balloons would see Lowe accompany the Army of the Potomac to the Peninsula and his reports to McClellan on the fortification of Richmond during June 1862 were of high quality. When deployed in static positions and in the right conditions, balloons could provide one of the most powerful surveillance tools available, but inherent problems would see them fail to become a fundamental part of Federal or Rebel intelligence. The adventures of Lowe and Bryan had already demonstrated the risks of free-flight as opposed

Thaddeus Lowe, Chief Aeronaut of the US Army Balloon Corps.

to tethered positions and they were found to be too cumbersome to transport and their utility heavily dependent on good atmospheric conditions. Unable to remain stable in high winds and unable to see in cloud or thick fog, they were very much a luxury item and even when they did fly, they had to rely on the intelligence acumen of their aeronauts. For the most basic information, such as reporting the location or movement of troops, Lowe and his comrades could be very effective. Rising high above the Virginia landscape to the east of Richmond on 29 May 1862, Lowe spotted a subtle shift in enemy numbers as he made his final ascent of the day as "the enemy have this afternoon established another camp … They seem to be strengthening on our left." That movement was the start of Joseph Johnston's positioning for the attack on the Army of the Potomac at the Battle of Seven Pines two days later. If Lowe's dispatch had shown the advantages of balloons, the following days illustrated their shortcomings. The high winds of an approaching storm would ground the aeronaut until the afternoon of the 31st, by which time he could be of little assistance to McClellan as the tactical demands of battle demanded real-time communications. Hours after fighting commenced, Lowe would report that "at noon I ascended at Mechanicsville and discovered bodies of the enemy and trains of wagons moving from Richmond towards Fair Oaks. I remained in the air watching their movements until nearly 2 o'clock when I saw the enemy form in line of battle, and cannonading immediately

The inflation of one of Lowe's balloons, the *Intrepid*.

commenced".[42] The utility of Lowe's information on the Rebel movement had been completely undermined by the speed at which he communicated it to his commander, but clearly he had not appreciated this as he stayed and watched Samuel Heintzelman commanding McClellan's left being assailed by Johnston.

Lowe was not a soldier and no amount of flying ability could compensate for his inability to report what he saw accurately or quickly. This would continue to undermine his effectiveness as a tactical intelligence weapon. His ORBAT reports were absent of any genuine detail and were instead limited to statements such as "several tents were visible about there and a number of bodies of men on parade."[43] This failing would eventually see Lowe and his balloons phased out. Joe Hooker, who had worked extensively with Lowe on the Peninsula, would be in command less than six months before he attempted to bring the Balloon Corps under army control and instil some genuine military utility. Disgusted at the interference of the military and

42   O.R. Series III, Vol. III, p.280.
43   O.R. Series III, Vol. III, p.263.

totally incognisant of his own part in his downfall, Lowe resigned. Without him, the Balloon Corps would not see further service beyond their existing emplacements around the Rappahannock, watching the Rebel stations around Fredericksburg. They would be the first witnesses to the commencement of the Gettysburg campaign, but would play no further part. This little-commented episode was one of the less progressive decisions made by Hooker and a blot on his record of advanced intelligence utilisation. After the War, an envious Edward Porter Alexander, who also understood the potential of the balloon, would question why the Federals chose to terminate their experiment with balloons so early.[44] Whether balloons could have played much of an active role in as fluid a campaign as Gettysburg, however, is questionable due to the logistical difficulties in their transportation.

The problem of the incorporation of civil-run innovations, such as balloon aviation, into a military structure would be one of the enduring challenges of the acceptance of new technologies. With such a small standing army prior to the outbreak of hostilities, both sides would rely heavily on skilled civilians, such as Lowe, given the insufficient time and resources to train army personnel properly. Unfortunately, in many instances these civilian institutions rarely appreciated the demands of a belligerent force and seldom possessed the inclination to adapt their systems and services accordingly. Perhaps nowhere was this tension more evident than in the most important innovation in military intelligence of recent years, new electric telegraph communications. Lowe had demonstrated one of the key tenets of intelligence: that, since the accuracy and thereby value of information depreciated quickly, the development of methods for increasing the speed and reach of communications would be of extraordinary importance. Of all methods of long-distance communication available to the army by the beginning of 1863, the telegraph was the most efficient, but also possessed the greatest difficulty of implementation in the battlefield.

The electric telegraph had been in commercial operation in America since the 1840s when Samuel Morse refined his signalling code. Lines were quickly strung up, often alongside railroads, linking major cities separated by hundreds of miles and by October 1861, telegraphic lines spanned the entire country. These lines were run by private companies, such as the American Telegraph Company and the Southwestern Telegraph Company, and required operators skilled in Morse code and equipment operation. At the outbreak of the War, there were already around 50,000 miles of telegraph wire already in place and over 10,000 people working in the industry. Like much of the technological advancements in ante-bellum American, most of the telegraphic network covered the North rather than the South, but it would take the shocking first defeat at Bull Run to stun the government into action to exploit this advantage. It was not until February 1862 that Congress approved the president's authority to requisition all and any telegraph and railroad lines and their staff.[45] Thomas S. Scott of

44 *Battles and Leaders*, Vol. III p.358.
45 O.R. Series III, Vol. I, p.879.

the Pennsylvania Railroad was subsequently appointed to establish control, a distinct conflict of interest for man who was later appointed Assistant Secretary of War and thereby given an administrative hand in the movement of men and materiel around the country.[46]

The problem for the Union, once it resolved to bring the telegraph directly under control of the army, was that the complexity of operating the telegraph system was such that it would need to lean increasingly on the civilian personnel network. This mixing of martial and social responsibility ultimately eroded its military efficiency. The opening battle had demonstrated the complications of controlling large bodies of amateur soldiers to the Federal high command, as well as highlighting the advantage held by the Rebels as a result of their twin armies and strategic base all being linked by telegraph. In the same month that the east and west coasts of America were connected by telegraphic lines, the Federals established the United States Military Telegraph Service to control the permanent telegraph lines, under the charge of the Secretary of War and attached to the Quartermaster's department.[47] However, despite its name, the Telegraph Service was not in fact a military operation, since it did not have the skilled personnel necessary to operate the lines. As such, the Telegraphic Service did not answer to the army and so its service to the commanders could often be severely curtailed by the whims of its civilian operators. Furthermore, the head of the Telegraph Service, Anson Stager (previously employed by Western Union) was based in Cleveland, while his deputy Thomas Eckert was normally to be found close to Secretary of War Edwin Stanton in Washington. Obsessed with the flow of communications, Stanton exerted almost complete control without coordinating with his generals. To the exasperations of the commanders, they would sometimes find themselves totally robbed of telegraphic utility by the autonomous actions of the personnel of the Telegraph Service. Arguably the chief beneficiary of the centralisation of the telegraph was Abraham Lincoln, who would "spend hour after hour with his War Secretary, where he could read the telegrams as fast as they were received and handed in from the adjoining room."[48]

While the Telegraph Service was created to run the established civilian network, the army was required to take up the mantle of developing a system that could be employed purely to support military tactical communications. With the demands to assume control of the existing structure came calls to establish a "flying field telegraph" system.[49] Eventually, permission was granted to create telegraph trains (including wire, batteries, skilled operators and so on) to enable the Army of the Potomac to install up to 20 miles of temporary line per day. Ad hoc field lines were fixed to twelve

46 Bates, David Homer, *Lincoln in the Telegraph Office* (New York: The Century Co., 1907), p.16.
47 Bates, *Lincoln in the Telegraph Office*, p.32.
48 Bates, *Lincoln in the Telegraph Office*, p.40.
49 O.R. Series III, Vol. I, p.376.

foot ash staffs at the rate of around two and a half miles per hour and control of this new function initially fell to the newly established Field Telegraph Service, as a unit of the Signal Corps. Although the telegraph had been in use for years, its application in war was still novel and while the wires were not a common sight for many of the troops, their existence around the battlefields was even more unusual. As can be expected with the amount of artillery used during the major engagements, wires were vulnerable to shrapnel and sabotage by marauding reconnaissance and cavalry units. Unfortunately, they were also the victim of their own troops' suspicions of the new wires strung up along the roadside. It would not be uncommon to see the Federal telegraph wire being cut by its own soldiers, convinced that "it was some rebel infernal machine." Once they realised that these cables were of vital military importance, however, and, more importantly, ran away from the front line towards headquarters, the men were quick to volunteer selflessly for extended guard duty.[50]

In keeping with the objective to formulate a more mobile system, for which the heavy equipment and specialist Morse code knowledge were ill-suited, efforts were made to introduce new technology to make the system more reliable and convenient. The leading innovator at the time was George W. Beardslee, who had developed the Beardslee Patent Magneto-Electric Field Telegraph Machine. Smaller and lighter than the usual telegraph machine, Beardslee's device did not require any special training for the operators to send and receive signals. The system generated magnetic currents that would synchronise alphabetic dials on the machines of the transmitter and receiver to spell out the messages. Since the in-built magnets also generated their own electric current, they dispensed with the need for heavy galvanic batteries to produce power. Critically, however, what they gained in mobility they lost in power and so the range of the Beardslee machines was far below that of their hefty Morse rivals.

The Confederacy, not as exposed to widespread telegraph use before the War, never felt the need to establish telegraph operations to assist its military efforts and the events of Bull Run

George Beardslee's Magneto-Electric Field Telegraph Machine, smaller and lighter than a Morse machine, but also less powerful.

50   Brown, Willard J., *The Signal Corps, U.S.A. in the War of the Rebellion* (Boston: U.S. Veterans Signal Corps Association, 1896), p.1177-178.

suggested that there was no problem that required fixing. Instead, since the War had also enforced the cessation of the southerly sections of the Southwestern Telegraph Company, the government of the Rebel portion was entrusted to Dr William S. Morris. Imperfect as it was, the Union did try and develop a centralised system for management of telegraph operations for the military, whereas the Rebel command merely expropriated the necessary services and equipment from the civilian structure whenever they felt the need. Unsurprisingly, this led to considerable tension between military and civilian authorities, but with the civil arm feeling the wronged party more often than not.

While the Union wrestled with the application of the telegraph for military use, another equally efficient, if slightly less powerful, communications system was being developed. Signalling, whether by lights, flags or other means, had been used to transmit very basic information between soldiers since the "time of Polybius."[51] By the mid-1800s, most European armies were already using a military signalling system based on Claude Chappe's semaphore, which used mechanical arms mounted on signal towers, raised and lowered based on a signal code to transmit messages. While this system was appropriate for a static, set-piece battle and had sufficient sophistication to transmit relatively complex messages, such semaphore equipment was heavy and cumbersome to transport. In 1856, a former military assistant surgeon named Albert J. Myer began experimentation on a system of portable flag signals, later nicknamed "wig-wag" signalling or "flag-floppers."[52] Myer has an active interest in signs and signals since writing his medical thesis on a system of sign language for deaf mutes and now he was determined to develop a system for efficient transmission of messages specifically for deployment by the military. Such a system would need to be light enough to be carried with an advancing army, but sophisticated enough to communicate detailed information between carriers.

What Myer developed was based on the principle of combining sets of signals (in this case, flag positions and movements) into a code for which certain

The godfather of American military signalling, Albert J. Myer.

---

51   *SHSP Vol XVI*, p.93.
52   Taylor, *The Signal and Secret Service*, p.6.

combinations translated into a definite meaning. In Myer's four-element code, movements of the flag to left or right of vertical in series would denote the numbers one to four; odd numbers would usually be signed by a movement to the left, so one wave to the left would denote '1' while two waves to the left would be '3'. Combinations of the numbers one to four would then denote specific letters or phrases, much like in Morse code. For instance, the letter 'A' would correspond to the number combination 1-1. Myer believed that codes sent on a four foot square flag hung on a twelve foot pole could be read at a distance of eight miles under normal conditions and up to 25 miles in very clear climatic conditions.[53] An added advantage of his system was that almost any form of hand-held flags or torches could be used. Signal officer Captain D. E. Castle would receive special mention for gallantry during the final day of Gettysburg for maintaining communication between Federal headquarters and General Henry Slocum's XII Corps under the most trying of circumstances: "His flagmen had also left with his signal equipments … Captain Castle quickly cut a pole, extemporized a signal flag from a bedsheet procured near by, and sent his dispatches through under a most galling fire."[54]

Ironically, when Myer wrote to the War Department requesting consideration of his new system, the Secretary of War at the time was non-other than Jefferson Davis, who would reject his proposal. Not to be put off, Myer applied again in 1857 with a more developed system and finally received approval to begin tests, despite a rather tepid review from an independent board of examination in Washington. The board was presided over by Lieutenant Colonel Robert E. Lee and its findings were that "such a system might be useful as an accessory to, in many circumstances, but not as a Substitute for the means now employed to convey intelligence by an Army in the Field, and especially on a Field of Battle."[55] During the summer of 1859, Myer continued to trial his communications system in Virginia, New York and Washington, aided by a certain Lieutenant Edward Porter Alexander of the Corps of Engineers.[56] By June 1860, the creation of the U.S. Army Signal Corps was passed into law and Myer himself was appointed a signal officer a few days later. Although the Signal Corps would help in revolutionising tactical intelligence transmission for the Union, the C.S.B. was actually created first and it was Edward Porter Alexander's work at the Battle of First Bull Run which demonstrated to both sides the potential of signallers as facilitators of both intelligence acquisition and transmission. It was not until March 1863 that Myer was formerly appointed as the head of the Office of the Chief Signal

53   Brown, *The Signal Corps*, p.93.
54   O.R. Series I, Vol. XXVII, Part I, p.206.
55   Raines, Rebecca Robbins, *Getting the Message Through, A Branch History of the U.S. Army Signal Corps* (Washington, Centre of Military History, 2011) p.6.
56   Alexander's brother James would be the first man to write a signal manual, two years before Albert Myer completed his.

Officer for the Union and thus the U.S. Army finally brought the creation of a Signal Corps into law, a month after the creation of the Bureau of Military Information.[57]

The real tragedy in the appalling neglect of the signal corps by the Confederate War Department was the failure to recognise the secondary value of signal officers as a source of intelligence acquisition. Due to the requirement to hold geographical positions of high visibility, signal staff quickly assumed the additional responsibility for observation, scouting and interception of SIGINT from the opposing signallers. Certain locations in the Eastern Theatre, such as Maryland Heights immediately above the strategic town of Harper's Ferry and Sugarloaf Mountain between Harper's Ferry and Point of the Rocks, became critical for both sides as military operations were conducted in the valleys below. Private battles would often be waged between the rival signal corps for command of these vital positions. As a relatively static battle fought over a limited area with undulating topography, Gettysburg would provide significant opportunities for both sides for effective deployment of their signallers if able to retain elevated positions, on which to post signal stations. But with the advantage of clear line of sight came the dangers of standing exposed to the enemy and their increasingly accurate firepower. To be a signal officer not only took skill, but also a huge amount of personal bravery to remain at their stations while battle raged around them and it was estimated that the ratio of killed to wounded in the Signal Corps was 150 percent.[58] Signal officers like Captain Castle would repeatedly be singled out for praise by their commanders for the shear guts they showed in facing up to perils of tactical signal operations. "Besides the officers already mentioned, who were conspicuous for their bravery and coolness under a galling fire," recounted Confederate General James Trudeau of Battery 1, which came under ferocious attack from Commodore Andrew Foote's gunboats during the battle for Island No 10 in the Mississippi, "I will mention Signal Officers E. Jones and S. Rose, who never left their posts one minute. While shot and shell were tearing everything to pieces, Signal Officer E. Jones had his flag-staff shot from his hands; he coolly picked up the flag and continued to communicate his message."[59]

Had Albert Myer been present when the two sides finally met at Gettysburg in early July 1863, he would have recognised a few old collaborators on his signal project, although they were by now dressed in grey and not present in an intelligence capacity.[60] With Alexander leading the development of signalling from the start of the War and having succeeding in sponsoring a practical system by the time of the first major battle, there was no reason why the Confederacy could not have established a tactical signalling system every bit as effective as Myer's. Sadly, the consolidation of

---

57   O.R. Series III, Vol. III p.954.
58   Raines, *Getting the Message Through*, p.29.
59   *SHSP Vol XVI*, p.96.
60   Edward Porter Alexander commanded James Longstreet's artillery, while Cadmus Wilcox was a division commander in Hill's Third Corps.

A detachment of signal officers at the battle of Antietam.

intelligence organisation within Richmond and Lee's own myopic planning ensured that the Army of Northern Virginia would face a shocking mismatch in communications by mid-1863. Even once the various corps had come to rest by 2 July, Lee's men continued to rely on couriers to pass messages and instruction, whilst a virtual web of communications had been thrown over the Federal army by the officers of the US Signal Corps, all of whom also provided an additional observation service.

Part of the reason why the signal officers assigned to the Army of Northern Virginia failed to provide robust communications support during the battle of Gettysburg can also be traced to one of the most serious problems with early military communications. There is no doubt that, with the widespread adoption of flag signalling and telegraphic transmission, there also arose increased opportunities for SIGINT. Since wigwag signalling required the operator to occupy a position where he could be easily seen, he would often also be in sight of the enemy soldiers or signallers as well. Given the enveloping nature of the Rebel positions around the Federal army at Gettysburg, elevated on the hills and ridges south of the town, during the battle it would be almost impossible for one Confederate corps to signal to another without being observed by his Federal counterpart. The same problem, but of a different nature, also existed for the telegraph. The fluid nature of the front line and the ever-present danger of cavalry raids that telegraph stations could often fall into enemy hands and certain skilled agents reported even directly tapping into telegraph lines to read communications. George Elsworth, a telegraph operator for Rebel cavalry officer John Morgan in Tennessee, described how "I took down the telegraph line and connected my pocket instrument for the purpose of taking off all dispatches as they pass through."[61] The following day, Elsworth commandeered a Yankee telegraph station in Lebanon, Kentucky and proceeded pose as the telegrapher for the Lebanon station and pump information from a Federal operator on the other end of the line. Hooker was later so concerned about the insecurity of the wires that he never communicated his plans to subordinates by telegraph "knowing as I do that they are so often tapped."[62]

The solution to both of these problems would be learned from the world of counter-espionage and the evolution of methods used by spies to hide sensitive communications. Basic encryption was nothing new and both sides soon adopted codes and ciphers to protect their important messages.[63] This, in turn, quickly led to a private war between the signallers to crack each other's codes. The Rebels, for instance, typically used a system known as the 'court' or 'Vigenère substitution' cipher, after its inventor Blaise de Vigenère, a 16th Century French diplomat in the court of Henry III. The Vigenère cipher used a 26 letter alphabetic square with each row starting one letter further down the alphabet (so the first line would start 'A', the second 'B', the third 'C' and so on). A 15 letter keyword or phrase would then be used both to encode and decipher the message. For much of the War, the Rebels used the keyword "Complete Victory" until early 1865 when it was replaced by an ominous new phrase: "Come Retribution."[64] The cipher systems of both sides, however, were far from perfect and messages often proved either too easy to crack or too hard to decipher. "The delay is so great in transmitting and deciphering dispatches in the cipher used by the signal corps," wrote Secretary Seddon to D.H. Hill in June 1863, "that I shall here after, when necessary to employ cipher, communicate with you in the following, viz: Reverse the alphabet, taking Z for A, Y for B, X for C, &c."[65]

---

61   O.R. Series I, Vol. XVI, Part I, p.774-5.
62   O.R. Series I, Vol. XXV, Part II, p.257.
63   Brown, *The Signal Corps*, p.132: General Order 8 enforced all official Federal reports to be sent in cipher.
64   Taylor, *The Signal and Secret Service*, p.16.
65   O.R. Series I, Vol. XXVII, Part III, p.918.

5

Lost Confidence in General Hooker

For all of the sophistication of the Federal intelligence system and the adoption of new technology encouraged by the fresh perspective of General Hooker, there could be no escaping the reality that good intelligence could not win battles, only soldiers and general could. Mr F.J. Hooker's first operation against Lee was a brutal lesson in practice over theory. With a reinvigorated army, the services of the newly authorised U.S. Signal Corps and the centralised interpretive intelligence power of the B.M.I. at his disposal, Fighting Joe was bursting with confidence as he planned his operation to break the Fredericksburg deadlock, smash through the Army of Northern Virginia and open the gates to Richmond. Lee had been dug in across the Rappahannock for the last eight months and had proved impervious to direct assaults across the river. Hooker, therefore, set about an ambitious plan to flank the Army of Northern Virginia by crossing five of his seven corps north of the Rebel position and then sweeping south, through the tangled terrain of the Wilderness, to crush Lee in a pincer movement as his residual corps struck directly from Falmouth, on the opposite bank. To complete the operation and ensure that the Rebel army was truly isolated, General George Stoneman, (a room-mate of Stonewall Jackson at West Point), would lead a "dragoon force"[1] on a deep cavalry raid to destroy the Orange & Alexandria railroad, which connected Lee to his supplies from the South.

The challenge was daunting. Rebel pickets and scouts monitored his fires and camps from the other bank and Jeb's troopers patrolled the river to the north. Any obvious move by the Army of the Potomac would surely be spotted well before it ever came close to Lee's position. By taking such an extended route north, Hooker's remaining I and VI Corps could be vulnerable should Lee launch an opportunistic attack if he learnt of the absence of the majority of the Federal army. Meanwhile, uncertainty on the location of Longstreet's corps meant that Fighting Joe was even more conscious of the need for accurate details on Lee's strength before he committed to any action. A general order was, therefore, issued to bring in as much information as possible for the B.M.I. to process: "It is the duty of all to see that every prisoner, deserter, contraband,

---

1   O.R. Series I, Vol. XXV, Part II, p 199.

or citizen, also all newspapers, communications, or other articles, wherever received, whether captured or coming from the enemy, are sent, without delay, to the provost-marshal-general, at these headquarters."[2]

It would not take long for the information to start flowing and a picture of what waited on the other bank of the river to come into focus. Cross-checking against information coming in from prisoners and deserters around Suffolk, Virginia, quickly confirmed that Longstreet had moved down to the Peninsula with around 35,000 men; the Army of Northern Virginia was effectively one corps short and the green light for the campaign could be given.[3] Although it may not have seemed to carry much significance at the time, included in General Order 40 issued to the Federal army on 10 April was a specific instruction on the conduct of officers overseeing picketing operations:

> The commanding general regrets that it has become necessary for him to repri-mand ... officers who send incorrect information from the picket lines ... Officers of outposts are expected to inform themselves accurately of all events tran-spiring in their vicinity, and those whose fears magnify trifling squads into large bodies of the enemy as richly deserve death as the base wretch who deserts his country s flag or his comrades in battle. It has been too much a practice, upon outposts and battle-fields, to send back reports and calls for re-enforcements, founded upon imagination or the tales of a frightened or cowardly shirk. The fate of battle may be changed by such reports.[4]

The key to the success of the first phase of the operation would be the first major counterintelligence success of the U.S. Signal Corps. As the intelligence war esca-lated in the wake of the establishment of the opposing signal services, it would not take long for Union signal officers T.S. Hall and P.A. Taylor to crack the Rebel code and start reading their enemy's messages. Inevitably, in early April, Captain Fisher of the Signal Corps intercepted a Rebel message, which confirmed that the Johnnies had themselves cracked the Union cipher.[5] Major Myer, in no doubt of what to do, instantly ordered Fisher to remain silent about his discovery and took the informa-tion straight to General Hooker. Myer recognised that the opportunity had arisen to create an unwitting Rebel double-agent. On 13 April, Butterfield sent a message to Henry Slocum and Daniel Sickles advising that "A large portion of General Stoneman's cavalry force have gone in the direction of the Shenandoah Valley, and will be absent some days."[6] The following day, Lee sent an urgent warning to General

2   O.R. Series I, Vol. XXV, Part II, p.197.
3   O.R. Series I, Vol. XXV, Part II, p.206-8.
4   O.R. Series I, Vol. XXV, Part II, p.197.
5   Brown, *The Signal Corps*, p.214.
6   O.R. Series I, Vol. XXV, Part II, p.204.

William E. Jones in the Valley that "I learn enemy's cavalry are moving against you in Shenandoah Valley; will attack Fitz. Lee in passing … General Stuart, with two brigades, will attend them. Collect your forces and be on your guard." Stoneman, however, was on his way south to attack the rail junctions around Richmond, not west towards the Shenandoah. Reacting to the fictional movement of the Federal cavalry, Lee promptly ordered Jeb Stuart to move up the Rappahannock to investigate and the dashing cavalier took up position several miles away from the river, around Culpeper Court House, from where he could block any westward dash by the Federal cavalry. Stuart's move created a 20 mile fracture in the Confederate defensive cordon in the area around Kelly's Ford. Testimony from prisoners and local citizens collected by Sharpe and his men quickly confirmed that Butterfield's trick had worked and by 26 April, Hooker was confident enough in his ORBAT to declare "We know the strength of the enemy in front."[7] Once the B.M.I. had confirmed that Jeb had opened up the hole at Kelly's Ford and that the Rebels' intention was instead focused on United States Ford to the south, the offensive was launched.[8]

Just as predicted, the Rebels were completely unaware of the movement of thousands of Federal soldiers until their pickets, sparsely strung along the upper Rappahannock, were swept away. While his soldiers were being thrown forward, Hooker also mobilised his intelligence infrastructure. From the skies above Falmouth, Professor Lowe (now "Chief of Aeronauts" as he was now supported by aeronaut E. S. Allen in his balloon, the Eagle) now reported directly to John Sedgwick.[9] Officers of the Signal Corps, under acting Chief Signal Officer Samuel Cushing, marched in step with the army to keep Hooker's corps in contact and provide valuable intelligence from the west bank. Once on the other side of the river, news of Hooker's movement quickly reached Jeb Stuart, but Rebel the intelligence network was several steps behind their opponent's. Stuart, Lee's leading intelligence asset, was still positioned miles away from the bulk of the army and, as Sergeant Bacon discovered, was too close to the enemy for safe courier communications. Having been alerted to the Federal movements on the evening of 28 April, Stuart sprang into action and a captured Belgian officer of the XI Corps alerted him to that fact that this was more than just a raid. This was a turning column of the V, XI and XII Corps and they were crossing the Rappahannock to close in on the Army of Northern Virginia.[10] Unfortunately for Stuart, he had no signal service available to him and instead would have to use the telegraph. More unfortunate still, with no military telegraph system and with the telegraph office closed for the night, Jeb would have to stew on his vital intelligence until the morning and so Lee would not learn of the Federal advance until the following day. At the same time as Jeb was waiting for the local telegraph office to open, the U.S. Signal Corps was

7   O.R. Series I, Vol. XXV, Part II, p.253-4.
8   O.R. Series I, Vol. XXV, Part II, p.273.
9   O.R. Series III, Vol. III, p.311.
10 O.R. Series I, Vol. XXV, Part II, p.761.

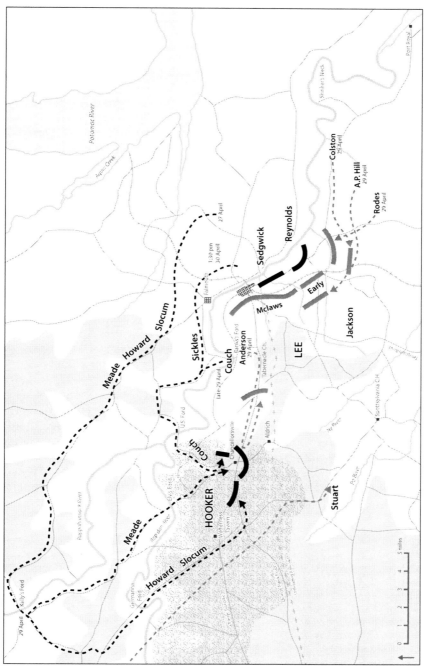

Map 2 Chancellorsville Campaign.

spreading its network of wires and signal officers out to extend over to the west bank of the Rappahannock.[11]

The Signal Corps was now using Beardslee's electromagnetic machines to transmit messages, thereby preserving control of the telegraph from the Telegraph Service, but their lack of range quickly started to tell and almost immediately they struggled to cope with the extended distances between the various station points. Assisting Cushing was none other than George Beardslee's son Frederick, a captain in the Signal Corps, but even he failed to establish a reliable connection. After several blackouts as Beardslee receivers registered no signal at all, by 30 April the Telegraph Service had taken over with their more powerful Morse system. Despite the disappointment of the Beardslee machines, the network of intelligence staff and infrastructure was soon feeding real-time tactical information back to General Hooker. To confuse the enemy further, the III and II Corps, which had been held back on the north bank of the river during the turning movement, now massed opposite Fredericksburg along with the I and VI Corps in a *ruse de guerre*. A massed movement of troops was spotted heading towards the river, but with the ultimate destination obscured by the low hills on the bank of the Rappahannock, Lee was forced to delay any definitive action until he knew where the attack would come from.[12] Fighting Joe had pulled off one of the most inconceivable operations of the War and "To have marched a column of fifty thousand men, laden with sixty pounds of baggage, and encumbered with artillery and trains, thirty seven miles in two days … is an achievement with few parallels."[13] Hooker had put his army within striking distance, but with the Rebels now conscious of their situation, the excellence of his operational planning needed to be matched by a similar quality of tactical leadership. Now the characters of the opposing generals would come to the fore.

On the brink of one of the most dramatic victories in American military history, Hooker suddenly stopped his march short of Lee's position and ordered the various columns of his army to concentrate at Chancellorsville, while further tactical information was sought.[14] Having halted his army, Hooker took the time to congratulate himself on the success of his daring operation, "the enemy must either ingloriously fly, or come out from behind his defences and give us battle on our ground."[15] However, the tangled foliage of the Wilderness was "a dense forest of not very large trees, but very difficult to get through … so that a man could hardly ride through it, and a

---

11   O.R. Series I, Vol. XXV, Part I, p.217.
12   Swinton, *Campaigns*, p.274; Colonel MacDougall described how Sedgwick utilised a ridgeline in front of the bridges over the Rappahannock to march his men repeatedly in full view of Lee's pickets to give the appearance that the whole Army of the Potomac was about to cross.
13   Swinton, *Campaigns*, p.273.
14   O.R. Series I, Vol. XXV, Part II, p.305.
15   Swinton, *Campaigns*, p.275.

Lee and Stonewall Jackson's midnight meeting before the attack of 1 May 1863.

man could not march through it very well with musket in hand."[16] Now aware of the danger, Lee did not wait: leaving Jubal Early in Fredericksburg to protect his rear from the threat of Sedgwick across the river, he pulled the remainder of his army round to engage the Federals.[17] Later that night, Lee and Stonewall Jackson held their famous midnight conference, witnessed by James Power Smith. Nobody knows what was discussed, but, between those two ultimate competitors, the option of retreat would not have been given much thought. With the instruction given to find away round to feel out Hooker's right, fate (or rather divine intervention), in the form of the Reverend Lacy and his connection to Charles Wellford, would intercede. Could Jackson's secret march make it past the watching pickets of Sickles, Slocum and Howard?

If good intelligence had contributed to the Army of the Potomac's success so far, the breakdown of that intelligence would conversely contribute to its defeat. During 1 May, the network of both land and airborne observers reported the movement of large numbers of Rebels towards Chancellorsville; Lee was choosing not to fly. Despite the threat to his left, which faced the Rebel army, Hooker was not ignorant of the

---

16   *Battles and Leaders, Vol III*, p.218.
17   Early had taken temporary charge of Richard Ewell's division of Stonewall's corps, while Ewell recovered from losing a leg in the defeat of John Pope at the Second Battle of Bull Run.

danger to his right flank, protected only by the thick undergrowth of the Wilderness. Having made an examination of the position, he dispatched a pointed warning to both Howard and Slocum that "The right of your line does not appear to be strong enough. No artificial defenses worth naming have been thrown up, and there appears to be a scarcity of troops at that point ... We have good reason to suppose that the enemy is moving to our right."[18] Typically, the cavalry would be given the responsibility of protecting the army flanks and scouting closer to the enemy, but with the bulk of his troopers still with Stoneman, on his raiding mission deep in Virginia, and the nearest cavalry to Howard four miles away, Hooker's right wing was unusually reliant on its pickets for tactical intelligence.[19]

Sure enough, Daniel Sickles' men soon spotted Stonewall's brigade marching straight past them, southwest down Wellford Furnace Road, away from Fredericksburg. This route would take them towards Howard's right flank, but also towards a possible line of retreat. The Federal reports were caught with indecision as the Rebels moved "rapidly from a point to the left of our position toward our right, with the evident intention of either passing around our right or of retreating."[20] Could the Rebels be evacuating after all? The answer came around 5:30 p.m. as 30,000 of Jackson's men came roaring out of the underbrush to smash into the 11,000 of Howard's corps.[21] Despite the repeated sightings of marching Rebels and the warnings to guard their flank, the XI Corps crumbled and fled in the face of Jackson's lightening attack with only the encroaching darkness and the mass of Hooker's main army stopping a full collapse. Agonisingly for Hooker, his warnings had been ignored and the tactical intelligence of the Rebel movement went unheeded or misinterpreted. Perhaps Howard's pickets still had the warnings of General Order 40 not to cry wolf going through their minds. Perhaps it was just cruel fate that the right of Howard's line was held by General Charles Devens Jr. Eighteen months earlier, Devens had led a small detachment across the Potomac River to attack a Rebel camp at Ball's Bluff, close to Leesburg, but there was no Rebel camp, only a clump of trees mistaken for rows of tents. Before Devens could pull his men back across to the safety, they were cut to pieces by the marauding Rebels. The disaster at Ball's Bluff would lead to the establishment of the Congressional Joint Committee for the Conduct of the War, to investigate this and other military disasters, and leave Charles Jr with deep reservations about the wisdom of acting in haste on the basis of limited intelligence.[22]

18   O.R. Series I, Vol. XXV, Part II, p.361.
19   *Battles and Leaders, Vol. III*, p.192.
20   O.R. Series I, Vol. XXV, Part I, p.633.
21   *Report of the Joint Committee* Part I, p.141.
22   Devens was not the only one to be profoundly shaken by Ball's Bluff. Among the Federal casualties was Colonel Edward Baker, a close friend of the President. Journalist Charles Carlton Coffin "I doubt if any other of the many tragic events of Lincoln's life ever stunned him so much as that unheralded message, which came over the wires while he

As the sun rose on 2 May, Robert Lee had around 15,000 men with him and another 12,500 with Jubal Early, but his daring had changed the nature of the battle.[23] From being caught between the jaws of the closing Federal pincer, he all but ignored the 22,000 men of "Uncle" John Sedgwick's VI Corps in Falmouth to create his own two-fronted attack on Hooker. Little did Lee know that his stake had just been doubled by his chief of staff, Robert Chilton. After the confusion over the attack orders at Malvern Hill, again, Chilton misinterpreted his commander's discretionary order for Early to judge whether the threat from Sedgwick was weakening (and if so to join him at Chancellorsville) or remain where he was to receive Sedgwick. Chilton delivered this instruction as a firm order and Old Jube promptly (and with no shortage of exasperation), began his march away from Fredericksburg to join the rest of the Army of Northern Virginia.[24] This communications failure gifted Sedgwick the perfect opportunity to strike hard against the feeble force left in the town, since he had been already been authorised to push his men across the river and launch his attack "if an opportunity presents itself with a reasonable expectation of success."[25] Unfortunately, Uncle John was not prepared just yet to put himself in motion and it would not be until the evening of 2 May that a direct order would force his hand. By then, the moment had been lost as Early returned to counter the threat.

Sedgwick's failure to exploit Chilton's intelligence blunder was unfortunate, but the Federals had still succeeded in engineering a battle on two fronts against a smaller opponent. In keeping with Lawley's description, the shock of Stonewall's attack had half-won the battle, but the Federals still had a significant advantage in numbers and Sedgwick remained poised to assault Fredericksburg from the east. Furthermore, although no one in the Federal ranks knew it, in the dying light of 2 May, Stonewall Jackson had been cut down by a volley of friendly fire from men of Dorsey Pender's North Carolina brigade, also killing two of Jackson's engineering and intelligence staff and wounding Ambrose Hill.[26] With strong leadership and good coordination between the disjointed legs of the army, a Federal victory was still there for the taking. Unfortunately, poor judgement and poor fortune would undermine Hooker's efforts on the second day of the battle, starting with the issue of an order by General Butterfield to John Sedgwick not to use flag communications across the river since "The enemy read our signals."[27] This order was made despite Butterfield being aware that the signal officers were now using a new Federal cipher, brought in after the fake transmission preceding Hooker's march.[28]

was beside the instrument on that mournful day, October 21, 1861." (Bates, *Lincoln in the Telegraph Office*, p.96).

23   Sears, *Chancellorsville*, p.239.
24   Dowdey, *The Wartime Papers*, p.465.
25   O.R. Series I, Vol. XXV, Part II, p.362.
26   *Battles and Leaders, Vol. III*, p.211.
27   O.R. Series I, Vol. XXV, Part II, p.384.
28   O.R. Series I, Vol. XXV, Part I, p.220.

Seemingly the same system that had unlocked the Rebel defence was now in danger of corrupting the Federal offence, amplified by the stuttering telegraph system. On giving the order to desist with signal communications, Hooker was unaware that Sedgwick had already crossed the river under cover of darkness. Now on the southern bank, the only reliable means of contact between the VI Corps and the rest of the army was the Signal Corps. It would not be until two signal officers, Captains Babcock and Gloshoki, tacitly began signalling to each other that communications between the two banks was restored by the morning of the 4th.[29] Meanwhile, Hooker would take a significant tactical decision that would resonate through to the battle of Gettysburg. Daniel Sickles, whose III Corps had become the front line of the Federal right flank following Howard's collapse, was ordered to pull his men back from the small clearing of Hazel Grove in order to concentrate his defensive force. Jeb Stuart, who had assumed command of Jackson's division after A.P. Hill had been incapacitated by shrapnel from an artillery shell, quickly filled the plateau with his 40 guns.[30] Sickles could do nothing but look on in horror as the Rebels proceeded to pound the length of the Federal line.

As if it could not get any worse for the Union army, during the crucial hours of the middle of 3 May, as the battle raged around him, Fighting Joe was barely conscious. Hit by a piece of masonry when a pillar of Chancellorsville House was shattered by a cannon ball, Hooker was concussed and unable to command. With the VI Corps ponderously threatening Fredericksburg, John Reynold's I Corps isolated north of Chancellorsville and no one able to seize the reins following Hooker's incapacitation, the Army of the Potomac was rudderless. Nothing, on the other hand, seemed able to stop the Army of Northern Virginia. Jeb had assumed control of the assault of the Federal right, following the loss of both Jackson and Hill, while Early's decisiveness ensured that no damage was suffered as a result of Chilton's mistake. While the Confederates were seemingly blessed with able leaders in abundance, should any one of them fall, the Federals languished until Hooker regained his senses.

In truth, even before Hooker's injury, the Army of the Potomac was contracting to a secondary defensive position to receive the Rebel attack, probably in the belief that Stoneman would undoubtedly have cut Lee off from his supply base by now. A ferocious attack on the rear of Lee's army from Uncle John could still lock the Army of Northern Virginia in the Union vice and leave him desperately short of provisions. It never materialised. Initially delayed by Early's holding force on Marye's Heights, the VI Corps failed to make any significant ground towards Hooker and by the 4th, Sedgwick had opted to take the defensive. After days of fierce fighting, Hooker ordered the retreat back across the Rappahannock and Lee, having completed surely his finest tactical achievement of his career, would be left to wonder how the Federals had got away. So an action that began with such spectacular operational

29 O.R. Series I, Vol. XXV, Part II, p.406.
30 Alexander, *Military Memoirs*, p.348.

The battle of Chancellorsville; in the foreground, Stonewall Jackson is fatally wounded.

success, largely due to expert usage of signalling and intelligence, was reduced to utter chaos by tactical mismanagement and faulty communications. The inquisition into how Hooker's forces could have wilted in the face of an inferior foe continued beyond the War and all the senior participants would have to answer to the Joint Committee. Central to the Committee's questioning was whether Hooker had been drunk during the fighting. This would explain the almost complete absence of leadership and his woozy behaviour during 3 May. Although he would be exonerated of that charge, Hooker supposedly later delivered his own verdict to Abner Doubleday: "I was not hurt by a shell, and I was not drunk. For once I lost confidence in Hooker, and that is all there is to it."[31]

Irrespective of the reasons why, Hooker had failed to follow up the success of his spectacular early manoeuvres and deliver the success his president craved. Instead of crushing the Army of Northern Virginia, the Federals lost over 16,500 men and reaffirmed the Rebel sense of superiority. Chancellorsville would become Lee's masterpiece. Like Antietam, he had taken on a significantly superior force, but this time he had recovered from desperate defence to lead an attack on two fronts and manufacture a stunning tactical success. The victory, however, was marred by the uncomfortable

31   Macartney, *Lincoln and his Generals*, p.154.

reality that it had come at punishing cost. Despite the greater quantum of Union casualties, the Confederates had lost almost 30 percent of their effective force, compared
to less than 20 percent for the Federals, and in Stonewall Jackson Lee had lost one
of his ablest and aggressive generals.[32] On hearing of Stonewall's injury, Robert Lee
quickly wrote him a message expressing that "Could I have directed events, I should
have chosen, for the good of the country, to have been disabled in your stead."[33]

The resurrection of the Army of the Potomac had been brought to a crashing halt,
but early signs of the potential effectiveness of the B.M.I. and the U.S. Signal Corps
gave a glimmer of hope. Their performance under the skilful guidance of Hooker
and Butterfield had opened up the seemingly impregnable Rebel defensive line and
continued to provide good tactical intelligence throughout the battle. It would be
unfortunate that teething problems with Beardslee's telegraph machine undermined
Federal confidence in own their communications system during a critical period
when coordination of Hooker's defence and Sedgwick's attack could yet have sealed
Lee's fate. Most disappointing of all was the performance of George Stoneman and
his dragoons, who summarily failed to make any significant damage to the Army of
Northern Virginia's supply lines during their raid. Poor weather and poorer leadership
would mean that Stoneman was not in position to hit the Richmond, Fredericksburg
and Potomac Railroad until 3 May and even then he proved incapable of doing the
job properly. To cause genuine damage, the Union cavalry needed to sever the rail link
north of Hanover Junction, where the RF&P Railroad separated from the Virginia
Central Railroad and where significant quantities of stores were depoted. However,
when Stoneman's troopers struck the rail lines, they did so south of Hanover and so
the Rebels were able to work around the damaged lines. All Hooker could do was
despair at the reports of Confederate trains continuing to run throughout 3 and 4
May, by which time the link to Richmond had been restored by the Southern engineers.[34] While alarm bells would ring throughout the Confederacy as to the ease of
the Federal cavalry raid through Virginia, "its military result, as bearing on the main
operation, was quite insignificant."[35]

In the halls of Washington there was no doubt as to the true result of the
Chancellorsville campaign. Lincoln had been loitering in the offices of the Telegraph
Service even more than usual and as news of his ignominious retreat filtered down the
wires, the president could only exclaim in anguish "My God! My god! What will the
country say! What will the country say!"[36] From Fredericksburg to Richmond could
be heard the creaking of the Sword of Damocles over Fighting Joe's head and rela-

32   Livermore, *Numbers and Losses*, p.98.
33   *Battles and Leaders, Vol III*, p.213.
34   O.R. Series I, Vol. XXV, Part II, p.416.
35   Swinton, *Campaigns*, p.302.
36   Brooks, *Washington in Lincoln's Time*, p.58.

tions between commander and president deteriorated so much that Hooker's removal had been all but sealed in early June. Only the general's close political ties into the cabinet, particularly Secretary of the Treasury Salmon Chase, persuaded Lincoln not to act unless Hooker himself offered his resignation. Fighting Joe would remain in charge, but his commander-in-chief's faith in his tactical ability was gone and with it came a tightening of his leash by a few notches. Hooker would now be even less able to counter an aggressive move from Lee.

6

The Iliad of the South

Once Davis and Seddon had given their blessing to Lee's daring new enterprise, the first order of business was to refit his army in the wake of the severe losses of Chancellorsville and prepare it for the new campaign. The Army of Northern Virginia had suffered around 13,000 casualties, but with the return of Longstreet's corps from Suffolk, their numbers were swelled to a total effective strength of around 75,000 men, the largest Rebel army since the defence of Richmond in 1861. To compensate for its increased size and the need for command flexibility to match the complicated operational plan, Lee reshuffled his army for the first time into three corps of three divisions each, (totalling 37 infantry brigades), based on his opinion that it was impos-

sible for any single general to handle a corps of over 30,000 men. Rather than look at ways of increasing his support staff and improving communications, Stonewall's Second Corps was instead divided to create a new Third Corps commanded by Ambrose Powell Hill. This restructuring also served the dual benefit of facilitating a more balanced shift north. The new Third Corps could hold Fredericksburg while the Second marched ahead to clear a path through the Shenandoah and the First held Hooker in check in central Virginia.

While new soldiers could be drafted in, one casualty of Chancellorsville would be much harder to replace: the commander of the Second Corps, Stonewall Jackson. His pugnacious brand of religiously-fuelled Confederate fundamentalism meshed well with

Commander of the new Third Corps of the Army of Northern Virginia, A.P. Hill.

Lee's own strong convictions and disregard for his opponents. Jackson's death led to the appointment of Richard "Old Bald Head" Ewell as commander of the Second Corps, ahead of more senior candidates such as D.H. Hill and Lafayette McLaws, a move that Longstreet believed was driven more by Robert Lee's preference for fellow Virginians than his abilities as a soldier. This view is unfair on Ewell, who was Jackson's most able subordinate in the Second Corps and so a natural successor to lead the men he had fought with since the Valley Campaign. Meanwhile, relations between D.H. Hill and Lee had been deteriorating for several months as Hill refused repeated requests to free up additional men to support the new campaign. Perhaps Longstreet's opinion of Ewell was driven more by a desire to undermine his credibility, since it would be Ewell and Old Pete who would also attract the bulk of the criticism for failing Lee during the battle of Gettysburg. Whatever Longstreet's concerns, Lee was clearly comfortable with Ewell's leadership and it would be the Second Corps which would lead the initial march towards the Potomac, supported by John Imboden's cavalry.

Further to the reorganisation of his infantry corps, Lee's only other significant structural change to the Army of Northern Virginia was to galvanise Jeb Stuart's cavalry division. Six brigades were brought together under generals Wade Hampton, Beverley Robertson, Fitzhugh Lee, W.H.F. Lee, Albert Jenkins and William "Grumble" Jones, with two additional brigades brought in during the campaign under Imboden. The rationale for this move, however, was defensive rather than offensive and not based on the need for augmented intelligence capability. Lee was concerned by the Union cavalry's growing size and he explained in a letter to President Davis that he needed an additional two divisions of horses or "some great evil will befall us if this state of things continues."[1] Throughout his detailed preparations for the campaign, Lee only had limited interest in investing in military intelligence to support his strategy and operations. With his bigger cavalry, his confidence in the tactical intelligence capacity of his army was high

Richard "Old Bald Head" Ewell, who assumed command of the Second Corps of the Army of Northern Virginia on Jackson's death.

---

1   O.R. Series I, Vol. XXV, Part II, p.740-1.

and only one new appointment could be argued to have had any significance for his intelligence resources. Major David Bridgford and his battalion were temporarily appointed to the provost guard, whose primary duty was to secure and process captured prisoners and deserters as well as protect against desertion.[2] Since they had direct exposure to enemy troops, the provost marshals would often also be charged with interrogation. The provost marshal of the Army of the Potomac was Marsena Patrick, one of those responsible for the creation of the B.M.I. and a powerful figure in the intelligence structure of the Union army. With the right instruction, Bridgford could also provide such a resource for obtaining ORBAT, especially as the two armies began to brush against each other in the latter stages of the campaign. This would have provided a far more rounded intelligence picture than could be produced by cavalry and pickets alone. Unfortunately, there is no evidence that Lee had any such a sophisticated role in mind for Bridgford and instead he was attached to Ewell's advance rather than his own headquarters.

In the final piece of preparation for the invasion, but one in which Lee would have no direct influence, Longstreet and Stuart dispatched their most trusted agents to Washington to begin independent espionage operations. Benjamin Franklin Stringfellow arranged to travel from Washington to meet Stuart near Salem, not too far north of Kelly's Ford where Hooker had crossed his army during his march to Chancellorsville. Thomas Nelson Conrad had an ear in the Federal War Department and was awaiting the development of operations, having volunteered to guide Stuart the next time he crossed the Potomac in order that Jeb "would dash into Washington with his whole command and make the White House his headquarters."[3] Harrison was told simply to catch up with the Army of Northern Virginia as soon as he had information of value, with assurance that "the head-quarters of the First Corps were large enough for any intelligent man to find."[4] Lee had already expressed his frustration at the absence of his own trusted agents like E. Pliny Bryan, but the fact that he did not seek to control or coordinate this spy activity gives an indication of how much he valued their input into his operational plan. Once his forces were in motion, his principal concern would be to manoeuvre them into a threatening position to force the Federals to meet him once he had consolidated his forces. His requirements in the early phases of his campaign, therefore, were limited to gathering information on Union strategy and operations, in case a sudden shift in sentiment triggered another march on Richmond. Like so many of the tactical engagements so far, Lee would seize the initiative and so have the distinct advantage of being able to dictate his own actions. His opponents, however, would have to constantly track his movements in order to establish his objectives before moving to engage him.

2   O.R. Series I, Vol. LI, Part II, p.721.
3   Conrad, *The Rebel Scout*, p.83.
4   Longstreet, *From Manassas to Appomattox*, p.333.

The Army of the Potomac had already been restructured on Hooker's arrival at the beginning of the year. The failure of Chancellorsville, however, had demanded both lives and careers and the approaching loss of thousands of nine month and two year volunteers precipitated significant reshuffling. Of greatest concern were the Federal cavalry and its dismal leader George Stoneman. Stoneman would avoid the ignominy of being dismissed by instead being granted medical leave to recover from severe haemorrhoids before being sent west. Appointed to lead the cavalry in his stead was General Alfred Pleasonton, who had commanded the residual cavalry left with Hooker at Chancellorsville and had acquitted himself adequately. Pleasonton was a

Benjamin Franklin Stringfellow, one of Jeb Stuart's spies sent to Washington before the Gettysburg campaign.

brash, arrogant bully, whose later testimony and writings on his campaigns gave the impression that he almost won the War singlehandedly. Stoneman had been given an offensive tactical role in May, but Pleasonton's primary duty in early June was in information gathering.

Unfortunately for Fighting Joe and Alfred Pleasonton, during the opening period of the campaign Lee held all the advantages, benefiting from his proximity to the benevolent geography of the Shenandoah Valley to protect his movements and his forces. As the Army of Northern Virginia moved away from their positions at Fredericksburg, so Hooker lost the benefit of his Balloon Corps and scouts around the Rappahannock. Unlike the purely military intelligence resources such as the cavalry, however, which required rest and refitting, Sharpe and the B.M.I. had never stopped monitoring the Rebels from across the river. A week before the first Johnnie soldiers left Fredericksburg for Culpeper, Sharpe submitted a general report summarising various information on Rebel activities and possible movements. Although little precise detail was included, the B.M.I. report included a prediction of an upcoming Confederate operation of "a campaign of long marches & hard fighting in a part of the country where they would have no railroad transportation. All the deserters say that the idea is very prevalent in the ranks that they are about to move forward upon or above our right flank."[5]

---

5   O.R. Series I, Vol. XXV, Part II, p.528.

By the first week of June, Sharpe's intelligence had been confirmed by information provided by spies in Virginia, such as Pleasonton's informant G. S. Smith, who
had been submitting accurate information on conditions around Fredericksburg since
the spring.[6] In spite of the disadvantages, from the outset accurate information on
Lee's intentions was forthcoming and agent Smith even stated to Pleasonton on 1
June that "one thing that looks very apparent to me, and that is, that this movement
of General Lee's is not intended to menace Washington."[7] Predicting the ultimate
destination of the Army of Northern Virginia, however, would be the primary challenge for Mr Smith and his colleagues. The challenge for the B.M.I., meanwhile,
would be how to verify these reports being amassed from non-military sources, such
as spies outside of their direct control. While Smith's assessment was broad but accurate, the following week information of a plot to seize Washington by Rebels dressed
as Federal soldiers would be reported by a "secret detective" in the employment of
General Robert Schenck.[8]

Fully cognisant of how difficult the intelligence task would be, Hooker issued
orders in early June to harvest as much information as possible, while the cavalry
was sent west to feel the enemy. The B.M.I. responded by pushing out their spies and
hoovering up any refugees, deserters and contraband for interrogation. The nature
of Lee's northward movement would mean that good communications between the
various strands of the Federal military could open up huge additional resources for the
B.M.I., if the information could be obtained. Supplementary input could be available
from indirect sources such as General Darius Couch, who had taken over command
of the Department of the Susquehanna in Harrisburg, following his resignation from
the Army of the Potomac. Couch had assembled a web of intelligence agents, who
had been pressed into service during the summer of 1862 to protect the rail roads
through Pennsylvania. One of larger of these spy groups was based around the area
of Cashtown and Gettysburg, led by local citizen David McConoughy. This network
would yield some vital information, but Couch reported directly to Washington and
was concerned purely with defence of the territory around the Susquehanna. For the
information from these groups to be of service to the Army of the Potomac, efficient
communication would have to be maintained by Hooker with both Washington and
(indirectly) Harrisburg, whilst the two major cities would also need to be constantly
linked by telegraph. All their information would need to be filtered through Sharpe's
team before it could be safely passed to Hooker.

Hooker has often been criticised for dithering during the early part of the campaign,
as if dazzled by some mesmerising sleight of hand by Lee, which allowed the Rebels
to disappear from his front, while starving him of inspiration on how to act. Between
Smith and Sharpe, it is true that there was accurate information being brought into the

---

6   O.R. Series I, Vol. XXV, Part II, p.196.
7   O.R. Series I, Vol. XXVII, Part III, p.3.
8   O.R. Series I, Vol. XXVII, Part III, p.54.

Provost Marshal's office from the very beginning, indicating an offensive move away from Fredericksburg, but there was nothing to give any clear indication of exactly what Lee was planning. "Hooker's balloons were on the lookout during the day time, and deserters and spies brought him information that changes were in progress, but their object and meaning remained a riddle."[9] Furthermore, Hooker and the Army of the Potomac were still under the yolk of the Lincolnian dichotomy. In fact, as early as the first week of June, Hooker had recognised the beginning of Lee's disengagement from the Fredericksburg front and correctly guessed his intention.

Despite their best efforts to disguise their movements, the commencement of the "Iliad of the South,"[10] which began with gradual retirement of first Longstreet's and then Ewell's corps on 3 June, was immediately spotted by the Yankee observation balloons and signal officers across the river and reported to Butterfield. Despite this knowledge, the Federal command had simply too much to lose by acting without strong substantiating evidence of the Confederate objective and did not have the sanction of Washington to mobilise the army, even though Lee was known to be in motion. On the morning of 5 June, Hooker sent a message to Lincoln to outline exactly the situation as he saw it:

> Yesterday morning appearances indicated that during the night the enemy had broken up a few of his camps and abandoned them ... this could be for no other purpose but to enable the enemy to move up the river, with a view to the execution of a movement similar to that of Lee's last year. He must either have it in mind to cross the Upper Potomac, or to throw his army between mine and Washington.

Hooker's lack of action during the early weeks of June, save for a cursory advance of Sedgewick's VI corps across a bridge to Fredericksburg to ensure that someone was still at home, can be traced back to his obligations to Washington rather than any doubts about Lee's aggressive intentions. Citing his instructions of 31 January, Hooker laid out his operational dilemma to Lincoln:

> I desire that I may be informed as early as practicable of the views of the Government concerning this army ... I am of opinion that it is my duty to pitch into his rear, although in so doing the head of his column may reach Warrenton before I can return. Will it be within the spirit of my instructions to do so?[11]

9   *SHSP Vol. XXXVII*, p.80.
10   Mosby, John, *Stuart's Cavalry in the Gettysburg Campaign* (New York: Moffatt, Yard & Co, 1908) p.103.
11   O.R. Series I, Vol. XXVII, Part I, p.30.

An attack into his residual force at Fredericksburg would have put Lee in a very difficult position, as he could not afford to continue to move away and allow Hooker to get between him and Richmond. However, Lee's understanding of the bifurcation of effective command of the Army of the Potomac between Hooker and Washington, as well as some basic counterintelligence measures, succeeded in preventing a disruptive attack by Fighting Joe. Within hours of Hooker's message, Lincoln had ruled out any plan to assault the rear of the retreating Rebels, illustrating the fear that Lee had instilled in the Union high command. While leaving the final military decision to Henry Halleck, Lincoln cautioned that Hooker should not take "any risk of being entangled upon the river, like an ox jumped half over a fence and liable to be torn by dogs front and rear, without a fair chance to gore one way or kick the other."[12] It was finally left to Old Brains to overrule his general on the basis that to move against a possibly entrenched force at Fredericksburg would be too great a risk, but that did not absolve Hooker of the obligation to track the Army of Northern Virginia and look for the opportunity to strike as it strung itself out between its base and its targets in Maryland or Pennsylvania.

Hooker was now left waiting to see what Lee was going to do in the knowledge that soon the Rebel army would likely be west of the Blue Ridges and beyond his reach before the final plan was revealed. As Marsena Patrick would note in his diary, "Hooker feels very bad – He is prohibited from crossing to Whip [sic] Hill and, like McDowell, is shut up to the defence of Washington."[13] Adding to Hooker's frustration, new reports from balloons on the north bank of the Rappahannock portrayed the arrival of several new camps leading Hooker to believe that the Army of Northern Virginia had been substantially reinforced. Although he could not hope to disguise the concentration of the bulk of his army away from Fredericksburg, some of General Lee's efforts at counterintelligence did produce results. Hooker's assessment of the situation to Major General John Dix on 12 June was impressively accurate, except for the fact that he believed that Army of Northern Virginia had been reinforced by D.H. Hill up from North Carolina. That Lee "has a numerical superiority over me"[14] was a false belief that would continue all the way through to the end of the Gettysburg campaign, with fateful significance.

To compound Hooker's problem, the lowering of his stock in Washington after Chancellorsville had meant a concerted effort was made by the War Department to diversify responsibility for the defence of the North. While the Army of the Potomac remained the major Federal army in the Eastern Theatre, it was not the only military force around Washington. Under the Union organisation, three separate departments remained independent from Hooker's command at the beginning of June 1863: Samuel Heintzleman's Department of Washington, protecting the capital; Robert

---

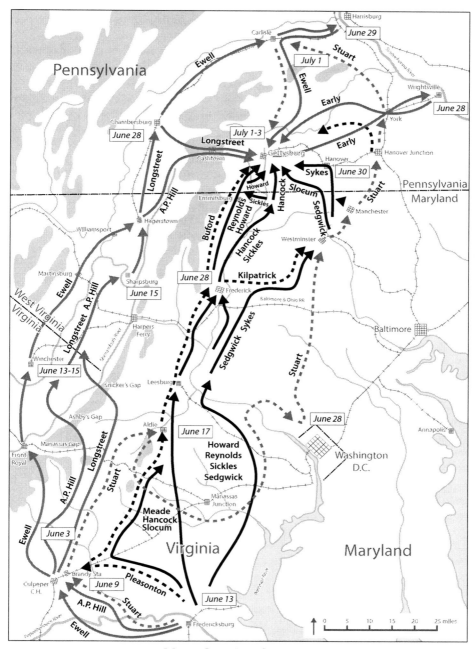

Map 3 Gettysburg Campaign.

Schenck's Middle Department, occupying the Federal-controlled area of northern Virginia, including Winchester (in the Shenandoah Valley) and Harper's Ferry; and General Dix, still holding the ground on the Peninsula taken by McClellan over a year before. In addition to these separate troops, and in light of the perceived danger of Lee's movements, on 11 June two new departments were instated. The Department of the Susquehanna, led by Darius Couch, was created to guard the logistical arteries around Harrisburg and the Department of the Monongahela, under General William Brooks, to cover the area of western Pennsylvania around Pittsburgh. Couch still had not forgiven Hooker for Chancellorsville and so now refused to have anything to do with the leader of the Army of the Potomac.[15] All of these separate commands reported directly to General Halleck in Washington, who, in concert with his commander-in-chief, had no intention of offering them up to the man who had lost his nerve when General Lee was at his mercy. As Lee's march took him towards the Valley, so he moved further away from Hooker's sphere of influence. In turn, Fighting Joe would become increasingly reliant on vicarious reports from Washington of events in western Virginia and Maryland. This situation would be made even more uncomfortable when a rampant Jeb Stuart started operating within striking distance of the Federal telegraph network.

Fortunately for the Army of the Potomac, Johnny Reb's skills at deception were no match for Billy Yank's new intelligence machine and the main victim in this intelligence war was poor Jeb Stuart. Almost immediately, things started to go wrong for the darling of Confederate tactical intelligence and for the next four weeks almost every step he took would see him on the losing end of a fight he did not even know he was in. Flushed with excitement at his new cavalry corps, the flamboyant Stuart organised a general review for the first week of June around Culpeper Court-House. Stuart set the date of 5 June for his big party, where he planned to parade all five brigades of his horsemen in a gloriously self-indulgent celebration of the Confederate cavalry (and its commander) before leaving on the greatest campaign of their careers. Unfortunately, Lee could not attend on the planned date, since he was still preparing matters for the rest of his army, but not to be put off that his beloved general had been delayed, Jeb simply organised another review to be held three days later.

The delay would prove a costly one, as the demand from Hooker to bring in all potential information meant that the Federals could not possibly miss the massive build-up of horse flesh half way towards the Blue Ridge Mountains. The same day as his original review, John Buford of Pleasonton's division reported the Rebel cavalry's presence at Culpeper and its reinforcement by Robertson, Jones and Jenkins.[16] The source of this information, "a refugee from Madison County," estimated the size of the enlarged cavalry at around 20,000; by the time that the Federals were ready to take action, this number had been refined to a more accurate 12,000 men (the true

15   *Battles and Leaders, Vol. III*, p.241.
16   O.R. Series I, Vol. XXVII, Part III, p.8.

number was closer to 10,000). Buford's information on the concentration of Jeb's troopers was confirmed by Sharpe, but again, while the raw data acquisition was good, the interpretation was still premature. Jeb's preparations for his grand review were wrongly interpreted as evidence of an impending major Rebel cavalry raid into Union territory.[17] Although Hooker was still grappling to put together the meaning of Lee's manoeuvres, he recognised a threat when he thought he saw one and immediately sent his cavalry on a peremptory strike to hit the Rebels and break up the attack before it started. Such a decision would not have been proscribed lightly; at the time of ordering the advance into Rebel-held Virginia, the Federal's only ORBAT information suggested that Pleasonton's force, even augmented by about 3,000 infantry, was significantly outnumbered. By sending one of his key operational and intelligence assets in an aggressive action against a foe acknowledged to be superior in both size and skill, Hooker not only indicated his willingness to take the initiative in disrupting Lee's plans, but also showed the confidence he had in his cavalry and the remaining part of his intelligence resources.

Federal intelligence had indicated that Jeb could be found around Culpeper and so Pleasonton was ordered to cross the Rapidan at Kelly and Beverly's Fords, due north east of the town, on 8 June.[18] But with Jeb's troopers having already retired north after the review, in preparation for commencement of their eventual advance towards Pennsylvania, it was a shock to both sides when the Federal cavalry burst out of the woods near Brandy Station early the following morning. Over the course of the day, the two cavalries merrily galloped amongst each other swinging sabres and firing carbines, but otherwise achieving very little. One of the largest cavalry battles in America would end with around 1,200 total casualties for both sides, representing a fraction of those actually involved. With little damage actually done, both sides withdrew and claimed victory.

Alfred Pleasonton, the new commander of the cavalry corps of the Army of the Potomac.

---

17 O.R. Series I, Vol. XXVII, Part III, p.35; Jones, *A Rebel War Clerk's Diary*, p.341.
18 O.R. Series I, Vol. XXVII, Part III, p.27.

The importance of the battle's role in intelligence gathering, however, would be fostered by Pleasonton's own testimony to the Joint Committee and then later by his extraordinary account in the *The Annals of War*.[19] Despite there being no record of it in the official reports of the time, Pleasonton would testify that he had been ordered on a reconnaissance in force by Hooker and that he had taken the Rebels completely by surprise.[20] These statements were confusing enough, since his initial opinion had been that "They [the Rebel cavalry] were aware of our movement, and were prepared,"[21] but he had even greater revelations in store. Following his "surprise" attack, Pleasonton was supposedly able to raid Stuart's headquarters and capture valuable papers, including Lee's orders for the Rebel cavalry to ride east and tear up the Orange and Alexandria railroad all the way to the Potomac. This would delay the Federals while Lee crossed the river at Poolesville and marched directly at Washington.

One would have thought that such an astonishing intelligence success would have been reported immediately to his commanding officer, rather than the vague testimony of two captured contrabands, whose intelligence was actually passed on. As it happened, however, Hooker need not have worried himself unduly, as Pleasonton also made it clear that his single-handed foiling of Lee's original campaign would cause the Rebel leader to revise his operational strategy completely. Only days after ordering the advance, Lee would instead apparently be forced to pursue his eventual course through the Shenandoah. In summing up his efforts at Brandy Station, and in light of the evidence of his successes, (sadly not shared with any of his commanders), it could almost be said that Pleasonton was magnanimous in his declaration that "the services of the nine thousand splendid soldiers of my command could not have been more brilliant or more important to the army and the country in their results."[22]

The Battle of Brandy Station would prove to be little more than a minor episode in the Gettysburg campaign and Lee would continue marching and Hooker would continue waiting. Despite the best efforts of Pleasonton later to burnish his actions as a resounding intelligence success for the Union, the Rebel cavalry quickly organised themselves to thwart Pleasonton's further efforts to observe the Army of Northern Virginia and Lee continued unmolested into the Valley. However, it would be the psychological effects of the battle that would have a much greater significance. The Federal cavalry crowed their way back across Rappahannock, having finally caught their Rebel counterparts by surprise and given them a stiff fight despite unequal numbers. In Rebel ranks, meanwhile, the lack of a clear victory could only be perceived to be a bad sign. "The surprise of Stuart, on the Rappahannock, has chilled every heart" reported J.B. Jones from Richmond. "The question is on every tongue—have

19   *The Annals of the War Written by Leading Participants North and South*, McClure, Alexander Kelly (ed.) (Philadelphia: Times Publishing 1879).
20   *Annals* p.449.
21   O.R. Series I, Vol. XXVII, Part III, p.38.
22   *Annals* p.450.

our generals relaxed in vigilance?"[23] A little over a month earlier, General Benjamin H. Grierson of Grant's cavalry had led his 1,500 "Butternut Guerrillas"[24] on one of the most devastating cavalry raids of the War. Running riot through Mississippi into Louisiana, Grierson's troopers sucked the Rebel troops away from Grant as he marched his army north towards Vicksburg. If the stock of the Federal cavalry was on the rise, poor Jeb Stuart was heading in the other direction and a storm of criticism greeted him from his own people, who "blame Stuart much for allowing himself to be surprised in his camp by Pleasonton, and call upon him to do something to retrieve his reputation."[25] The supremely self-confident Jeb was not used to this kind of treatment from the Yankees or his own people and was doubtless still effected by the battle when Lee called on him for a major intelligence mission two weeks later.

Brandy Station represents a metaphor of the opening phase of the campaign: the two forces faced each other through their cavalry, but with neither able to extract any significant benefit. Operating in Virginia and with only a skeleton force in the Valley, the best chance for Hooker to continue to pull in information lay with his cavalry. If they could get amongst the Rebel corps, they had a chance of picking up potential informants, while penetrating into the Shenandoah might give clues as to an intended crossing point of the Potomac. To cross east of Harper's Ferry would put Lee dangerously close to both Washington and Baltimore and give Hooker considerably less time to plan his defence. Following the course of the Valley and crossing around Sharpsburg would suggest that Lee intended to move into the Cumberland Valley and so a target in Pennsylvania was the likely final objective. The Federal high command repeatedly stressed the importance of gaining information on what was already evident to be a major invasion by General Lee. Sadly, the newfound confidence in the Federal cavalry's own abilities did not immediately translate into results for General Hooker. The difficulty of this assignment, however, should not be underestimated. It must be remembered that the opposing general in this operational intelligence battle was one of the supreme cavalry officers of his generation, now stung into additional vigilance by Brandy Station and with significantly more troopers at his disposal. The Rebels had proved themselves masters of the land between the Blue Ridge Mountains and the Potomac and Pleasonton would only have about a week before their soldiers topped the mountain passes and disappeared into the Shenandoah.

In fact, the Federal cavalry leader did do a reasonable job of acquiring valuable information, but he was a fighter not a thinker and his desire to loose the sabre constantly undermined the effectiveness of his positive intelligence work. Coupled with his innate misunderstanding of the importance of his role, Pleasonton's inability to interpret correctly the information he acquired before reporting would cause

---

23 Jones, *A Rebel War Clerk's Diary*, p.345.
24 So called since they dressed in brown, Confederate home-made clothing.
25 O.R. Series I, Vol. XXVII, Part I, p.41.

exasperation among his superiors. Sometimes, it seemed, he had not even taken the time to consider what he was writing, On 10 June, he relayed accurate information from a contraband from Stuart's service, picked up at Brandy Station, that Longstreet, Lee and Ewell had all been at Culpeper on the day of Stuart's review, but that A. P. Hill had been left in Fredericksburg in case the Federals launched a strike from across the river. Less than five hours later, Pleasonton would report the testimony of another contraband, who would put Hill at Culpeper as well during the review.[26] This differing information on the whereabouts of Ambrose Hill was transmitted with no attempt to explain the contradiction or highlight that the two reports did, however, agree that at least two of the three Rebel corps had moved and that their objective was believed to be Pennsylvania. If this lack of interpretation between two very similar sources was not enough, only a day later Pleasonton submitted yet another completely inconsistent statement to Hooker and Butterfield, putting Ewell back at Fredericksburg with Hill.[27] As more and more information was reported to him, so the poor cavalry commander became increasingly overwhelmed. Reporting both to Hooker and to the Secretary of War only served to spread the confusion during the early operational phases of the campaign, while attracting even more criticism. Halleck lost little time in criticising the intelligence from the cavalry as "very contradictory."[28]

There was no doubting that Pleasonton and many of his colleagues did not appreciate the art of information interpretation, which defined Stuart as such an effective intelligence agent for the Rebels. Fortunately for Washington, the cavalry was only one of the multiple intelligence acquisition resources being drawn upon by Hooker and all the information provided was fed into the B.M.I. rather than being dumped on to the commanding general. A critical failing of Pleasonton was his naivety in ascribing equal value to testimony from escaped slaves and prisoners as to his own agents or scouts. G.S. Smith, who had been one of the first to detect Lee's movements, again correctly reported the whereabouts of Ewell and Longstreet on 13 June,[29] but only a day later Pleasonton confidently reported the testimony of a black runaway who placed Lee, Longstreet, Ewell and Early marching in a single column towards Harper's Ferry. "I believe this man's report," was Pleasonton's cursory analysis.[30] Butterfield, however, did not and reported to General Halleck that Hill was still occupying the heights above Fredericksburg and that Lee had not yet moved from around Culpeper, but would be heading for the Valley. The source of this information was "Two of our best scouts"[31] and it was this form of more sophisticated intelligence that Hooker craved. "When will you hear from your scouts?"[32] was the blunt demand

26   O.R. Series I, Vol. XXVII, Part III, p.47.
27   O.R. Series I, Vol. XXVII, Part III, p.62.
28   O.R. Series I, Vol. XXVII, Part I, p.42.
29   O.R. Series I, Vol. XXVII, Part III, p.80.
30   O.R. Series I, Vol. XXVII, Part III, p.101.
31   O.R. Series I, Vol. XXVII, Part I, p.41.
32   O.R. Series I, Vol. XXVII, Part III, p.81.

from the chief-of-staff, but Pleasonton was unable to answer. Although he did not yet know it, his main reconnaissance party led by Colonel Duffié, which had been sent to get into the Valley through Thoroughfare Gap, had been surrounded at Middleburg.

In the absence of any of his own scouting work, Pleasonton would have to continue relying on a patchwork of hearsay information collected from unreliable civilians. In an effort to stop the fountain of nonsense from his cavalry chief, Hooker sent John McEntee, one of Sharpe's best operatives, to join Pleasonton in an effort to add the interpretive skills of the B.M.I. with the acquisition capability of the Federal cavalry. The instructions to Pleasonton could scarcely have been clearer: "After you have examined any prisoners, deserters, or contrabands brought in, the general desires you will give him [McEntee] a chance to examine all of them, and desires that all information may be communicated with great promptness, and directs that you leave nothing undone to give him the fullest information."[33] Sadly, Hooker's envisioned marriage was not a smooth one and would not be long before McEntee was being used as nothing more than a scout. The head of the Federal cavalry had still not learnt the importance of processing of information before transmission.

33   O.R. Series I, Vol. XXVII, Part III, p.170.

7

Long Marches and Hard Fighting

The engagement at Brandy Station and the confirmation that Lee had pulled most of his forces north of the Rappahannock had put the Federals on high alert, but it would take the accumulation of much more information to satisfy Hooker and Washington as to what action to take. Only a month beforehand, one of the deadlocked armies facing each other across the river had surreptitiously pulled their force out of their entrenchment successfully flanked the other. The same thing could be happening again in reverse. The wires between Hooker, his intelligence resources and Washington hummed with reports, cross-checks and bold conclusions, some more accurate than others. Fighting Joe's intelligence machine was coming alive and, although Lee has stolen the march to put himself out of easy range, if he made any mistakes and revealed his plan too early, the Federals would know quickly. To add to the efficiency of the Union system, Hooker authorised the Signal Corps to report to his corps commanders since "It is found that telegraphic communications often fail at a time when most needed."[1] At least some of the lessons of Chancellorsville had been learnt.

As Hooker spurred his intelligence machine into action, the Rebels were struggling to get theirs in order. Lee had not cracked down on the Southern press, as Hooker had on his own, and by 9 June a Richmond newspaper confirmed that he was in motion. Lee perhaps overestimated the power of his own counterintelligence when he moaned to James Seddon that "I think the enemy had been mystified as to our movements until the publication of my dispatch to the Department of the cavalry fight,"[2] but he was right to point out that these leaks were a problem. During the first two weeks of June, while the cavalries probed each other and the B.M.I. tried to mobilise into Virginia, all that was known for certain was that the Army of Northern Virginia was on the march and anywhere in the North could be a target.

Whatever prompted Hooker's final decision, the order was given on 14 June for Uncle John Sedgwick to pull back across the Rappahannock and the headquarters of

1   O.R. Series I, Vol. XXVII, Part III, p.86.
2   O.R. Series I, Vol. XXVII, Part III, p.886.

the Army of the Potomac to be moved to Fairfax Courthouse, squarely beside Washington. While he moved directly north, and "in the absence of any specific information as to the objects, movements, and purposes of the enemy," John Reynolds was given charge of the right wing of the Army of the Potomac, (consisting of his own I Corps, George Meade's V and Howard's XI) and told to coordinate with the Cavalry Corps.[3] By taking such an ostensibly defensive position, it is clear where Hooker believed his duty lay now Lee was in motion. Perhaps his sudden decisiveness could be ascribed to an individual piece of intelligence, such a particular piece of testimony from Charley Wright, a former black servant in Stuart's employment. Both Pleasonton and McEntee reported contraband witnesses confirming that

General John Reynolds, the commander of the I Corps and chosen by Hooker to lead the right wing of the Army of the Potomac.

both Ewell and Longstreet were with Lee in Culpeper Court House, indicating that the bulk of his army had moved west towards the Shenandoah, rather than taking a more direct route around the Rappahannock. In truth, it was more likely that the weight of evidence of Lee's movements forced Hooker to act, rather than any single piece of decisive information and that the collaborative effort of his cavalry and scouts, tied together by the B.M.I., gave him the accurate picture he needed to determine his next course of action.

With these first tentative actions of the Federal response, so began the next phase of the campaign and a raising of the stakes of the intelligence battle. The news that the Army of the Potomac had started its retraction towards Maryland, electrified the North and prompted the president to issue a proclamation demanding 100,000 militia. As the new Departments of the Susquehanna and Monongahela came into being, Andrew G. Curtin, the Governor of Pennsylvania, issued a stark warning to his citizens that "The State of Pennsylvania is again threatened with invasion, and an army of rebels is approaching our border."[4] Out went the call for volunteers to fill the ranks and Couch and his colleagues north of the Potomac reinvigorated their intelligence operations.

---

3   O.R. Series I, Vol. XXVII, Part III, p.72-3.
4   O.R. Series I, Vol. XXVII, Part III, p.145.

So far, Lee's plans had been going well; his corps had withdrawn smoothly from Fredericksburg without inciting an aggressive response from the Federals, other than the brief exchange at Brandy Station. Even that high-spirited little rumpus, however, had not apparently given away his ultimate objectives. Now, the bulk of his army would be further from Richmond than Hooker was and, during this critical phase, the Rebels too required good operational intelligence to confirm whether Lee's gamble on Lincoln's control over Hooker had paid off. Both cavalries now struggled to gain superiority as Pleasonton probed Stuart's screen to catch a glimpse of what the Army of Northern Virginia was up to and Jeb likewise fought to throw the Federal troopers back and make his own reconnaissance. At certain times, the Army of Northern Virginia was strung out across over 100 miles west of the Blue Ridge Mountains, but the inability of Pleasonton to acquire definite information about its movements in the Valley and the disruptive activities of Ewell's advanced party clouded the picture for the Yankees. The subdivision of the Army of Northern Virginia made the task of correctly tracking it almost impossible and the Federals would have to draw on the full power of their intelligence service to keep up. Pointed orders were again sent out to Pleasonton to get into the Valley, while General Julius Stahel with the Department of Washington was charged with spreading the net over the area north, around Manassas.[5] Anticipating a likely flood of unprocessed and probably contradictory information, the interpretive capacity of the B.M.I. was brought to the fore. The generals were directed to send all deserters and contraband to the office of the Provost Marshal, where Colonel Sharpe was waiting to pump them for information. While Sharpe remained at headquarters, his agents like John McEntee were sent right to the front to be as close as possible to the action.[6]

Only the capability of the B.M.I. and Hooker's staff managed to keep him in touch with Lee, as the Confederate general's operation strategy started to pull at the seams of the Federal military. During the second half of June, as the threat moved closer and closer to the Northern states, so would panic threaten to overwhelm the War Department and further split Washington's response between strategic and operational demands. Rather than following Ewell directly into the Valley through Thornton's Gap as had been reported,[7] James Longstreet led his First Corps on a provocative line east of the Blue Ridges. By keeping Longstreet within range of the Yankee front, Lee had hoped to draw Hooker out of Virginia and into Maryland and thereby bring the War out of his beloved homeland.[8] With the Federal headquarters moved to Fairfax in a clear covering move, however, Lee resigned himself to his frustration and ordered Longstreet to cross into the Valley. With Hill having already crossed the mountains,

5   O.R. Series I, Vol. XXVII, Part III, p.75.
6   O.R. Series I, Vol. XXVII, Part III, p.86.
7   O.R. Series I, Vol. XXVII, Part I, p.39.
8   O.R. Series I, Vol. XXVII, Part II, p.306.

after being called forward following the Federal withdrawal from the Rappahannock, by 20 June the last of the Rebel army disappeared from Hooker's sight.[9]

The Army of Northern Virginia was passing the point of no return and any delay in sweeping the Federals out of the Valley could see Lee's divided army caught between the mountains and the river, while Hooker fell on him from behind. To scramble any signals as to his true intentions and prepare for his army's arrival in Maryland, Lee ordered an advanced shock force of Imboden's and Jenkin's cavalry to cross the Potomac "to effect a diversion favorable to operations in the Valley, increase the ranks of your brigade, and collect horses and cattle for the army."[10] While the Rebel cavalry under Stuart, positioned with Longstreet, had assumed the task of providing the necessary screening across the gaps in the Blue Ridge Mountains, Imboden's cavalry party caused a storm of alarm as soon as they crossed the river. With only one division in Winchester and Daniel Tyler in Harper's Ferry as the last Federal military forces between Lee and Pennsylvania, Federal information acquisition on the vanguard of Lee's army was now largely in the hands civilians. Couch and Curtin were already breathless with anxiety at the possibility of the War coming to them and, as soon as the first Rebel horsemen splashed their way on to the north bank of the Potomac, a flood of non-military sources poured unconfirmed information into the government offices in Washington. On 16 June, the same day that Halleck would assert

that there was no clear evidence of a substantial Rebel presence in Maryland, Couch reported from Harrisburg that 20 – 25,000 Rebels could be holding positions as far north as Chambersburg, Pennsylvania. Witnessing the deluge of raw and unverified information, Butterfield exclaimed, "Cavalry enough is reported to have appeared to fill up the whole of Pennsylvania and leave no room for the inhabitants."[11]

For a former soldier, General Couch should have realised his obligation to obtain reliable intelligence for the War Department, rather than filling the telegraph wires with confusing hysteria. Fortunately, Lincoln and Stanton's eyes were not yet on Pennsylvania, but on a far more immediate problem. Newly

General Darius Couch, who quit the Army of the Potomac to assume command of the Department of the Susquehanna.

---

9   Longstreet, *From Manassas to Appomattox*, p.341.
10 O.R. Series I, Vol. XXVII, Part III, p.878.
11 O.R. Series I, Vol. XXVII, Part III, p.163, 174-5; O.R. Series I, Vol. XXVII, Part I, p.45.

promoted Dick Ewell was revelling in the honour of leading the first prong of the invasion and now was his chance to repay the faith of his commander. Between him and Shepherdstown, his designated crossing point of the Potomac, stood the single Federal garrison at Winchester, under the control of Major General Robert Schenck's Middle Department. Leading the defence of Winchester was General Robert Milroy, whose haughty treatment and "outrages" against Virginia's citizens had made him a particular target for the Confederate army.[12] "We hope he may not be taken alive," General Butler commented to Arthur Fremantle "but if he is, we will not shrink from the responsibility of putting him to death."[13] On 13 June, a scout of General Benjamin Kelley, leader of the First Division of the Middle Department, reported a warning from local citizens that Lee was surrounding the town. Daniel Tyler dispatched an urgent warning to Milroy to pull back towards Harper's Ferry, but it never got through; the Rebels had cut the telegraph between the Union outposts and Winchester's fate was sealed.

With the fight now being taken up in the Middle Department, but with Hooker and the Army of the Potomac obediently sat guarding Washington, Lincoln and Halleck were left in a difficult position if Winchester was to be saved. Having refused to allow Hooker to take charge of those troops in the Valley, the president now asked him if he could smash his way through Lee's army to save them, just after the Army of the Potomac had repositioned itself to cover Washington in order to satisfy the president's desires for security. Almost as if in a deliberate attempt to drive his commander to despair, only nine days after blocking Hooker's request for a pre-emptive strike at Lee, Lincoln enquired "If the head of Lee's army is at Martinsburg, and the tail of it on the Plank road between Fredericksburg and Chancellorsville, the animal must be very slim somewhere. Could you not break him?" Fighting Joe could barely restrain himself, now that his commander-in-chief was asking him to throw his army in a wild attack at the enemy to save the very troops that he had been expressly forbidden to touch. With almost treasonous sarcasm the general answered "Will the President allow me to inquire if it is his opinion that Winchester is surrounded by the rebel forces?" before laying out his reasonable logic that without a firm idea on the location of all of Lee's corps, he ran too great a risk of stumbling into a surprise attack.[14]

There was no way that Hooker would be able to intercede before Winchester fell unless Milroy and his comrades made a determined stand, but this did not seem to stop him from making his point as to the perceived ridiculousness of Washington's disaggregation of both command and intelligence while Lee rampaged towards Pennsylvania. As it happened, Robert Milroy had no intention of making a stand and managed to evade Ewell's embrace and make it to Harper's Ferry, but only by leaving about half his men (almost 4,000) behind at Winchester; with them, the last vestiges of Federal presence in the Valley evaporated. Halleck was enraged by Milroy's

12   O.R. Series II, Vol. V, p.807.
13   Fremantle, *Three Months in the Southern States*, p.214.
14   O.R. Series I, Vol. XXVII, Part I, p.39-40.

capitulation and instructed Schenck pointedly: "Do not give General Milroy any command at Harper's Ferry. We have had enough of that sort of military genius."[15] In truth there was very little that could be done to save the town without the intervention of the Army of the Potomac, but while Halleck raged, Lee rejoiced. Winchester had fallen easily and his army had a clear path to Pennsylvania.

As the final week of June began, the War had come to the people of Pennsylvania. On 23 June, one patriotic citizen of Adams County, Henry Honn, drew a line across the Chambersburg pike road on the outskirts of Cashtown, west of Gettysburg, and promised to kill the first Rebel he saw crossing it. Within an hour, he had shot dead his first Jonnie as Imboden's troops duly stumbled across Honn's invisible border.[16] The Rebels would find no peace in Pennsylvania, only "hard fighting."

The fall of Winchester left no doubt that Lee had a major invasion in mind, since the city would be needed as his secure base in the Valley, while he coordinated with Richmond. Hooker, however, was not of a mind to leap to any conclusions and continued to play a patient, if perhaps not happy, game until the intelligence compelled him to issue orders. Union scouts and spies continued to be sent out to locate and assess the enemy forces, while Pleasonton repeatedly pressed Stuart at the mountain gaps. In a rare piece of genuine cooperation between the cavalry and the B.M.I., a detachment of spies under Bureau agent Milton Cline moved with General David Gregg's 2nd Cavalry Division as they attacked Stuart at Aldie on 17 June. While the troopers were engaged, Cline and his men managed to get through the Confederate line and into the Valley below, where they would examine the Rebel army almost as far west as Salem.[17] At the same time, the U.S. Signal Corps were deployed in positions along the eastern ridges of the Valley to provide observation where possible and cover failures in the telegraphic system, which had begun to manifest themselves again. The Federals knew how vital the work of the Signal Corps could be to the upcoming operation and Special Order 112 crystalised the need to occupy and hold Sugar Loaf Mountain, a vital part of the communications chain between headquarters at Fairfax Station (linked by telegraph to Washington) and Maryland Heights, above the key crossing-point of Harper's Ferry.[18]

As well as Sugar Loaf, a detachment of signal officers was sent to the Heights to join General Tyler, who had withdrawn his men from Harper's Ferry on the suspicion that it would be next on Ewell's menu. These specialist officers immediately set about scouting the southern banks for Rebel troops; as the Rebel army approached the river, so they marched into the Federal intelligence web. Within a day, deserters had been brought in from the Eleventh Tennessee, who revealed that Ewell's corps

15   O.R. Series I, Vol. XXVII, Part III, p.124.
16   Scott, William A., *Battle of Gettysburg* (Gettysburg, 1905) p.1-2.
17   O.R. Series I, Vol. XXVII, Part III, p.266.
18   O.R. Series I, Vol. XXVII, Part III, p.152.

was around Williamsport and preparing to cross the Potomac and move on the Ferry. As Tyler started to feed accurate information acquired from the signal officers back to Washington, Hooker was at work spreading the signal corps further up the Blue Ridges and on to South Mountain, where the Shenandoah Valley gives way to the Hagerstown and Cumberland Valleys of Pennsylvania. Like Sugar Loaf, the signal station on South Mountain was a key intelligence asset and its importance moved both Hooker and Albert Myer to single it out. Myer would stress its security to replacement Chief Signal Officer, Lemuel Norton, while the commander of the army would personally instruct John Babcock to move his people there "to overlook the valley beyond, and see if the enemy have camps there."[19]

By 20 June, the Federal high command had a chain of observers and scouts waiting along the spine of the Virginia and Maryland mountains, all of this interconnected by flag and telegraph communication as far north as General Couch in Harrisburg. Meanwhile, spread around the countryside south of Harrisburg, around Cashtown and Gettysburg, Couch's citizen spies under David McConaughy were already scouting for information, assisted by Thomas Scott's engineers of the Pennsylvania Railroad Company. For once, home advantage was with the Union and they would make it tell. The flow of accurate information into his headquarters could not have come any earlier for Fighting Joe, who was starting to show the strain of management of the Army of the Potomac as both an offensive operational military organ and a defensive strategic one. "He acts like a man without a plan and is entirely at a loss what

to do," was Marsena Patrick's damning verdict in mid-June. "He has treated our 'Secret. Service Department' (headed by Col. Sharpe) which has furnished him with the most astonishingly correct information with indifference at first, & now with insult."[20] Whether Hooker was being genuinely rough with Sharpe is uncertain, but there is no doubt that he had become reliant on him. The importance of the Bureau of Military Information to collate and analyse so many disparate sources of unverified information into useable intelligence can scarcely be overstated. Sharpe and his men were not only running their own agents such as Cline and McEntee, but also supporting Butterfield and Patrick

Provost Marshal of the Army of the Potomac
General Marsena Patrick.

19   O.R. Series I, Vol. XXVII, Part III, p.225.
20   Sparks, *Inside Lincoln's Army*, p.261.

in the collection and interpretation of a mass of raw information. Every conceivable source was collected, from the keen eyes of Tyler's soldiers perched about Harper's Ferry to the untrained opinion of Dr. H. Seller from Williamsport.[21] Anything could prove the key to determining Lee's location and direction, but only if it could be verified and evaluated.

With both armies now in motion and coming into proximity, intelligence losses were inevitable and a diversification of resources would be key to maintaining continuity. Pushing his intelligence operatives out on to the fringes of Hooker's army put them directly in the path of the Rebel scouting parties and cavalry, who were also hunting for information. John Babcock would have a close scrape with a marauding band of Rebel cavalry, who dashed into Frederick sending local inhabitants and the U.S. signal officers fleeing from the tide. "I suppose I must got too," mused the imperturbable Babcock to George Sharpe, but no wailing Johnnies could put him off his task and their attack on Frederick "may prove beneficial for me, as I can learn much on returning after they have left."[22] While Babcock may have escaped the clutches of Lee's army as it spread its feelers into Maryland, one of his intelligence colleagues was not so lucky. Major William Stirling and Chief Acting Signal Officer Captain Benjamin Fisher were resting at the house of Mr Birch at Little River Turnpike close to Aldie when they were interrupted by some unwelcome intruders. A group of Mosby's Partisan Rangers, led by John Mosby himself, politely joined the party and requested the pleasure of the Federal officers' company back to their lines. Despite being dressed in full Confederate garb, Mosby and his men had ridden straight through a column of the Army of the Potomac to penetrate deep into Federal territory. As well as relieving Hooker of one of his senior intelligence staff, Mosby also helped himself to certain dispatches to Pleasonton, tipping off the Rebels as to plans for a Federal cavalry advance towards Aldie.[23] Fisher was acting under orders from Hooker to establish a signal station at Snicker's Gap and his surrender would see the appointment of Lemuel Norton as Chief Acting Signal Officer for the rest of the campaign. His capture so far from Lee's closest troops reveals the determined, but also increasingly desperate, nature of the Rebel scouting. The loss of one of their senior intelligence staff, however, resulted in no discernible interruption in the work of the Federal intelligence service.

Such breaches of security were to be expected as the mobile armies thrust and parried across the rural plains of Virginia, but what would drive Hooker and his superiors to despair was the unwelcome intervention of the media. This time, however, Hooker's volatile relationship with the journalists from the Northern newspapers circulating around his camps was about to generate something positive for the Federal

---

21   O.R. Series I, Vol. XXVII, Part III, p.227.
22   O.R. Series I, Vol. XXVII, Part III, p.74.
23   Mosby, John, *Mosby's War Reminiscences* (New York: Dodd, Mead and Company, 1898) p.167.

army. Fighting Joe was well aware that their reports eventually found their way into the hands of his opponents as a source of strategic information and so the opportunities for counterespionage could not be resisted. "Have the newspapers announce that I am moving on to the James River line. It will mask my real movements in these parts,"[24] Hooker instructed Stanton on 16 June, before he made his move from Fairfax Station. Little did he know that Lee was already too far out of reach for the Confederate intelligence services to alert him to any press reports of Union movements, but the message would be duly received in Richmond.

Not content with assisting Fighting Joe's cunning misdirection, however, once again the Northern newsmen overstepped their perceived boundaries. Just as Lee was starting to reveal his desperation for positive intelligence, the *New York Herald* leaked news of the real movements of the Army of the Potomac on 18 June. Hooker exploded with rage and read the riot act to the agent of the Press Association in Washington, L.A. Gobright.[25] For once, even General Halleck would express some sympathy for his commander, citing his own problems with the media during his time in command of the Western theatre. But if Hooker valued the information served up to the enemy at "millions of money,"[26] Lee had no means to pay the bill. As soon as he left his initial base of operation at Culpeper on 16 June, his communications with Richmond began to stretch. Any useful information acquired in Washington, and transmitted via the Secret Line to Richmond, would be subject to an increasingly long delay before it could reach him – if it could reach him at all. Tactical intelligence would increasingly lose its accuracy and relevance as the time taken between acquisition and receipt lengthened and so Davis's intelligence resources would cease to become a viable option for the Army of Northern Virginia.

Meanwhile Pleasonton's aggression, whilst continuing to undermine the efforts of Butterfield and the B.M.I. to generate positive intelligence for Hooker, had a similar counterintelligence effect on the Rebels. The third week of June may have marked an apex in the hysteria in Washington and Pennsylvania, but, unbeknownst to Lee, it also marked the end of his brief period of operational intelligence superiority. His army would be crossing the Potomac River at a point close to Sharpsburg, where the bones of thousands of his soldiers still littered the fields around Antietam creek. If he was to avoid being surprised again, he needed positive information on the Federals. "I have heard nothing of the movements of General Hooker either from General Stuart or yourself," Lee complained to his war horse, General Longstreet, "and, therefore, can form no opinion of the best move against him."[27] In the absence of accurate information, Lee was unhappy with Longstreet's move west of the Blue Ridge Mountains, which drop him out of contact with the Army of the Potomac. This criticism was

24   O.R. Series I, Vol. XXVII, Part I, p.47-8.
25   O.R. Series I, Vol. XXVII, Part III, p.192.
26   O.R. Series I, Vol. XXVII, Part I, p.52.
27   O.R. Series I, Vol. XXVII, Part III, p.900.

perhaps unfair given that maintaining the mystery surrounding the movements of his army was key to keeping Hooker in check. "Lee is in as much uncertainty as to our whereabouts and what we are doing as we are to his,"[28] Daniel Butterfield correctly surmised. With Imboden already in Pennsylvania and the vanguard of his army less than a week away from committing to crossing the Potomac, Lee's own intelligence system, based primarily around Jeb Stuart, had not been able to furnish him with the intelligence he needed. So far, progress up the Valley had been as good as Lee could have wished for, but with Ewell moving past Winchester, his mind was filled with concern as to where the Federal army might be.[29] If Mr F.J. Hooker had made an aggressive move to block Harper's Ferry, he could bottle the Army of Northern Virginia up in the Shenandoah or isolate and crush the Second Corps before Longstreet or Hill could come to its aid.

Although Lee and many of his contemporaries would later focus their criticism on the cavalry's absence from the army's side as battle approached, the problems of Rebel intelligence acquisition had begun well before Stuart left on his raid. The operational strategy of the Gettysburg campaign had been founded on the presumption that Hooker and Lincoln would be too concerned by any potential threat to Washington to move aggressively to halt the Rebel march before all three corps were safely across the Potomac. Although such an extended move would realistically put General Lee beyond communication with Richmond, he was confident that his superiority in positive and counter-intelligence, through his cavalry, would maintain his advantage and keep him fully apprised of any movements of the Army of the Potomac in good time to make any tactical changes. Should any additional information come through from other sources, then it could serve to augment Jeb's work. What Lee had not counted on was Alfred Pleasonton and the newly inspired Yankee cavalry, spurred on by repeated goading from Hooker and Butterfield and complemented by the added analytical dimension provided by the B.M.I. While Hill was racing to catch up with the First and Second Corps, Jeb Stuart, rather than galloping between the two armies to keep tabs on the Yankees, was desperately trying to keep Federal eyes out of the Valley. For consecutive days at Aldie and then Middleburg, sharp clashes between the Rebel and Federal horsemen seemingly produced no positive result for either side. Then, on 21 June, Pleasonton struck Stuart again at Upperville. Once again, the Union cavalry failed to break its way through Jeb's screen, for which history would judge Pleasonton an intelligence failure, but again the Rebels had failed to appreciate the greater game. "The attempts to penetrate the mountains have been successfully repelled by General Stuart with the cavalry,"[30] boasted Lee to President Davis on 23 June, but he was wrong. As Jeb and Pleasonton swapped sword swipes and bullets at Upperville, Milton

---

28   O.R. Series I, Vol. XXVII, Part III, p.174.
29   O.R. Series I, Vol. XXVII, Part III, p.905.
30   *SHSP Vol. XXXVII*, p.86.

Cline and his band of scouts slipped back over the pass and headed straight for Sharpe with accurate and timely information on the Rebel army in the Valley. "The line of the enemy's infantry begins between Piedmont and Rectortown, and runs thence toward Front Royal, where there is considerable force," reported Sharpe to Butterfield, two days after Upperville. "Divisions of Pickett and Hood lying in rear of Snicker's Gap, in position to defend it. Three companies of infantry at Millwood, opposite Ashby's Gap, and the rest of Longstreet's corps between Front Royal and Winchester."[31]

While Stuart struggled to protect the right flank of his army from the pugnacious Pleasonton, he turned to his most trusted subordinate, John Singleton Mosby, whose "information was always accurate and reliable,"[32] to assist in filling in his intelligence duties. In Jeb's absence, it was Mosby who was prowling the middle ground of Virginia and probing the Federal lines for intelligence and it was Mosby who had penetrated Federal lines to pick up Fisher and Stirling. It is possible that the capture of Fisher's dispatches from Hooker to Pleasonton, confirming that the Federal cavalry commander was also being supported by three brigades of infantry, justified Stuart's decision to remain on the defensive and hold the mountain gaps rather than conduct further reconnaissance.[33] At this point, although Stuart's inability to provide tactical intelligence was a serious cause for concern, it did not mean that Robert Lee was completely ignorant of the situation. Messages to Richmond on 18 June make it clear that the general knew that Hooker was alert to his movements and preparing to begin his pursuit.[34] Now, it was more important than ever to gain knowledge of the Federal activity. As Lee's frustration grew with the lack of information at his disposal, so did the pressure rise on his most trusted intelligence officer. As Pleasonton called off his assault on Upperville, Stuart rode to meet Lee, who was stationed with the First Corps at Paris, Virginia. Later that day, Lee issued orders to Jeb Stuart (via General Longstreet) to take decisive action. He was directed to ride out into Maryland and to move up to Ewell's right flank to shield him from any Federal attacks and keep him informed of any movements by Hooker.

Robert Lee's orders to Jeb Stuart would precipitate the most critical intelligence event in the operational phase of the Gettysburg campaign for the Army of Northern Virginia and one that would highlight the lack of diversity in the Confederate structure. Lee was committing to send his major intelligence asset out of reach of his army for an unspecified period, when he suspected that the Army of the Potomac were about to move. The potential consequences of Stuart's failure or capture were enormous: Lee would be marooned between Maryland and Pennsylvania without his favoured means to monitor Hooker's approach. As if the stakes were not high enough, once again General Lee's lackadaisical style of management only served to lengthen

---

31   O.R. Series I, Vol. XXVII, Part III, p.266.

32   O.R. Series I, Vol. XXVII, Part II, p.692.

33   McClellan, H.B., *The Life and Campaigns of Major-General J.E.B. Stuart's Cavalry* (Boston: Houghton Mifflin, 1885), p.306.

34   OR Series I, Vol. XXVII, Part II, p.296.

his odds of success. His order of 22 June was born of the reality that no one in the Rebel camp had a clear understanding of what Hooker was up to; "Do you know where he [Hooker] is and what he is doing? I fear he will steal a march on us, and get across the Potomac before we are aware." However, rather than directing Jeb to go and find out, Lee instructed him to undertake a mission with multiple objectives, including to "take position on General Ewell's right, place yourself in communication with him, guard his flank, keep him informed of the enemy's movements, and collect all the supplies you can for the use of the army."[35] The need to provide intelligence only came fourth on the list, but the execution of the entire operation was contingent upon the actions of the Federals. There is no record of the discussions between Lee, Stuart and Longstreet before the order was issued, but it is questionable whether Jeb fully appreciated what priority Lee wanted him to place on these various tasks. For days, he had fearlessly blocked every aggressive Union strike against the First Corps and now he was being asked to do the same for Ewell's Second. Perhaps the release of General Order 72 the day before, providing for procurement of new supplies as the army crossed into enemy lands, may also have inadvertently put Stuart's mind on to the importance of finding fresh resources for the troops.[36]

His orders received, Stuart called in Mosby to confer on the best possible route to achieve Lee's proscribed objectives. More than anyone on the Confederate side, Mosby understood the positioning of the Federal army and the local geography. Mosby was of the opinion that Hooker was stuck on the defensive and so the best option was to pass between his dispersed corps and cross the river at Seneca. As General Winfield Hancock's II Corps still held Thoroughfare and Hopewell Gaps, south of Aldie, Stuart decided to swing down and pass through Glasscock Gap, before wrapping northward round Hancock to rendezvous with Mosby at Gum Springs. The Gray Ghost, meanwhile, would continue his aggressive harassing and reconnaissance activities while he waited for Stuart to cross the Federal lines. This was a slight adjustment to Lee's expected plan for Stuart, which would have seen him take a more direct route straight across Hopewell Gap. Clearly Lee was not abreast of the latest tactical intelligence on the enemy. Mosby wasted no time in mobilising and marched in his full colours right through the Federal ranks and across Bull Run. Convinced that Hooker was not moving, he sent another dispatch to Stuart to assure him that his passage was clear.[37]

News of Hooker's inertia had, by this time, also reached Lee and so he issued a second order on 23 June, based on the understanding that the Federal army had not moved against him. Jeb now had two sets of discretionary orders from his commander based on two sets of contingencies, but both stressing the need to get to Ewell's side, while foraging for supplies and feeding him with operational information. This latest

35   O.R. Series I, Vol. XXVII, Part III, p.913.
36   Nesbitt, Mark, *Sabre and Scapegoat* (Mechanicsburg: Stackpole Books, 1994) p.56.
37   Mosby, John, *Mosby's War Reminiscences*, p.174-5.

order also included an aside to inflict "all the damage you can," to the enemy as he went.[38] These two orders and their subsequent execution became the focal point of the intelligence debate around the Gettysburg campaign, led principally by the Rebel protagonists as they sought to shed blame and point fingers. Men like Charles Marshall of Lee's staff, would later accuse the flamboyant cavalry officer of directly contravening Lee's orders by setting off on his ride even though he knew that the Army of the Potomac was in motion. Conveniently, this charge dissolved Robert Lee of any culpability for Stuart's actions. Speaking after the war, Marshall would delight in telling a shocked dinner party audience that he had tried to have Jeb court martialled for disobedience after the conclusion of the campaign, but that Lee would not hear of it.[39]

Whatever the opinions on culpability, the immediate consequences for Lee were that he was left with only two cavalry brigades and without Jeb Stuart. His remaining troopers were those of Beverly Robertson and Grumble Jones, whilst Imboden and Jenkins brigades were still moving in advance with Ewell. If there could be any accusation of dereliction of duty levelled at Stuart, it was in regard to his selection of raiding party. Longstreet had requested that Jeb at least "order General [Wade] Hampton … to report to me at Millwood,"[40] hoping that he would not take all the cream of his cavalry corps with him on the ride. Stuart, however, had no intension of either leaving Hampton or taking either Robertson or Jones, for whom he had minimal respect. Instead, he left them clear instructions to guard Ashby and Snicker's Gaps, watch the Federals and then to join up with Lee once the enemy had moved away.[41] As Jeb rode out of his headquarters on the night of 24 June, Lee was left with the intelligence capacity of his pickets, the casual observations of any local sympathisers and the rump of his cavalry, currently immobilised by the opposing Federal army. Before any charges could be made against Stuart, it is difficult to see past Lee's own intelligence planning, at a time when receipt of accurate information was paramount. The question has to be asked as to why he chose to send Jeb away at all, let alone on a prolonged ride to link up with his most northerly corps. Clearly, Lee was unaware of the success of the Federal intelligence agents in piercing his cavalry screen, otherwise he would have questioned Mosby's assertion that the Army of the Potomac would remain rooted in front of Washington. Instead, Lee believed that his troopers would have the freedom of the eastern side of the Blue Ridge Mountains to pick their way through the Federal corps and sweep north, wreaking general havoc, before linking up with Ewell. Meanwhile in Washington, Benjamin Stringfellow and Henry Harrison had independently begun their perilous journeys to link up with their commanders. While Stringfellow headed due west to join Jeb at Salem in Virginia, Harrison went north through Maryland. It would be days before either was heard from again.

---

38   O.R. Series I, Vol. XXVII, Part III, p.923.
39   *SHSP Vol. XXXVII*, p.95.
40   O.R. Series I, Vol. XXVII, Part III, p.915.
41   O.R. Series I, Vol. XXVII, Part III, p.927.

In keeping with their accusatory analysis of the rest of the Gettysburg campaign, the Southern historians completely ignored the Union contribution to the failure of Stuart's mission. At the same time as Lee was preparing his infamous instructions, the combined efforts of the Federal cavalry, the U.S. Signal Corps and the B.M.I. were stiffening Hooker's resolve to act. As was characteristic of Federal intelligence under this Union general, it was the all-source nature of mutual corroboration that made the difference. While Babcock dodged the Rebel intrusions into Frederick, General Tyler continued to supply observation and scouting intelligence from Maryland Heights as the Rebel corps neared their Potomac crossing. Meanwhile, Pleasonton's relentless harassing of the Rebel cavalry positions was not as valueless as many, including his own superiors, suspected as he had facilitated Milton Cline's return. There was no doubt now where the Rebels were heading, but with three corps spread across the approaches to Maryland and Imboden's cavalry already running riot in Pennsylvania, it would unrealistic to expect any single source of information to be able to elucidate a complete picture of the Rebel advance. Instead, it was the sheer weight of evidence that finally made up Hooker's mind. An erroneous report from Babcock on 24 June placed the entire Army of Northern Virginia through Martinsburg on the Potomac, despite Sharpe's report of the previous day, passing on Cline's information that Longstreet was still about two days march from the river, between Front Royal and Berryville. This information on the First Corps was confirmed by Tyler, although not before another hysterical message from Couch to Lincoln stating that the whole Army of Northern Virginia was already across the Potomac.[42] Meanwhile, at Berryville that very evening, General Lee was confidently explaining of the situation to Isaac Trimble: "We have again out-manoeuvred the enemy, who even now don't know where we are or what are our designs. Our whole army will be in Pennsylvania the day after to-morrow, leaving the enemy far behind, and obliged to follow us by forced marches."[43]

Lee was right in some respects, but he had failed to grasp the underlying significance of his own prediction. Over the course of the previous week, Hooker had stewed over the ever expanding portfolio of evidence that Lee was not threatening Washington, but without yet satisfying

General Isaac Trimble, who accompanied Robert Lee during the campaign.

42   OR Series I, Vol. XXVII, Part III, p.285-6, 295.
43   *SHSP Vol. XXVI*, p.119.

himself, much to exasperation of Lincoln and indeed his own staff. For all the difficulties of contrasting information, Marsena Patrick (the closest of Hooker's staff to
the B.M.I.) harshly criticised Hooker's lack of direction in his diary on 19 June: "We
get accurate information, but Hooker will not use it and insults all who differ from
him in opinion – He has declared that the enemy are over 100,000 strong – it is
his only salvation to make it appear that the enemy's forces are larger than his own,
which is all false & he knows it."[44] Could Fighting Joe have been paralysed by Lee's
bravado again? The answer came on 25 June. With the definitive confirmation that the
Rebel army was moving away from his front at Washington and about to cross into
Maryland, Hooker finally gave the orders to give chase. Again, Reynolds was ordered
to organise and lead the right wing of the army, composed of the I, III and XI Corps,
and speed across the river to seize the South Mountain passes opposite Frederick and
keep Lee from heading for Baltimore.[45] Once there, Reynolds would link up with
John Babcock and the Right Wing could fan out to find Lee with the full breadth
of its intelligence capability.[46] The remaining corps would march north in Reynolds'
wake and cross into Pennsylvania to concentrate around Middletown and Frederick.

As part of this general movement, Winfield Hancock's II Corps was ordered from
Gum Springs to Edwards Ferry on the banks of the Potomac. This route took him
directly across Stuart's intended path through Glasscock Gap as recommended by
Mosby. Jeb Stuart, already cursing his luck for the rain storms, which had slowed
his progress so far, was now cut off from direct contact with the Army of Northern
Virginia. Stuart himself maintained that this was no accident and that to pass through
the Federal lines and reunite with the Army of Northern Virginia on the other side
of the Potomac was always his intention.[47] Whether by accident or design, Stuart
was now faced with a choice: turn back and reunite with Lee to inform him that the
Federal chase had begun; or send a courier with the news (in the hope that it made
it through enemy lines) and carry on north around the Federal army until he found
Dick Ewell somewhere in Pennsylvania. The previous year, he had faced a very similar
decision on the Peninsula and his boldness in circumnavigating McClellan's vast army
won him the acclaim of Lee and the Confederate nation. Now Jeb was being excori-
ated in his own nation's press as the man who had been surprised and bested by, of all
people, Alfred Pleasonton. When considering what was going through the head of the
dashing Rebel cavalry officer as he considered his next move, it is impossible to ignore
the psychological pain of a bruised ego. Whether it was on account of his vanity,
disobedience or complete misjudgement of the situation (and there is no shortage of
commentators willing to offer their opinion on which was more prevalent), Stuart
chose to continue his ride and circumvent the Army of the Potomac, while following

44   Sparks, *Inside Lincoln's Army*, p.261.
45   O.R. Series I, Vol. XXVII, Part III, p.307.
46   O.R. Series I, Vol. XXVII, Part III, p.312.
47   O.R. Series I, Vol. XXVII, Part II, p.692.

Lee's directive to cause as much disruption as possible while behind enemy lines. He would not make contact again with Lee until the morning of 2 July once battle was well and truly joined, exhausted from riding 210 miles in only eight days.

Whatever the true underlying objective of Jeb's ride, there is no doubt that Hooker's orders to move and the decisiveness of the Federal march caught the Rebels by surprise. Stuart was now prevented from a quick reunion with his line by moving west of Centreville and, therefore, forced to swing even further east into Maryland. With Hancock now strung out on his left, he was also rendered completely impotent from an intelligence perspective. Had Stuart sought to take a moment to consider his run of luck so far, perhaps he would have re-assessed the chances of one of his couriers making it through the Yankee line. Needless to say, Jeb's final dispatch to Lee warning of Hooker's pursuit never reached its destination; he was completely isolated. Jeb's two planned reunions with his own intelligence sources were also foiled: Benjamin Stringfellow did not reach Salem in time to meet Stuart, but was captured by the Federals and taken to Washington, not to reunite with Stuart until after the campaign;[48] meanwhile John Mosby, probably the best informed of all Lee's intelligence agents at that time, was left high and dry on the eastern side of the advancing Union army as the II Corps marched on his intended rendezvous location of Gum Springs. The brave and dutiful Gray Ghost was exactly the sort of man Lee needed in Jeb's absence, but Mosby reported directly to Stuart and since there was no centralised Confederate operational and tactical intelligence system, he could not be plugged into either Lee's information network or that of Richmond. Both Stuart and Mosby were effectively lost to the Confederacy for the next week.

By 26 June, Jeb's raiding party and his residual troopers under Robertson and Jones were the last Confederates left in Virginia. Lee was now 175 miles from the intelligence hub of Richmond. Although, his communications with Davis were already at breaking point, it did not mean that Lee was completely without options. In his defence of Jeb's actions during the campaign, John Mosby rightly questioned why Lee did not seek to utilise the resources still at his disposal, primarily the residual cavalry of Robertson and Jones or even Jenkins. Imboden was still busy ripping up the Federal infrastructure around the Ohio to Baltimore Railroad close to Harrisburg, but Jones and Robertson were still only a handful of miles south, docilely watching as the Union forces pulled away from their positions in the mountain gaps. Both cavalry officers disobeyed Stuart's directions to move up in support of the Army of Northern Virginia, once it was clear that the Federal army was on the move, and it was not until Lee's orders of 29 June to consolidate his forces in Pennsylvania that Robertson and Jones finally made an effort to rejoin him. They did not arrive until 3 July, the day after Stuart returned from his marathon ride, and just in time to be of no service to Lee either before or during the battle.

48 McClellan, *Life and Campaigns*, p.336.

Although his motivation for not calling up his remaining cavalry sooner will remain one of the mysteries of the campaign, it is likely that Lee simply did not have the level of trust in his other cavalry officers that he did in Jeb. Marshall believed that Lee's personal relationship with Stuart obscured his professional judgement and that "General Lee was excessively fond of Stuart... he possessed a most noble and lovable nature."[49] This view, however, grossly simplified the trust that had developed between the commander and his de facto chief of intelligence. Lee was naïve to believe that there was no risk that Jeb would fail in his mission, but the greater crime was to have left himself so devoid of any alternative means of gathering information as Hooker's pursuit began. At the same time that Robert Lee was stripping himself of his cavalry, Fighting Joe was reinforcing his.[50] As Alfred Pleasonton pushed on towards Frederick, he was joined by a third division under General Judson Kilpatrick.[51]

By placing the Federal army between himself and Richmond, Lee had inverted the natural Confederate operational advantage and turned his situation into one of exterior lines of communications and logistics. Rather than seeking to augment his positive intelligence acquisition power, Lee's response was to revert again to bluff and diversion to exploit Washington's paranoia of its own defence and force the Army of the Potomac to hesitate. The same day that Lee issued his refined order to Jeb, he finally sent a request to Davis stating that "those under General Beauregard, can be employed at this time to great advantage in Virginia. If an army could be organized under the command of General Beauregard, and pushed forward to Culpeper Court House, threatening Washington from that direction, it would ... effect a diversion most favorable for this army."[52] With his positive intelligence capacity reduced, Lee would try and compensate by increasing his counterintelligence. If Jeb could begin the panic by cutting his usual destructive swath through Maryland, the paranoia in Washington would cause Lincoln to hold Hooker's response longer. Unfortunately, there was a joker in the pack. Occupying the Peninsula still, over a year after McClellan's landing, was General John Dix and his 30,000 men. Any aggressive moves by Dix during Lee's march north would send Davis into an equal panic for the safety of Richmond as could be expected of Lincoln and Washington. The door had been opened for Dix, a political appointee rather than a professional solider, when George Pickett's division was brought up to join Longstreet before the campaign began.[53] With some encouragement from Halleck, he started a small expedition on 18 June up the York River to around 20 miles east of Richmond, but it would be nearly a week before he could gather any kind of serious threat.[54]

---

49   *SHSP Vol. XXXVII*, p.95.
50   *Annals*, p.452.
51   Kilpatrick had earned the nicknamed "Kilcavalry" after his seemingly unquenchable desire to prove the effectiveness of modern guns in shredding his reckless cavalry charges.
52   O.R. Series I, Vol. XXVII, Part III, p.924-5.
53   O.R. Series I, Vol. XXVII, Part I, p.34.
54   O.R. Series I, Vol. XXVII, Part III, p.206.

The plan for General Beauregard to be brought up from the Carolinas and assemble his force around Culpeper Court House was communicated to the Confederate commander-in-chief in three messages sent between 23 and 25 June. The distance between the headquarters of the Army of Northern Virginia and the Rebel capital was such that it would take five days for the messages to arrive home. Davis and Adjutant-General Samuel Cooper, startled at the request given the late notice for such a risky manoeuvre, rejected Lee's plan out of hand, citing recent developments east of Richmond and the renewed success of Grant in the West. Cooper added to his missive a strong warning to Lee: "I would suggest for your consideration whether ... you might not be able to spare a portion of your force to protect your lines of communication."[55]

General John Dix.

In a wholly predictable irony for the Rebels, the replies of both Cooper and Davis were indeed intercepted before reaching Lee. Before it had even reached Pennsylvania, the Army of Northern Virginia was effectively cut off from its strategic intelligence headquarters and even if Cooper's message had not been seized by the Federals, it would still not have reached Lee in time to change the course of the campaign or the ensuing battle. As Hill and Longstreet's troops completed their Potomac crossing to meet up with Ewell at Hagerstown, Lee had no idea as to the precise whereabouts of his enemy. He was on a collision course with the Federals and expecting a potentially decisive holding action from Richmond, which would never come.

Agonisingly for Lee, the last communications he received from Richmond revealed that Hooker had trumped him again. In the days leading up to Lee's decision to order Stuart out, the Confederate wires came alive with reports of a new threat to the east of the capital. Pickets reported a Yankee force of 20,000 was assembling at Yorktown; John Dix had finally got himself together to move in force.[56] Most worrying of all, these troops were supposedly re-enforced with troops from the Army of the Potomac;[57] Hooker's little game of counterintelligence with the Northern Press

---

55   O.R. Series I, Vol. XXVII, Part I, p.76.
56   O.R. Series I, Vol. XXVII, Part III, p.912.
57   O.R. Series I, Vol. XXVII, Part III, p.911.

had duly been picked up by the C.S.S.B. and was now sewing panic in Richmond. Although the anxiety over the threat from the Peninsula was short-lived, and the Northern press would soon change their reports of a bold Federal advance under Dix to that of wholesale withdrawal of troops from the frontiers of the Peninsula (and even Kentucky) back to Washington, Dix's threat had come at exactly the wrong time for the Army of Northern Virginia. General Lee was in no doubt that this was a bluff and that Washington would never sanction such an aggressive advance while he was bearing down on Pennsylvania. He was also certain that the man to take Richmond would definitely not be John Dix. As he said his goodbyes to Old Dominion, Lee repeatedly begged Seddon and Davis to see through the masquerade and permit him to utilise some of the troops scattered round the Confederacy in idle defensive positions. Lee's continued badgering was quite out of character, but "So strong is my conviction of the necessity of activity on our part in military affairs, that you will excuse my adverting to the subject again, notwithstanding what I have said in my previous letter of to-day."[58] While he may have been a masterful military tactician, he had been undone by his own political manoeuvring and Mr F.J. Hooker's little trick. By not informing the War Department from the beginning of his plans for Beauregard, he had allowed Hooker to beat him to the punch and the "army in effigy" that Lee had desired was instead now dressed in blue and massing along the Pamunkey River east of his own capital. Just as Lee predicted, Dix's offensive would prove, in the words of D.H. Hill, "not a feint but a faint,"[59] but it ensured that the Army of Northern Virginia would be alone in threatening the North as the campaign moved towards its climax.

The damage of Hooker's little scheme, however, would go beyond merely upsetting Lee's operational plans. While the Johnnies washed themselves in the waters of the Potomac, the C.S.B. and William Norris would be focused on events east of Richmond and not north of Washington.[60] Norris, who had become increasingly frustrated by having the dubious distinction of being the only staff officer in the War Department still only at the rank of major, had spent much of the previous weeks touring Virginia as escort to Arthur Fremantle.[61] As such, he had precious little time to devote to overseeing covert intelligence operations, in spite of the importance of Lee's campaign. To compound the problem, another conflict would further compromise the Rebel intelligence effort. While its principal army was operating in Union lands, the Confederate Signal Bureau was about to undergo an attempted coup by its rival, James Milligan's Independent Signal Corps. One of Milligan's acolytes, R. A. Forbes, formulated charges against Norris for no less than revealing the Confederate

58   O.R. Series I, Vol. XXVII, Part III, p.931.
59   O.R. Series I, Vol. XXVII, Part III, p.972.
60   O.R. Series I, Vol. XXVII, Part III, p.927-8, 939.
61   Canan, H.V., *Confederate Military Intelligence* (Maryland Historical Magazine Volume 60, Baltimore: Maryland Historical Society 1964), p.45.

code to the enemy whilst being drunk aboard a flag-of-truce boat at the end of May.[62] Norris would eventually be cleared of these charges by a court of inquiry, but an internal squabble among its core intelligence services could hardly have come at a worse time for the Rebellion, so far into its greatest gamble of the War.

On the night of 28 June, while the First Corps rested close to Chambersburg, Longstreet's chief-of-staff, G. Moxley Sorrell, was trying to get some well-earned rest when he was awakened by his provost guard. They had captured a suspicious-looking civilian dressed in smart, but distinctly travel-worn clothes, who had been trying to infiltrate the camp claiming to work for General Longstreet. Despite his dishevelled appearance, Sorrell immediately recognised the man as Longstreet's spy, Henry Harrison, and rushed off with him to find Old Pete.[63] After a long trek from Washington, Harrison had indeed found the First Corps with relative ease and the information he brought would reshape the entire campaign. Only the day before, Harrison reported, three Union corps had taken their positions at Frederick and another two had reached South Mountain, less than 50 miles southeast of where they now stood.[64] Finally, the Confederate high command had a timely and highly accurate picture of the Federal pursuit, including the chilling news that Hooker had already been marching on them for four days. Longstreet lost no time in dispatching Harrison to Lee to tell the general his information. If Fighting Joe knew the location of the Rebel corps and, more specifically, that Dick Ewell was still separated (menacing York and Harrisburg), he would have the option of either sealing off the Second Corps and crushing it between his force and Couch's Susquehanna militia or striking directly at Lee while he was short of numbers.

That same evening, in his headquarters, Robert Lee was still unaware of his poten-tially desperate situation. Despite the troubling lack of word from Stuart, General Lee was satisfied with his progress up to that point. All his forces were now safely into Pennsylvania, a reserve army was hopefully under orders to march from the Carolinas to menace Washington and Hooker was still lagging somewhere south of the river.[65] "Our army is in good spirits, not over fatigued, and can be concentrated on any one point in twenty-four hours or less," Lee confided to Isaac Trimble.

> I have not yet heard that the enemy have crossed the Potomac, and am waiting to hear from General Stuart. When they hear where we are they will make forced marches to interpose their forces between us and Baltimore and Philadelphia. They will come up ... broken down with hunger and hard marching ... strung out on a long line and much demoralized, when they come into Pennsylvania.

62   Gaddy, *William Norris*, p.174.
63   Longstreet, *From Manassas to Appomattox*, p.324.
64   Longstreet, *From Manassas to Appomattox*, p.347.
65   *SHSP Vol. XXXVII*, p.228; Alexander, *Military Memoirs*, p.379.

I shall throw an overwhelming force on their advance, crush it, follow up the success, drive one corps back on another ... and virtually destroy the army.[66]

While Harrison was informing Old Pete of the rapid advance of the Yankees, Lee was formulating his final preparations for marching on his chosen operational objective of Harrisburg. The final, decisive battle he had longed for was close at hand. Then came the arrival of Harrison and the bursting of Lee's bubble. Not only did the spy completely revise his understanding of the Federal chase, but at last the feebleness of his intelligence-gathering and communications position must have dawned on him. If Hooker had crossed the Potomac on the 25th and yet he had heard nothing from Jeb, then his most trusted scout must either be marooned, captured or dead. Furthermore, if Union troops were in Frederick, then they were closer to Williamsport and Shepherdstown than he was and so his communications line to Richmond must be all but cut. Lee immediately abandoned his designs on Harrisburg and resolved to consolidate his army east of South Mountain and out of the Cumberland Valley.[67] Orders were immediately issued for Longstreet and Hill to march due east of their positions and for Ewell to march south in the direction of Cashtown and Gettysburg. As Abner Doubleday would later describe it: "The head of the serpent faced about as soon as its tail was trodden upon."[68]

An apologist for Rebel intelligence could regard the events of 28 June as justification for its structure. Although obviously not as sophisticated at the B.M.I., built on the twin pillars of scouting and espionage while one function was misfiring, (as the premier scouting agent was undertaking a "useless, showy parade"),[69] the key intelligence sought by Lee was nevertheless still acquired by the Rebellion spies. To accept this argument, however, would be to give far too much credit to the architects of the Confederate intelligence system and perhaps far too little credit to the spy himself. Henry Harrison represents almost a *deus ex machina* figure in the history of the Gettysburg campaign: arriving seemingly from nowhere to dispense such vital information, only to disappear (almost) from the story altogether. His incredible ability to slip through the tight Federal lines and locate Longstreet's headquarter within three days of learning of the Federal crossing was not widely appreciated and those who did tried to use the incredible nature of his feat as evidence that he could not possibly have existed. In fact, Harrison was not the only Rebel spy with vital information in Maryland. Thomas Nelson Conrad had been observing the Federal reaction to Lee's invasion and realised that Washington was almost undefended as the War Department focused the Union forces on attacking the Army of Northern Virginia. With the information of the Federal capital's vulnerability, Conrad set off for Pennsylvania; but

66   *SHSP Vol. XXVI*, p.121.
67   O.R. Series I, Vol. XXVII, Part II, p.307.
68   Doubleday, *Chancellorsville and Gettysburg*, p.65.
69   Sorrell, *Recollections*, p.163.

his mission was not to find Lee, rather to locate Jeb Stuart and offer to guide him on a devastating raid. Despite his detailed knowledge of the tactical situation, especially as he bounced his way through the Federal corps in Maryland, Conrad made no attempt to find the senior commander. Instead, having missed Stuart at Rockville, the "chaplain-scout" made for Baltimore, in the hope of catching him there.[70]

John Mosby would later baldly state that "No spy came to Chambersburg."[71] Mosby instead believed that Lee had already decided to concentrate around Gettysburg, but this assertion came as part of a wider defence of the performance of the Rebel cavalry. With the Gray Ghost's agenda to defend the misfiring Jeb Stuart, he can hardly be relied upon as an impartial witness. By the time of Harrison's appearance, the Confederate tactical intelligence apparatus was a shambles, with limited skirmishing and scouting power and the remains of its cavalry strung out from Ashby's Gap to the Susquehanna River. Harrison's was the last piece of tactical information that General Lee received until word reached him of General Pettigrew's encounter with John Buford's 1st Cavalry Division on 30 June, the precursory shots of the battle that Lee had been planning for six months. Meanwhile, to the east, intelligence reports poured into the Federal command from almost all conceivable sources, including the Federal cavalry, its signal officers, professional and civilian spies, Pennsylvania residents and intercepted Rebel communications and soldiers.

Observing the stark contrast between the intelligence positions of the Union and Confederate armies as June gave way to July, it is telling to note that Mosby's disbelief in the existence of Henry Harrison was based on the quality of the information he had brought. Along with his report on the location and direction of the Union army, Harrison announced a truly extraordinary change to the administration of the Army of the Potomac, which had occurred only that day and which Mosby denied could possibly have been discovered so quickly. Perhaps better than any other event during the campaign, the Federal drama of 28 June defines the superiority of their intelligence system. Early that morning, only three days before the battle would begin, General George Gordon Meade, commander of the Federal V Corps, was awoken in his camp by Colonel James Hardie of Halleck's staff in Washington.[72] Meade's reaction to Hardie's unexpected arrival says much about the man himself: a former military engineer and veteran of the Mexican War, Meade had been a solid professional throughout the War and performed with dedication, if not quite distinction, in each of the major engagements of the last twelve months. For all his ability, however, Meade was a fractious and sensitive man, quick to anger and not without his own brand of egotism – although not quite in the league of McClellan or Hooker. As he stared up at Halleck's man, Meade assumed that Hardie was there either to relieve him of duty or arrest him, although he was not exactly sure what he might have done to warrant

---

70   Conrad, *The Rebel Scout*, p.83-6.
71   *SHSP Vol. XXXVII*, p.227.
72   *Battles and Leaders, Vol. III*, p.241.

such treatment. Instead, Hardie handed over a communication from President Lincoln informing him of his appointment to command of the Army of the Potomac.[73]

Unbeknownst to the rest of the army, the previous days had witnessed a fierce argument across the telegraph lines between General Hooker and Washington. With all of Lee's forces now confirmed to have made it into Maryland, and his own numbers being eroded as men reached the end of their service periods, Hooker demanded permission to assume control of the troops left at Harper's Ferry, still under command of General Schenck.[74] The struggle between Hooker and Washington for overall control of the Federal troops in the Eastern Theatre had reached its crescendo and under the weight of the Lincolnian dichotomy, Joe had finally run out of fight. At 3:00 p.m., Halleck received a message from Hooker: without the ability to command all the troops in his front, he no longer

General George Gordon Meade, who assumed command of the Army of the Potomac only three days before the start of the battle.

felt able to undertake his sworn duty to protect both Washington and Harper's Ferry and so he tendered his resignation. If Marye's Heights had done for Ambrose Burnside, Maryland Heights was the end of his successor. It took only five hours for the War Department to confer with the president and accept gratefully Hooker's offer. As if to record their moment of triumph for all posterity, Halleck's orders to Meade included brief, but explicit, emphasis that "All forces within the sphere of your operations will be held subject to your orders. Harper's Ferry and its garrison are under your direct orders."[75]

To take such drastic action, with Lee loose in Pennsylvania and the armies sure to collide in the coming days, was little short of extraordinary. Of all people, Alfred Pleasonton would be moved to point out the hypocrisy of his own government for

73   O.R. Series I, Vol. XXVII, Part I, p.61.
74   O.R. Series I, Vol. XXVII, Part I, p.59.
75   O.R. Series I, Vol. XXVII, Part I, p.61.

breaking their pledge "never to swap horses when crossing a stream."[76] To assume command in the midst of a desperate chase was one thing, but to take over from a man as sensitive to intelligence losses as Joseph Hooker made Meade's task even more challenging. In an excellent piece of judgement, taken in conference with Meade's trusted chief engineer Guvenor Warren, despite their mutual distaste Meade decided to retain Daniel Butterfield and Hooker's staff. This decision would keep the B.M.I. and the rest of Fighting Joe's intelligence apparatus in place, at least until the end of the battle.

It is arguable that the true value of this resource, especially the B.M.I., can be seen not by what happened during the transition of leadership of the Army of the Potomac, but by what did not happen. For all Hooker's genius in the organisation of such an advanced intelligence structure, his paranoid desire for secrecy resulted in an equally counterproductive information blackout for his subordinates. Meade would later testify in front of the Joint Committee that he had no knowledge of the operational or tactical movements of either his own army or that of the enemy. "General Hooker, left the camp in a very few hours after I relieved him" Meade declared, "I received from him no intimation of any plan, or any views that he may have had up to that moment."[77] Within 24 hours of assuming command, however, Meade had been fully informed of the tactical situation and was able to issue decisive orders. It would be an ignominious end to the career of General Hooker, who had done so much to restore the pride of the Army of the Potomac and who should have been credited with the creation of the world's most sophisticated military intelligence machine. Instead, he would forever remain: "General Joseph Hooker, the defeated of Chancellorsville."[78]

76   *Annals*, p.458; as if to compound the irony, Lincoln purportedly coined the phrase on hearing of his nomination for a second presidential term, which he would win by beating another general of the Army of the Potomac, George McClellan in 1864.
77   *Report of the Joint Committee*, Part I, p.329.
78   Beckett, *The War Correspondents*, p.119.

8

A Collision of Two Armies

After weeks of marching, 28 June marked the end of the operational phase of the Gettysburg campaign and the start of the tactical. From this moment on, the emphasis of the intelligence acquisition process shifted from monitoring the enemy in order to discern his objectives to locating him and formulating an engagement. During the course of the day, as Meade was guided through the huge volume of information gathered since the Rebels crossed into Union territory, it became clear that the Rebel advance was a full-scale invasion of the North and thus protection of Washington and Harper's Ferry was no longer the priority. The intelligence passed on by the B.M.I. led to an immediate shift in Federal planning as the new commanding general resolved to bring on the battle with Lee and "relieve it [the North] from the devastation and disgrace of a hostile invasion."[1] Meade's initial assessment of the position of the Army of Northern Virginia sent to Washington (via Harrisburg as Stuart had cut direct telegraph communications) was impressively accurate. In a bitter irony for its creator, the replacement of Hooker with Meade represented an ideal environment for the B.M.I., since the best intelligence service in American military history now had a suitably decisive commander. Armed with full information on the tactical situation, Meade quickly stepped into the role of leader of the army and focused on the immediate task of making contact with Lee's scattered forces. Rather than seeking to strike, however, Meade the engineer would look to draw him into a battle where the Federals could assume the defensive in a suitable environment.

By this stage of the War, senior generals had learnt the penalties of taking the offensive against well-set opponents. Fredericksburg and Antietam were timely reminders of just how much punishment could be meted out by a smaller force, if established in a strong defensive position. Fighting Joe would put his finger on the issue when he testified to the Joint Committee that, aided by new weaponry, "those acting on the defensive can commence killing at a more remote distance and can kill faster."[2] Such

---

1   O.R. Series I, Vol. XXVII, Part III, p.374.
2   *Report of the Joint Committee*, Part I, p.145.

a position presented itself about 16 miles south-east of Gettysburg along Pipe Creek, between Manchester and Middleburg. The small creek was banked by steep ridges blocking the routes to Winchester and Baltimore, on which a defensive line would be almost impregnable to attack. "His first idea was to take advantage of the lay of the ground,"[3] would be General Grant's later criticism of Meade and the thought of digging in, while the Army of Northern Virginia broke itself along those high banks, seduced the new commander. A defensive posture, however, could not be maintained indefinitely and both Lee and Longstreet were fully aware that Lincoln would not let Meade delay long if the Army of Northern Virginia continued to loiter on Federal soil.

As the new commander of the Army of the Potomac weighed up the need to find Lee with his desire to fall back to Pipe Creek, the only serious error that leaked into Meade's intelligence in the critical few days before the start of the battle was the continued overestimation of the size of Lee's army. Meade had accepted the view that the Army of Northern Virginia was composed of around 92,000 infantry with 270 guns and 6,000 to 8,000 cavalry. This figure was almost a third higher than reality and this erroneous belief in his inferiority of numbers would continue to affect Meade's tactical decision-making throughout the rest of the campaign.

Regardless of the intelligence provided to him prior to the commencement of the battle, on the morning of 1 July, Lee had achieved almost everything that he had set out to do. Although he had been prevented from undertaking an attack on Harrisburg, he had successfully drawn the Army of the Potomac out of their defences and into the open field of battle. Moreover, on the first day, he could be expected to hold a considerable numerical advantage as his three corps were already concentrating on Gettysburg, while the Union's six corps were still widely scattered and Meade hesitated between attack and defence. As the armies started to assemble around the town, the opportunities for the acquisition of intelligence would be broadly the same for both sides. The opposing topographical features of the Seminary and Cemetery Ridges provided ample scope for both commanders to monitor the movements of his opponent. Prisoners, offering the chance to collect vital ORBAT information, would be captured in numbers so great that both sides would struggle to cope with them. The only element which would not provide a significant role after the opening morning would be the cavalry. With the armies so close, they would not play a significant part in tactical information gathering during Gettysburg, but would instead be left to play their part in an over-looked clash on 3 July. Victory would be in the grasp of the commander who utilised his tactical information best.

Utilising these various means of generating information would be largely dictated by the actions of the commanding generals. Lee, as usual, would assume the offensive as soon as he saw the progress being made by Hill and Ewell's corps on the first afternoon. Meade, having been denied the chance to take a defensive position at Pipe

3   Macartney, *Lincoln and his Generals*, p.167.

Creek, quickly realised the potential of Gettysburg's rolling hills and consolidated to repel the Rebel attacks. Lee would require good observational reconnaissance and scouting to identify weaknesses in the Federal line, combined with detailed ORBAT from prisoners and deserters. As he stressed in his official report, his tactics would revolve around a coordinated offensive to pull the Federal defence apart by pressuring discrete sections of their line in order to open up gaps for his men to pour through. For Meade, the defensive actions of the first day could be maintained by utilising the imposing protection offered by Culp's Hill and Cemetery Ridge, unless Lee ceased attacking him or if the opportunity to counter-attack presented itself.

Two days before Henry Harrison had managed to smuggle himself across Union lines and back to the First Corps, Boston journalist Charles C. Coffin, travelling with the Army of the Potomac, filed a report predicting that "If Lee advances with nearly all his forced into Pennsylvania, there must be a collision of the two armies not many miles west of Gettysburg."[4] Almost at exactly the same time as Coffin was sending his prescient article, Robert Lee was discussing the impending climax of his campaign and apparently "laid his hands on the map, over Gettysburg, and said hereabout we shall probably meet the enemy and fight a great battle."[5] For a man with such astonishing apparent foresight, and he was not the only combatant to claim it,[6] he was woefully ill-prepared when the shooting started. James Longstreet had a slightly different opinion and believed that the battle of Gettysburg was "was totally unexpected on both sides."[7] In support of Old Pete, there was no shortage of commentators who would also describe the battle as a meeting engagement or an "accidental collision,"[8] and not even John Reynolds, at the vanguard of the Army of the Potomac, knew with any certainty on this Wednesday morning that one of the greatest battles of the entire Civil War was about to start. To say that the battle was totally unexpected by both sides, however, does a gross disservice to the Federal intelligence work of men like John Buford, Aaron Jerome and George Sharpe. Although it can be said that neither commander truly predicted the start of the battle on 1 July, it is not true that both forces stumbled into each other blindly or accidentally.

As the armies came together, Meade had mobilised his entire intelligence machinery towards the front so that, should the enemy be found, his decision-making could be based on the best available information. John Buford was sent out as part of an advanced cavalry force of General Reynolds to find Lee in the vicinity of Cashtown. He was accompanied by scouts, Signal Corps officers and telegraphic engineers. With John Reynolds were members of the B.M.I., now primarily tasked with providing

---

4   Andrews, J. Cutler, *The North Reports the Civil War* (Pittsburgh: University of Pittsburgh Press, 1955), p.406.
5   *SHSP Vol. XXVI*, p.121.
6   Pleasonton would also claim to have tried to alerted Meade of an inevitable clash at Gettysburg (*Report of the Joint Committee*, Part I, p.359).
7   *Annals*, p.453.
8   *Battles and Leaders*, Vol. III, p.251.

ORBAT information on the Rebels. The brief affray with Pettigrew on 30 June encouraged Buford's natural belligerence and, bolstered by information provided by B.M.I. scout Edward Hopkins and Aaron Jerome of the U.S. Signal Corps (ensconced on the steeple of the local college), he moved his division forward four miles out of the town to receive any return by the enemy the following day. There is no doubt that the Federal army had engineered a superior intelligence position for themselves, but for all the assistance that this superiority granted them throughout the next three days of battle, it had its most profound effect on the first day. In the ever-humble opinion of his superior Alfred Pleasonton: "Buford's judgment in believing he would be attacked in heavy force on the morning of the 1st of July, and going out four miles to meet it the night before, was what saved to us the position. Had he waited an attack at Gettysburg, he would have been driven from the place before any support could have arrived."[9] Whilst Pleasonton overlooked the role that the good intelligence work of his support staff played in Buford's decision-making, it is difficult to argue with his conclusion of the excellence of his subordinate's interpretation and implementation of that intelligence. With advanced knowledge of the presence of the Rebel army in his vicinity, Buford was able to take the initiative, with the understanding that three Federal corps were within half a day's march and he had the communications at his disposal to mobilise them immediately. As Buford himself put it, "By daylight on July 1, I had gained positive information of the enemys position and movements, and my arrangements were made for entertaining him until General Reynolds could reach the scene."[10] The first of the Rebel corps had been found at last.

The contrast between Buford and Henry Heth could not be more profound. Like all the subordinates in Hill's Third Corps, he had been left to rely upon his scouts, pickets and cavalry for tactical information on the whereabouts of the enemy. This information was duly brought on 30 June by James Pettigrew who, the story goes, had been

John Buford, whose decisive action on the evening of 30 June would define the first day's fighting at Gettysburg.

9 *Annals*, p.454.
10 O.R. Series I, Vol. XXVII, Part I, p.927.

sent to Gettysburg to find shoes, where he briefly engaged Buford's cavalry before pulling back. Captain Louis Young of Pettigrew's staff later claimed that they had been warned of the presence of the Federal army before they even reached Gettysburg. As the men of Pettigrew's brigade rode towards the town that afternoon they were intercepted by two men coming in the opposite direction. One of them was none other than Longstreet's spy, Henry Harrison.[11] Two days after delivering the decisive information that brought both armies to that quiet corner of Pennsylvania, the Rebel spy was again one step ahead of his superiors. Pettigrew's information, sadly, was not accepted by Heth or Hill, who had just returned from a meeting with Lee, where the latest location of the Army of the Potomac was agreed to be about 20 miles south of Gettysburg at Middleburg. Just as Hooker had initially struggled to keep up with the various strands of Lee's army as it threaded its way through Virginia and Maryland, so too had Lee failed to follow Meade's dispersal of the Army of the Potomac. Buford's cavalry were instead interpreted to be local militia and so Hill approved Heth's request to move more aggressively against Gettysburg again the following day. In Young's opinion, "The spirit of disbelief had taken such hold, that I doubt if any of the commanders of the brigades, except General Pettigrew, believed we were marching to battle, a weakness on their part which rendered them unprepared for what was about to happen."[12]

When judging the decisiveness of the disparity in intelligence between the two armies on the first morning, it should not be forgotten that even the best intelligence does not automatically win battles. Despite the Confederate's almost complete ignorance of the true situation, they had the advantage that their orders to consolidate on the area had been given more than a day earlier and the confluence of so many roads from all major local towns into Gettysburg meant that

General James Johnson Pettigrew of the Second Corps. His opinion of the Federal troops in Gettysburg was ignored by his superiors.

11   *Histories of the Several Regiments and Battalions from North Carolina in the Great War 1861-'65 Vol. V* (Goldsboro: Nash Brothers, 1901)(hereinafter referred to as the *HSR*) pg 115 and possibly also the same as referred to by Fremantle (Fremantle, *Three Months in the Southern States*, p.252).
12   *HSR*, p.117.

their mobilisation to the battlefield would be swift. Unlike Lee, whose army was all converging on the same general location, the scientifically minded Meade was still "dreaming Pipe dreams"[13] and holding his corps to the south in the hope of luring his opponent to him. Deficient in tactical information they may have been, but as Hill ordered the divisions of Henry Heth and Dorsey Pender to march on the 3,000 troopers of Buford's cavalry brigade, the Rebel situation was vastly superior and would only get better still as Dick Ewell approached from the north.

As Heth's advanced column moved on Gettysburg a few hours after daybreak and started to exchange fire with the enemy cavalry, there was great surprise when these local 'militia' started to fight back hard. It would not be until later that afternoon, in conversation with Arthur Fremantle, who had arrived with Longstreet, that the sickly Ambrose Hill would comment on the uncharacteristic stiffness of the Federal resistance.[14] The realisation of their tactical misunderstanding was never articulated better than by Hill's own soldiers on spotting the black hats of the Iron Brigade. By refusing to accept the more accurate intelligence supplied to him by his scouts and brigade commanders the previous day, Hill had sprung a trap entirely of his own making. While Hill and Ewell (and later Lee) were reacting to what they saw developing in front of them, Reynolds and Howard (and later Meade) had been furnished with well-acquired and interpreted intelligence from Buford and his Signal Corps support. Meade, therefore, understood the situation exactly and knew that the rest of the Army of Northern Virginia was on the way. If they could be held for a few hours, the Army of the Potomac could organise to lure them to Pipe Creek or fight them where they stood.

The stubbornness of the Federal opposition that so surprised Ambrose Hill not only stemmed from the understanding that this was the decisive engagement that had been brewing since early June, but also the knowledge of where reinforcements were coming from. As Aaron Jerome observed the action from the cupola of the Lutheran

General Henry Heth, a division commander of Hill's Second Corps, who did not believe that the Army of the Potomac had caught up to the Rebels.

13   Scott, *Battle of Gettysburg*, p.8.
14   Fremantle, *Three Months in the Southern States*, p.254.

Seminary, he was watching not just for the butternuts soldiers marching from the east and north, but also his brothers in blue hurrying to the scene from the southwest. As Buford traded the first blows with Heth and Pender's divisions in the morning, the appreciation of when reinforcements would arrive was key to holding his position. What the Rebels did not understand on the morning of 1 July was that they were in a race. Buford and Reynolds had been anticipating this situation for days and it would be the men of the I Corps, rather than their leader George Meade, who would commit the Army of the Potomac to the battle.

If they had understood that the Federals were rushing to secure a strong position before being forced out of town, perhaps Hill, Ewell and Lee would have acted with a similar determination to the foes they so disrespected. While poor Dick Ewell would set himself up for fierce criticism after the battle by allowing himself the discretion afforded him by Lee's order to attack Culp's Hill, Reynolds was in quite the opposite frame of mind. Once he was sure that it was Lee's army, his courier was left with no such ambiguity as he was sent off to inform Meade of the situation "Don't spare your horse, never mind if you kill him."[15] While Reynolds lay dying from a Rebel sharpshooter's bullet and as Oliver Howard's XI Corps arrived on the field, Butterfield was in Meade's headquarters in Taneytown completing a draft order to pull the army back towards Pipe Creek, in the event that Lee took the offensive. While the nature of what was unfolding remained a mystery to Meade, he still had every intention of avoiding battle in Pennsylvania and so stayed any instruction to move his remaining corps towards Gettysburg. Although never issued, since the vortex of combat developing around Gettysburg would suck in the remainder of his army within hours, the Federal commander would regret ever requesting the drafting of his "Pipe Creek Circular".

So determined was the counterattack from the first arriving Federal support that Hill was very nearly thrown back to Chambersburg. In the end, it was the timely arrival of Old Bald Head from the north that halted the implosion of the Third Corps. Rodes division of the Second Corps arrived just in time to return the favour that Hill had bestowed on Ewell at Antietam the previous year and halt the Federal progress. Once Jubal Early had joined the fight by around 2:30 p.m., the four Rebel divisions outnumbered the two Yankees corps by over 5,000 men and the weight of Rebel troops inexorably shoved the Federals off their initial lines on the ridges west of Gettysburg.[16] As Lee and Longstreet arrived to survey the battleground around 1:30 p.m., they quickly recognised that Hill and Ewell had the smaller Union force on run. The blessing was given for the general engagement that Lee been so careful to caution his commanders against in the days before. But, the Rebels were already falling behind in the tactical

15   Meade, George, *The Life and Letters of George Gordon Meade*, Vol. II (New York: Scribner's, 1913), p.36.
16   Longstreet, *From Manassas to Appomattox*, p.357.

race. Swift messages sent to Taneytown meant that by 1.10 p.m. on the first day of the battle, Butterfield was dispatching orders to General Hancock of the II Corps to proceed to Gettysburg and take command, with Reynolds having fallen. By 6:00 p.m. on the same day, Meade had determined to commit to battle; the entire Army of the Potomac had been mobilised to the fight within twelve hours. Once the Rebel assault had failed to dislodge the Federals at the end of the first day's fighting, the odds began to shift dramatically in Meade's favour.

In contrast, although Lee elected to commit to the fight much earlier, his unusual indecisiveness betrayed his lack of confidence in his understanding of the tactical situation. While Meade had embraced the intelligence apparatus established by his predecessor, admittedly with little other option, Lee had stripped himself of his. On 30 June, Stuart was at Hanover, roughly equidistant from Gettysburg as Taneytown, still circumnavigating the Army of the Potomac and dragging an eight mile long Union wagon train, which he had snaffled on the fourth day of the raid in compliance with Lee's orders to disrupt the Federal war effort.[17] Exhausted by a week of hard riding and fighting, he was on his way to meet Jubal Early at York, completely unaware that Old Jube had already been ordered to rejoin the rest of the army around Gettysburg. As the Federals were solidifying their position on Cemetery Ridge, Stuart reached York only to find that the Second Corps had already gone and so, believing the army to be heading in the direction of Shippensburg, dispatched two of his staff, Major Venable and Captain Henry Lee, out to find them. While Robert Lee was still blind at his front, Jeb was galloping around Pennsylvania trying to find him.

Meanwhile Lee, lauded for his skill in utilising tactical intelligence, was relying on scraps and reluctant to issue firm orders to Ewell and Hill to attack while the strength of opposition on the hills was still unknown. Lee did not have the luxury of time to consider his options before dispatching his orders since he arrived with the fight ongoing and so was compelled to afford discretion to his corps commanders. These orders were further complicated by the problem of controlling his scattered corps with limited communications resources and such a small administrative staff. With the piecemeal arrival of Hill, Ewell and Longstreet on the first day and the mincing of the Third Corps in the early exchanges, organisation was lost almost immediately. As if this was not enough, it should not be forgotten that the Army of Northern Virginia was now in the untried three-corps configuration with two brand new corps commanders in Hill (still in his sick-bed) and Ewell at the helm.

The Rebel's poor intelligence dogged them throughout the first day and Ewell's progress in particular, having reached the foot of Culp's Hill on a tide of fast-retreating Yankees, was blighted by poor and confusing reports. The seizure of the hill was critical to stopping the Federals occupying a strong defensive line, but faulty information

---

17   O.R. Series I, Vol. XXVII, Part II, p.694.

from General William "Extra Billy" Smith[18] of enemy movements on his flank caused Ewell to stall his initial advance, only for those enemy troops to be revealed as his own men. Meanwhile, early reconnaissance of the hill led Ewell to believe it to be unoccupied, a mistake quickly revised as the bullets started to whistle around them. The attack was halted and then abandoned entirely when a captured Federal courier revealed a message from General George Sykes to Henry Slocum advising of the Federal V Corps' imminent arrival.[19] Sykes, who had actually stopped about four miles from Gettysburg and who would not arrive at the field until around 7:00 a.m. the following morning, was completing a punishing two day march, covering 47 miles in the stifling summer heat. None of the combatants knew it at the time, but as the light failed on the first day of July, so too was the sun setting on Lee's chances of success. Confederate military strategy demanded that opportunities be sought to isolate portions of the Union army in order to orchestrate engagements where they would have numerical advantage. By early afternoon, Lee had stumbled into exactly that position, but he had lacked the eyes to see it.

By not realising the race that they were in, not only did the Confederates leave it too late to take advantage of their superior numbers, but they could not stop the Federals securing a strong defensive line along Cemetery Ridge. Just as the Army of Northern Virginia had inverted their natural strategic advantages by invading the North, now they surrendered the tactical advantage by assuming an outside line in an arc around the hills south of the town. As they had flooded back through Gettysburg, the Federal army had wrapped itself around the twin anticlines of Culp's Hill and Cemetery Hill and along the spine of Cemetery Ridge (over the critical thoroughfares of Baltimore Pike and Taneytown Road linking the town to Meade's headquarters at Taneytown) and down to the two small hills of Big Round Top and Little Round Top. This became the 'fish-hook' defensive line. "Our exterior lines were about five miles in length, and to move from point to point required long, round about marches, often exposed to the enemy's view," was Edward Porter Alexander's assessment of the Rebel situation on 2 July, once the Federals were positioned. "Their force would allow 25,000 infantry and 100 guns for each mile of line. Ours would allow but 13,000 infantry and 50 guns per mile."[20]

The failure to drive the Federals away from Culp's Hill and Cemetery Ridge ensured that the battle would not be won for the Confederacy that day and the situation they faced at dawn on 2 July could not have suited their tactical intelligence resources less. For the next two days, Lee would attempt to coordinate a series of synchronised attacks on differing points in the Union line relying primarily on courier communications. Meanwhile, his opponents could observe his every move and then report almost

18   Extra Billy was so nicknamed for the extra fees he used to command as a mail contractor before the War.
19   OR Series I, Vol. XXVII, Part II, p.446.
20   Alexander, *Military Memoirs*, p.387.

instantly to their commanding general. Doubleday estimated that Lee took three times longer to communicate with his corps commanders than Meade and the Rebel's curved line ensured that any flag signals between Lee (positioned on Seminary Ridge) and Ewell (facing Culp's Hill) could be read by the enemy. The officers of the U.S. Signal Corps instinctively understood the opportunities that the Federal position offered and were quick to exploit them. By mid-morning of 1 July, Jerome's position in the cupola had been supported by another station at Gettysburg courthouse to provide information to General Howard, as he marched up from Emmitsburg. After the fish hook line had been established, by 11:00 a.m. on the 2nd, the men of the Signal Corps had occupied every suitable high position on the Federal side of the field. To augment communications between these stations and the commanders, throughout the first day, wires were strung out across the Union positions and, by sundown, telegraph lines connected Meade's operational base at the small farmhouse of Lydia Leister on Cemetery Ridge all the way past the Round Tops to Emmitsburg.[21] This would have been achieved sooner, but the smoke from the battle prevented quicker installation. Surveying the scene from the town on the second morning, Lee realised the gravity of his situation: "the enemy have the advantage of us in a shorter and inside line and we are too much extended. We did not or we could not pursue our advantage of yesterday, and now the enemy are in a good position."[22]

---

21 O.R. Series I, Vol. XXVII, Part I, p.202.
22 *SHSP Vol. XXVI*, p.125.

9

"Did You Get There?"

The first night was a short one and the Rebel generals were up before 4:00 a.m. to plan the day ahead. They may have lost the chance to whip the Federals in one day, but in the Confederate camps the result was still almost a foregone conclusion. Arthur Fremantle reported that "the universal feeling in the army [of Northern Virginia] was one of profound contempt for an enemy whom they have beaten so constantly, and under so many disadvantages."[1] The Army of Northern Virginia had been arranged essentially as they had arrived at the field, with the Second Corps spread to the north and east around Culp's Hill, the Third occupying the Rebel centre and Longstreet's men stretched to along the southern sections of Seminary Ridge. Now, with a Federal force finally in front of him to attack, but with its size and exact position still unknown, Lee needed good tactical information to plan his assault.

In his official report, Lee claims that the strength of the Federal army was unknown to the Confederates on 1 July and every effort was made to gain accurate ORBAT information "to ascertain the numbers and position of the enemy."[2] This sweeping statement, however, ignores the reality that Lee had also severely restricted his capacity to overcome this uncertainty a week earlier. On 1 July over 5,000 Federal prisoners were taken by the Rebels, but without the tools to process the prisoners, which Butterfield and Patrick had established at Taneytown for Meade, the information generated was poor. The Confederates had no ability to coordinate the wholesale processing of prisoners since David Bridgford's provost guard battalion had been left behind in Winchester. This potentially crucial source of ORBAT intelligence was denied to Lee through his own poor planning during the campaign. Without the means to analyse the various regiments of enemy soldiers as they fell into his hands, Lee had no accurate way of measuring the progress of the Federal army as it came together on the field. Colonel Armistead L. Long, Lee's military secretary, advised his commander during the night of 1 July that "only two or three corps of the enemy

---

1   Fremantle, *Three Months in the Southern States*, p.256.
2   O.R. Series I, Vol. XXVII, Part II, p.307-8.

are up," but in fact 43 of 51 Yankee brigades were up and in position by early the next morning.[3]

With Jeb still absent and despite the thick early morning fog, Lee ordered a reconnaissance of the enemy lines by his senior topographical engineer, Captain Samuel R. Johnston, who was about to write himself his own piece of the Gettysburg legend. Johnston was a trusted engineer with the Army of Northern Virginia, who had completed several previous missions for Lee and was held in high esteem. Dispatched around 4:00 a.m. and assisted by Major John Clarke, he rode across to the Federal left flank, up Little Round Top and back to Lee's position at Chambersburg Pike behind Seminary Ridge by around 7:30 a.m. Or so he claimed. As Johnston explained his route and described the complete absence of meaningful Federal presence that he encountered, Lee pointed to the Round Tops anchoring the southernmost point of the Union line, "Did you get there?" Yes, confirmed Johnston, and the hills were clear of Yankees.[4] If this was true, Meade had forgotten to lock his back door and the Rebels had been gifted a potential position on Cemetery Ridge from which, it was believed, Rebel artillery could enfilade the Union lines. Here was another Chancellorsville in the making.

Lee saw the plan instantly: a surprise attack could put a Rebel force up on to the closer of the two hills, Little Round Top; a coordinated assault by Ewell on Culp's Hill could then squeeze Meade in a pincer. His trusted old war horse, General Longstreet, would provide the main strike force, marching north up the Emmitsburg Road (along the foot of Cemetery Ridge) to hit the perceived southern lip of Federal line and roll it up while seizing the high ground of Little Round Top. Meanwhile, Ewell would lead a synchronous attack on the Union right to prevent Meade from freeing up reserves and repelling Longstreet's approach. By Lee's usual standards, this plan was reasonably simple, save for the difficulty of managing a dual offensive between two points separated by the enemy force occupying elevated ground. These intricacies were of little concern to the old general, however, since he would not play a part in the actual execution of these manoeuvres, but leave it to his corps commanders. During the entire day's fighting, one of the most important of his military career, Fremantle estimated that Lee gave only one message and received one report.[5] Unlike Meade, who by then had taken the field and positioned himself in the centre of the action to plug himself into a courier and flag communications network that had spread throughout his scattered corps, Lee would not be playing an active part in events as they unfolded and therefore gave no thought to a dedicated communications system for his army.

How Johnston and Clarke managed to miss Buford's troopers bivouacked around the Peach Orchard at the foot of Cemetery Ridge, two regiments of Geary's division

---

3   Alexander, *Military Memoirs*, p.300.
4   Hyde, Bill, 'Did You Get There? Capt. Samuel Johnston's Reconnaissance at Gettysburg' (*The Gettysburg Magazine*, Issue 29), p.86-93.
5   Fremantle, *Three Months in the Southern States*, p.260.

of the XII Corps, the officers of the Signal Corps on the crest of Little Round Top or the III Corps arriving along the Emmitsburg Road was to say the least puzzling. Johnston's previous record of competent service would indicate that dereliction of duty or deceit was highly unlikely, but perhaps in the thick fog that shrouded that July morning, which did not lift until around 10:00 a.m., it would have been perfectly possible for the two horsemen to have slipped in between the isolated Union positions and climb the larger of the two hills, Big Round Top, by mistake. Whatever the truth in Johnston's observation, the decision had been made. Further reconnaissance from Lee's Chief of Artillery General William Pendleton, who briefly established a good observational position on the Fairfield Road, did nothing to refine the initial understanding.[6] Lee made his interpretation and issued his orders by 11:00 a.m. The Federal left was 'in the air' and Old Pete would roll them up.

In keeping with the principles of the intelligence ladder, tactical information had the shortest expiry date and so it would be unwise for any commander to assume that his enemy would remain static for any prolonged period. It was already nearly four hours since Johnston had returned and before he would set out, Longstreet insisted on waiting another hour for General Evander Law's Alabama Brigade of Hood's division to come up from picket duty at New Guilford. By now, every Federal corps was present at the field except for Sedgwick's VI, which had been held in position by Meade around Manchester, in case the Pipe Creek plan was still possible. Uncle John was only given orders to hurry to Gettysburg at 7:30 p.m. the previous evening; by around 5:00 p.m. on the 2nd, they had completed the marathon march of 34 miles to arrive along Baltimore Pike, behind Cemetery Ridge. Even if Longstreet had set off immediately when ordered, it would have been wise to have acquired some additional information on the latest status before launching his attack, in case any significant changes to the enemy position required some improvisation. No effort had been made by Lee or Longstreet to establish a permanent observation point, however, to advise on the Federal movements and later analysis of the incident would focus instead on the First Corps' delays in commencing their attack.

Almost from the outset Longstreet's march was a shambles, a fact that his critics would quickly link to his disagreement with Lee's proposed tactics in favour of his own view of circumventing the Federal position. Longstreet too believed in the benefits of fighting from a position of defence and interposing the Army of Northern Virginia between Meade and Washington would force Meade to initiate an attack. His orders having been received, however, Old Pete's duty was to get his corps in to position without being seen. The principal concern during his march towards the Emmitsburg Road was the prying eyes of the pesky Yankee flag-floppers up on Little Round Top. To guide them safely under the noses of the signalmen, Captain Johnston himself was ordered to the front of Longstreet's column. If any of the Confederate generals had any scepticism as to the accuracy of Johnston's reconnaissance, their suspicions were soon to be realised. At about 1:30 p.m., Lafayette McLaw's leading division stumbled into an exposed position beyond Black Horse Tavern. The soldiers of the First Corps did not need a Federal code book to understand that the furious flag-waving from Signal Officer Captain James Hall on Little Round Top meant that they had been spotted and Federal headquarters would soon know. Had McLaws or Longstreet known the Federal cipher, however, they might have been intrigued by Hall's report; the signal officer identified around 10,000 Rebel troops, but reported them moving across the Federal line from left to right and not towards it.[7]

While the First Corps were blundering their way towards the Yankees, a dishevelled and exhausted figure rode up and presented himself to the commander of the Army of Northern Virginia. Jeb Stuart, who had spent the previous hours besieging the town of Carlisle, twenty five miles north of Gettysburg, had finally returned to the army. After

General Lafayette McLaws of the First Corps.

eight long days of riding and fighting, dragging their captured wagon train and 400 prisoners, Jeb and his men were close to collapse and had been reduced to sleeping in the saddle.[8] On arrival, they were too late and too tired to affect the day's plans and so were sent off by Lee to guard Ewell's left flank until a more active role could be determined.

Once McLaws and Hood had finally dragged themselves to the Emmitsburg Road it was almost 3:30 p.m., nearly eight hours after Johnston had reported back to Lee and four and a half hours since orders had been issued. According to Johnston, the road ahead lay clear for Longstreet to march on an oblique angle on Cemetery Ridge and the Round Tops. What greeted them however, as if to mock their ignorance of the real situation, were 11,000 thousand Federals of Daniel Sickles' III Corps sprawled across Emmitsburg Road. Lafayette McLaws instantly recognised the situation and the threat, three times requesting that Longstreet reconsider Lee's orders for the Rebel

7   O.R. Series I, Vol. XXVII, Part III, p.488.
8   O.R. Series I, Vol. XXVII, Part II, p.696.

attack since "the reconnaissance on which they were based had been faulty." McLaws later claimed that he had repeatedly requested permission to accompany Johnston on his mission, but had been denied. Whether McLaws' presence would have made a difference is a moot point, but ultimately he did not lay the blame with Lee's engineer. "All this resulted from defective and deficient organization of our staff corps; not from anybody's fault, but from the force of circumstances. We read since the war that there was an abundance of reconnoitering on our left, but very little, if any, on our right."[9]

How Sickles came to be there was the subject of similarly heated debate among the Federals. As the V and III Corps arrived at the battlefield throughout the morning, Meade deployed them to shore up his line along Cemetery Ridge. Having brought Geary's division of the XII Corps across from the Round Tops to support the defence of Culp's Hill, Daniel Sickles was ordered to the left of Hancock's II Corps to cover up to the crest of Little Round Top. Sickle's men had been called up by Meade at 7:00 p.m. the previous day, but poor courier work meant that the order was not received until 2:00 a.m., resulting in the III corps not arriving until about seven hours later and thus avoiding Captain Johnston's earlier reconnaissance. For Daniel Sickles, whose hatred of George Meade would extend well beyond the end of the War, this assignment was not to his liking. The general felt the proposed position, covering uneven and wooded ground between the ridge and the hills was not tenable. To add to the problem, Alfred Pleasonton had taken the extraordinary decision to relieve John Buford's two cavalry brigades guarding Sickles' left, without instructing anyone to replace them. Emmitsburg Road had been left unprotected.[10] After repeated requests for Meade to review his position, Sickles took it upon himself to act and, in magnificent fashion, led his men about three quarters of a mile forward of the Federal line to create his own personal salient.

Meade had been too concerned with what was happening on his right to worry unduly about what Sickles was up to, but the ghosts of Chancellorsville

General Daniel Sickles, leader of the III Corps whose actions during 2 July nearly led to the destruction of his entire corps and who would viciously attack Meade's leadership after the battle.

9   *SHSP Vol. VII*, p.75-8.
10   O.R. Series I, Vol. XXVII, Part III, p.490.

were about to revisit the Army of the Potomac. Almost exactly two months before, Stonewall Jackson had marched his men right past three of Hooker's corps and through the dense thickets of the Wilderness to hammer into Oliver Howard's XI Corps and collapse the Union left. Just as Howard's pickets had wrongly interpreted the movement of Jackson's corps as a retreat, Signal Officer Hall's report of 1:30 p.m. wrongly assumed that the Rebel column of Longstreet's First Corps was moving away from their intended target and so no preparations were made to receive the eventual charge. In the aftermath of Stonewall's shock attack of 2 May, Sickles had been forced to look on in horror as the Rebel artillery occupied his previous position of Hazel Grove and then pounded the Union line. Whether still haunted by that experience or whether he was just seeking a stronger artillery position, as he later claimed, Daniel Sickles picked an unfortunate movement, which put him directly in Longstreet's way. Having spent four hours getting into position to execute Lee's orders, Old Pete was not open to suggestions to change the script now. Despite the Rebels' blundering march towards Cemetery Ridge, Sickles' men seemed detached, unsupported and completely unaware of the danger. Perhaps their stealth had been successful after all. Either way, Longstreet was not in the mood for improvisation and so the First Corps would just have to go straight through them.

After the tumult of the first day's fighting, one would be tempted to think that a night of reflection and planning would see both armies recover their poise and direction. However, the battle of 2 July would prove to be an equally distasteful mix of shoddy intelligence and poor decision-making. Captain Johnston's reconnaissance early in the morning had been unquestionably faulty, leading Lee to the false conclusion that the Round Tops were undefended and that a march up Emmitsburg Road could precipitate the seizure of a position on Cemetery Ridge. As McLaws and John Bell Hood's divisions burst out of the woods and into the open in front of the III Corps, Little Round Top was vacant and Meade's left flank was indeed unprotected. Had Longstreet bowed to McLaws' badgering and amended Lee's order to allow the bulk of his force to swing round Sickles, the high ground could have been taken and Meade could have been rolled up. The main threat to the First Corps' march was the signal station placed on Little Round Top, in perfect location to observe any moves against them, which it duly did as Johnston and McLaws stumbled into the open at Black Horse Tavern two hours earlier. However, Captain Hall misinterpreted the Rebel movements and incorrect intelligence was reported back to Meade. Longstreet's clandestine march had in fact been a complete success and the only impediment was Daniel Sickles, whose own extraordinary decision-making was made without any tactical basis or permission from his commander. While it is right to contrast the comparative excellence of the Federal intelligence service against the paucity of the Confederate system, Lee's orders of 11:00 a.m. had become a self-fulfilling prophesy as the Federals were found to be completely unprepared for his main attack. Like Chancellorsville, the path was open for a surprise assault to smash into the Federal flank and open the battle on two fronts.

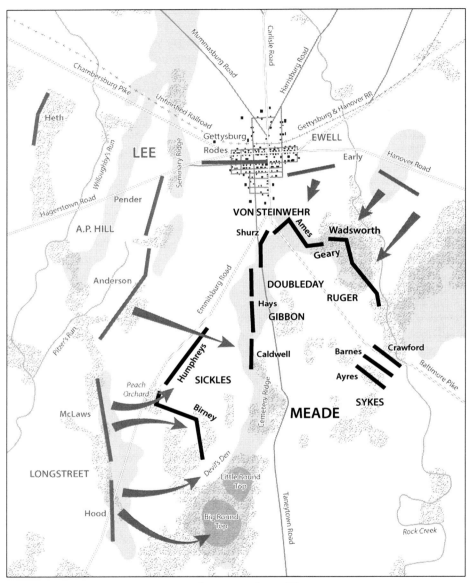

Map 4 Gettysburg Second Day.

But this was not Chancellorsville and when the attack came, terrible as it was, the Union tactical intelligence machine moved into another gear. By 3:30 p.m., the First Corps had arrived in the woods at the foot of Little Round Top, in front of the rocky outcrop known as the Devil's Den and hidden from view of all, except Captain James Hall. Experienced in identifying enemy troops, even those obscured from immediate view, Hall saw the threat and ordered his flagman, Sargent J. Chemberlin, to signal General Meade and alert Daniel Sickles. Meade had sent his chief engineer Gouverneur K. Warren over to examine the peculiar events on his left, who reached Little Round Top just before McLaws and Hood had fully revealed themselves. Warren would state in a letter written nine years after the battle that his military instincts overcame him on seeing that Little Round Top was "the key to the whole position" and that the woods in front of Sickles provided perfect concealment for enemy troops. On ordering a rifleman to fire an exploratory shot into the woods, he was not surprised that his instincts were confirmed and several thousand Rebel troops suddenly turned and "revealed to me the glistening of gun-barrels and bayonets of the enemy's line of battle, already formed and far outflanking the position of any of our troops." Hall's testimony, however, is somewhat different: not being versed to spotting concealed soldiers, Warren at first refused to believe the signal officer's report of the imminent danger until a Rebel shell burst overhead and wounded the engineer in the neck. "Now do you see them?" demanded Captain Hall.[11]

However the message was passed, as soon as Warren understood the danger, his decisive action and that of those around him, was critical in the defence of Little Round Top and the repulse of Longstreet's attack. Warren sent a dispatch to Meade to alert him to the danger, who in turn ordered Sykes to take his V Corps over to the left to meet the emergency. By this time, Longstreet's assault was under way; while Hood's division spread right to tackle the rocky approach of Little Round Top, McLaws was hacking into the left of Sickle's salient through the Wheat Field and Peach Orchard in front of Trostle's Farm, where the III Corps had centred themselves. To complete the envelopment, Longstreet's men were joined by one of Hill's division, under Robert Anderson, striking against the right side of the salient at the centre of Cemetery Ridge, still occupied by Hancock's II Corps. Warren's forthright actions were matched with good-fortune; as the V Corps approached, a rider was sent to find General James Barnes of the 1st Division with an order to occupy Little Round Top immediately, but ran into Colonel Strong Vincent. Without hesitation, Vincent commandeered the order and hurried his 3rd Division of 20th Maine, 16th Michigan, 44th New York and 83rd Pennsylvania up to join Hall. Vincent would not live long enough to see his men survive and then break Hood's charge, but instead the honours for the desperate defence of Little Round Top would fall to Colonel Joshua Chamberlain of the 20th Maine. Through a combination of great determination, courage and superlative post-war public relations, Chamberlain ensured that his name

---

11   Brown, *The Signal Corps*, p.366-7.

Confederate dead around the Devil's Den.

would forever be associated with the defence of Little Round Top, while the actions of men like his namesake Sargent Chemberlin would fall into obscurity.

As Hood's Texans were pushed off Little Round Top, Hill's brigades were threatening to plunge through the gap in the Federal line created by the dislocation of Sickles' salient from the II Corps on their right. As Andrew Humphrey's 2nd Division succumbed to the Rebel hammering, only desperate fighting and good staff work prevented the butternuts levering open the Yankee line and pouring through. As increasing emergency became apparent, so more troops from the V Corps were distributed across the Federal left to shore up the defences and prevent catastrophe. Desperate as this defence was, it was also effective and when the guns fell silent, all that was left of the Confederate offensive against Cemetery Ridge were the positions in the Peach Orchard and Devil's Den still held by Longstreet's men and thousands of dead and wounded soldiers.

If the fighting on the Federal left was battle at its most visceral, the coordinated attack on Culp's Hill was tactical execution at its most embarrassing. "The official reports are a painful record," wrote Alexander "of insufficient comprehension of orders and inefficient attempts at execution, by officers each able to shift the blame of failure upon other shoulders than his own."[12] Ewell duly commenced his bombardment of Culp's Hill in sync with Longstreet's advance at around 4:00 p.m., but with discretion to move his troops only if he thought such an action might be profitable, Old Bald Head held back for another two and a half hours. When the attack came, it was disjointed and piecemeal, with Ewell struggling to coordinate his division commanders efficiently and the growing darkness only hindering matters further. Battling up the steep and rocky slopes of Culp's Hill against the entrenched defenders must have seemed like a Sisyphean task for the men of Edward Johnson's division, until they suddenly stumbled into an entire line of empty Federal trenches. During the maelstrom of the attack on their left, Slocum had directed General Alpheus Williams to lead his 1st Division of the XII Corps away from the far right of the Union line and across to assist Hancock. Williams, who had assumed temporary command of the XII Corps in Slocum's absence, duly abandoned his trench line next to those of General George "Pap" Greene's 3rd Brigade, with instructions to John Geary to cover his old position with the rest of his 2nd Division. What Williams did not know was that Geary had also been ordered to move to the left and so now Greene was alone as Johnson's division of Rebels attacked. Should they be successful, not only would the Rebels have secured a position on Culp's Hill, but their angle of attack would put them only yards from Baltimore Pike, a vital artery of the Federal position. The lateness of the hour and the skill of Pap Greene prevented greater damage from the farcical Federal performance on Culp's Hill on the 2nd, while the questions would quickly flow as to how Ewell and Early were not able to exploit their enemy's confusion further. The latitude afforded to Ewell by Lee had resulted in two ineffectual assaults on Culp's Hill during the first two days, with only a toe-hold in the Union line to show for it. Unfortunately for Old Bald Head, even this would be prised from his grasp by an efficient pre-dawn counter-attack by the troops of the XII Corps to retake their entrenchments on the morning of 3 July.

12   Alexander, *Military Memoirs*, p.408.

10

A Plan Unchanged

The vicious fighting of 2 July would yield limited success for the Confederacy and the coordination that Lee had demanded of his corps commanders had not been forthcoming. Despite the shortcomings of Johnston's reconnaissance at the beginning of the day, Lee's tactic to strike against the Federal left and centre proved to be effective and came extremely close to succeeding, courtesy of Sickles' bizarre decision to disconnect himself from the Federal defensive line. Similarly, his plan to pressurise different points of the Union defensive line had nearly worked as Alpheus Williams' march from his Culp's Hill trench to Cemetery Ridge accidentally opened up a sizeable gap for Dick Ewell. As Lee pondered his actions for the following day, alone in his headquarters, if he hoped to crack the Army of the Potomac with yet another coordinated attack, he would not be able to do so without addressing the root of his problem and investing himself in good tactical intelligence and better communication. However, there is no evidence that Lee either desired or had the capacity to obtain this intelligence, even though he still had plenty of opportunity to do so. During the course of the first two days, so many thousands of prisoners had come into Rebel hands at such a fast rate that General Harry Hays, a brigade commander in Jubal Early's division of the Second Corps, would complain that "the prisoners taken ... by my brigade exceeded in numbers the force under my command." Marsena Patrick would record on the last days of the battle that he had his "hands full" looking after 2,000 prisoners in Taneytown, but in contrast, "we succeeded in checking the disorder & organized a guard."[1] At the same time, on Harry Hays' side of the line, "The prisoners sent to the rear, being under charge of no guard, escaped in the darkness."[2]

Instead of good ORBAT intelligence, Lee would chose to rely on testimony from his generals acquired in the smoke and confusion of battle. As Johnston had shown, scouting these battle lines was extremely challenging, even for an experienced engineer, and so it was not surprising that the information Lee received from the second

---

1   Sparks, *Inside Lincoln's Army*, p.267.
2   *SHSP Vol. VIII*, p.231-4.

day's fighting was dangerously deficient. As Hill's men battered against Humphrey's 2nd Division, General Ambrose "Rans" Wright of Anderson's division broke though and believed himself to have made the crest of Cemetery Ridge, reporting that "We were now complete masters of the field, having gained the key, as it were, of the enemy's whole line."[3] This convinced Lee that his tactical instincts had been correct and that Meade would break if he could be pressured sufficiently; a hard strike directly against Cemetery Ridge, again supported by demonstrations from Ewell but this time preceded by a huge artillery barrage, would open up the Federal centre for a combined attack by Stuart from the rear. As Lee would later put it, "The general plan was unchanged."[4]

His main attack would be led by General George Pickett of the First Corps and his three brigades of nearly 6,000 men, supported by an additional six brigades of the Third Corps under James Pettigrew (standing in for the injured Heth) and Isaac Trimble (having replaced General William Dorsey Pender, fatally wounded on 2 July). Further notional support was also available from a few of Anderson's brigades. In all around 13,000 Confederate soldiers would make the assault. Their target would be designated by a small clump of trees in the centre of Cemetery Ridge, an area occupied by John Gibbon of Hancock's II Corps. The problem was, however, that Wright had not punctured the Federal line nor made it on to the ridge. Lee was composing his tactics on the mistaken belief that Meade was weak in the centre. Had Wright actually commanded the Federal line, he might have noticed an additional 16,000 thousand soldiers of Sedgwick's VI Corps stationed in reserve, who had by then arrived at the field and slotted in along Taneytown Road. The largest corps in the Federal army had been placed right in the middle of Meade's forces, ready to meet any emergency that might arise. If the Army of Northern Virginia had been able to process its prisoners with the efficiency of the B.M.I., Lee might have realised that so far Meade had committed only two brigades of his V and none of his VI Corps.

George Pickett of the First Corps, who would lead one of the most famous charges in American military history.

3   O.R. Series I, Vol. XXVII, Part II, p.623.
4   O.R. Series I, Vol. XXVII, Part II, p.320.

Once again, as Lee postulated his next move, the contrast between his operations and those of his adversary could not be starker. As Lee sat alone, General Meade brought his corps commanders (or their substitutes in cases like Daniel Sickles, who had been wounded during the day's action) together in a council of war at 9:00 p.m. to discuss the results of the battle so far and the plans for tomorrow. The twelve senior commanders were posed three simple questions: whether to maintain their position, whether to remain on the defensive and if so for how long. The overwhelming vote was to stay and fight, but not to assume the offensive. Robert Lee rarely had time for such open discussion of tactics during battle and in the bitter aftermath of what he thought had been a successful canvassing of his senior generals, Meade would appreciate why. His neutral stance in the meeting, (George Meade did not cast a vote or offer an opinion) coupled with his ordering of the Pipe Creek Circular would leave him open to later attacks that he shrank from his responsibility to face Lee and only the fortitude of his subordinates prevented an ignominious flight from the field. None other than Daniel Sickles would have the chance to testify first in front of the Joint Committee, so the seeds of Meade's alleged weakness were sewn well before the head of the army would have the chance to answer them. He would be painted as dithering and cowardly, ultimately even without enough backbone to propose his own plan against the chorus of subordinates, (although less than 24 hours later Meade would apparently find the spine to dismiss supposed insistent pleading from his commanders to attack Lee once the final Rebel advance had been repelled). No shortage of witnesses would be found to counter the charge of cowardice against Meade, but Sickles would continue his vendetta long after the battle in a series of newspaper reports under the pseudonym "Historicus," castigating Meade while praising himself.[5]

Even if Meade did not give his voice to the council, it is highly unlikely that he ever considered retreating from Gettysburg, since he was too well informed of the situation on the evening of 2 July to have given up such a strong defensive position. Meade was an engineer at heart and, although he had favoured the location of Pipe Creek before the battle, he appreciated the advantages that he held with the fish hook line along the hills of Gettysburg. At 8:00 p.m., an hour before the generals came together, Meade sent a message to Halleck to report on the day's fight and to clarify that "I shall remain in my present position to-morrow, but am not prepared to say, until better advised of the condition of the army, whether my operations will be of an offensive or defensive character."[6] Having already informed his general-in-chief of his decision to stay, Sickles' suggestion that Meade was looking for any excuse to pull back and avoid the fight rings hollow.

Whatever his motives for calling the council, the basis for their discussion and ultimate decision was founded on their confident appreciation of the tactical situation. None of the attendees had any false impressions about how roughly handled they had

---

5   O.R. Series I, Vol. XXVII, Part I, p.127-8.
6   O.R. Series I, Vol. XXVII, Part I, p.72.

George Meade (standing) and the council of war on the evening of 2 July, which voted
overwhelmingly to stay and fight.

been by the Rebels over the previous two days, but they were comfortable that their
numbers and position were enough to continue to repulse anything that Lee threw at
them. After the battle, both Sharpe and Babcock would later claim that their work in
processing around 1,600 Rebel prisoners from 100 regiments captured by the end of
the second day would prove the decisive factor in influencing the council to stay and
fight.[7] Arriving at Meade's headquarters about an hour before the council convened,
the B.M.I. men gave their ORBAT report, indicating that all of the Rebel divisions
had been in action except for George Pickett. This suggested that Lee had no further
tricks up his sleeve and any final attack would have to come from the fresh troops of
the First Corps stationed on Meade's left.

Later in the evening, similar inspiration would also be attributed to the arrival
of Captain Ulrich Dahlgren. The young cavalry officer had been leading a party of
Federal troopers, supported by B.M.I. scouts (including the indefatigable Milton
Cline), when they intercepted a Confederate mailbag from a detachment of Rebel
cavalry in Greencastle. Inside the mailbag were the dispatches from Samuel Cooper and
Jefferson Davis rejecting Lee's request for a secondary force to be brought up to threaten
Washington. Whatever else happened in the coming days, Meade could now be certain

7   John C. Babcock Papers, Library of Congress.

that the Army of Northern Virginia was on its own. Unlike Sharpe and Babcock, news of Dahlgren's mission would appear in the *New York Tribune* the following day and the young man would later receive personal thanks for his intelligence work from President Lincoln, (although a cynic might make note that Dahlgren's father was a Rear Admiral and chief of the U.S. Navy Bureau of Ordnance).[8] Again, just as with the operational intelligence that had brought them to Gettysburg, it is more likely that the B.M.I. and Dahlgren's work formed part of the overall intelligence picture that convinced Meade not to take the extremely risky and demoralising step of retreating in the face of an extremely aggressive opposing force. Meade's confidence was such that he even predicted to General Gibbon that Lee's offensive would be against his position. "Well, general, I hope he does," was John Gibbon's reply, "and if he does, we shall whip him."[9]

Before the sun rose on the battlefield on 3 July both commanders had made up their minds as to the final act of this hideous play. Pickett's unused division, with their additional brigades borrowed from Heth and Pender, would lead the charge, while Ewell threatened on the right to keep Meade entertained and Stuart pressed the rear ready to sweep into the Union line as their defence started to crumble. Meade, conversely, would sit tight and await Lee's next move, comforted by the logistical and communications advantages of his interior lines and with the untouched VI Corps positioned to meet any threats. A little after daybreak, General Lee left his headquarters about four miles from the front to deliver his orders and inform Longstreet that, once again, he would be given the honour of leading the attack.[10] Unlike his opponent, Lee had no interest in conferring with his subordinates and was already "impatient of listening and tired of talking."[11] Rans Wright had apparently exposed the weakness in the centre of the Union line, seemingly indicating that Meade could not possibly have his whole army up. An overwhelming force concentrated against that same point would surely break the last of the Federal resistance; the end was finally in sight. "The enemy is there, and I am going to strike him," Lee exclaimed, indicating at Cemetery Ridge with his fist.[12] He had led his army over 200 miles from Fredericksburg into enemy territory, chosen the ground and now it was time to smash "those people" out of his way. The general plan was unchanged.

Old Pete, on the other hand, was little short of horrified at the bluntness of the plan, since "the column would have to march a mile under concentrating battery fire, and a thousand yards under long-range musketry … the conditions were different from those in the days of Napoleon, when field batteries had a range of six hundred yards and musketry about sixty yards."[13] Unlike his commander, he believed that the events of the previous day had demonstrated the Federal strength, not weakness and in the

8   *SHSP Vol. VIII*, p.523.
9   Meade, *The Life and Letters*, p.97.
10   Alexander, *Military Memoirs*, p.415.
11   Longstreet, *From Manassas to Appomattox*, p.387.
12   *SHSP Vol. V*, p.68.
13   Longstreet, *From Manassas to Appomattox*, p.386.

absence of any guidance from Lee, no effort had been made to prepare his troops overnight for another assault. Longstreet also had very little idea of the true strength of the Army of the Potomac, but the concept of ordering so few men to march across roughly a mile of open ground against a well-set enemy holding an elevated position was madness.

> I have been a soldier, I may say, from the ranks up to the position I now hold. I have been in pretty much all kinds of skirmishes, from those of two or three soldiers up to those of an army corps, and I think I can safely say there never was a body of fifteen thousand men who could make that attack successfully.[14]

Old Pete had no need to justify his record to Lee and was no coward in the face of a strong enemy position. Only a year earlier, he had taken a major role in the attack on Malvern Hill. In disturbingly similar circumstances at the climax of the Seven Days Battle, Lee's army had confronted the Army of the Potomac and its uncoordinated frontal attack wrecked itself on that low Virginia hillside, laced with Federal guns. To soften up the Yankees before making the charge on Malvern Hill, Lee had decided to concentrate a massed fire on their position, but this had failed to make any impact and his men were chewed up by Henry Hunt's artillery on their approach. Seemingly the only lesson that the greatest tactician of the War had learned from that experience was that bigger must be better: since the Yankee was no match for his Southern adversary, it must have been a deficiency of artillery, which was to blame. This time, therefore, Hunt and his comrades would feel the full force of the Rebel batteries before Lee unleashed Pickett.

The charge would, therefore, be preceded by one of the largest artillery barrages of the entire War focused on the opposing brigades and batteries on Cemetery Ridge. Once Pickett's men were drawn up, the First Corps' guns, now under the charge of Edward Porter Alexander (having taken over from J. B. Walton), would silence the enemy artillery and soften up the targeted Federal positions. Unfortunately, again, Lee's lack of tactical intelligence on the Federal composition and deployment undermined his planning. Not only did his proposal pit a small strike force against a numerically superior enemy in a favourable defensive position, but the placement of the Rebel guns had not been undertaken with any prior thought towards achieving the maximum damage. If the fish hook formation gave one advantage to the Rebels, it was the opportunity to mass artillery opposite its acute angles in order to enfilade the Union line. Rebel guns had indeed been positioned near the town at the northern end of the battle field, which could have fired down the length of Cemetery Ridge, but a lack of coordinated reconnaissance meant that no one in Lee's army appreciated this logistical gift. "Not a single gun was established within a thousand yards, nor was a position selected which

---

14   *Battles and Leaders, Vol. III*, p.343.

enfiladed the lines in question,"[15] complained Alexander in his memoirs. Whilst the Lee of Chancellorsville had been obliged to utilise every tactical advantage to overcome his disabilities in numbers and position, the Lee of Gettysburg had left his tactical playbook unopened in favour of liberally applied blunt force. The only motive Longstreet could later find to explain his commander's attitude during the third day was that "he was excited and off his balance ... and he labored under that oppression until enough blood was shed to appease him."[16]

Up on Cemetery Ridge, Frank Haskell was enjoying a moment of mundanity in between the savagery. After the early excitement of Ewell's extrication from the trenches on their right, the morning of the 3rd was spent in preparation and nervous anticipation. By noon, around a large pan of chicken and potatoes, several of the senior generals of the Army of the Potomac had gathered, including Meade, Gibbon, Pleasonton, Hancock and John Newton. As the sun reached its zenith, the generals allowed themselves to relax. Meade and Gibbon both instructed their provost guards to return to their regiments in order to have every fighting man at the front. Captain Farrel, head of John Gibbon's provost guard, "a quiet, excellent gentleman and thorough soldier," received his orders and left the party to execute his instructions. "I never saw him again," wrote Haskell. "He was killed in two or three hours from that time, and over half of his splendid company were either killed or wounded."[17]

Frank Haskell of John Gibbon's division of the II Corps, an eye-witness to the carnage of 3 July.

At almost exactly 1:00 p.m., the peace was broken by a single enemy shell bursting over the ridge; it was a signal gun for the start of the final offensive action in Lee's Gettysburg campaign. The Rebel artillery of 172 guns opened up and started to rain down shell and solid shot on Meade's army for a full hour. For Frank Haskell and the Union generals, it was a shocking event: "Who can describe such a conflict as is raging around us? To say that it was a summer storm, with the crash of thunder, the glare

15   Alexander, *Military Memoirs*, p.418.
16   Longstreet, *From Manassas to Appomattox*, p.384.
17   Haskell, *The Battle of Gettysburg*, p.92.

of lightening, the shriek of the wind, and the clatter of hailstones, would be weak."[18] In comparison to this conflagration, the artillery exchanges of the battles of Second Bull Run, Antietam and Fredericksburg seemed little more than "holiday salutes." Alexander's adversary Henry Hunt, however, knew better than to waste his ammunition in a long-range duel when an infantry attack was surely coming and so he kept his reply to a minimum. On the opposing side of the field and already weighed down with the honour of sending his corps into battle again, James Longstreet instructed Alexander that it was now his responsibility to give final sanction to Pickett's Charge, based on the artilleryman's assessment of the effectiveness of his bombardment. Alexander was not about to have the buck passed to him to cancel Lee's entire plan for the third day and instead he responded to Old Pete after about 25 minutes of fire that unless he moved fast Pickett would not have the continued support of artillery.[19] "General, shall I advance?" demanded the impatient Pickett, straining to plunge into the battle. The old war horse could not even summon the resolve to give the verbal order but merely bowed.[20] Longstreet would later confide to Alexander: "I do not want to make this charge. I do not see how it can succeed. I would not make it now but that Gen. Lee has ordered it and is expecting it."[21]

Pickett's Charge, one of the most celebrated infantry attacks in American military history and the culmination of Robert Lee's month-long campaign into Pennsylvania, would last a little over 40 minutes. Before the clock reached 4:00 p.m. on the afternoon of the 3rd, the Confederate assault had been shredded by the combined musket and artillery fire of a Federal force that had fully prepared itself to receive them. General Hunt did not need the B.M.I. to assist his preparations to welcome George Pickett; during the morning of the final day, the massing Rebels were clearly visible to the watching Federal observers and Hunt had plenty of time to position his guns to wreck the approaching infantry before they came into close quarters. Moreover, unlike Lee, he was not going to give up any tactical advantages afforded by the formation of the attack. With such a relatively limited force concentrating on a small point in the Union line, the oblique angle at which the ridge ran north east from the Confederate front meant that Hunt could direct his guns on the Federal left under Freeman McGilvery (along the Plum Run line behind the Peach Orchard) and Benjamin Rittenhouse (now commanding Charles Hazlett's battery on Little Round Top) to enfilade Pickett's men as they marched forward.[22] The crushing artillery fire from the guns to the right of the men of the First Corps was matched by the ferocious volleys of musket and rifle into the Third Corps' lines. Despite the fire, the

18   Haskell, *The Battle of Gettysburg*, p.98.
19   Alexander, *Military Memoirs*, p.423.
20   Longstreet, *From Manassas to Appomattox*, p.392.
21   Alexander, *Military Memoirs*, p.424.
22   *Battles and Leaders, Vol. III*, p.374.

Rebels performed with astonishing bravery, crossing the open ground and numerous fences while wheeling in on Gibbon's position. The concentration of so many attackers towards such a small point meant that the pressure put on the defenders of the I and II Corps was desperate, but the weight of Northern firepower and reinforcements was irresistible. For combatants and witnesses alike, the conclusion to Lee's final attack was horrifying: "Only the Angel of Death could present such a scene."[23]

The final Rebel attack cannot be described as anything other than a total failure. A shell-shocked George Pickett, reacting to an order from Lee to prepare his division for possible Federal counter-attack, could only cry in despair "General Lee, I have no division now."[24] Based on the sparse and unverified intelligence acquisition from the second day, the planning of Pickett's attack was myopic and, yet again, the execution of a coordinated offensive on multiple points never materialised. Ewell, having been beaten to the punch by Williams snatching back his works earlier in the day, never got started. Jeb's attack against the rear of the Federal line was repulsed by the concerted efforts of, among others, a young George Armstrong Custer of Kilpatrick's division. The shock at the speed of the Rebel collapse was overwhelming for both commanders. As Robert E. Lee witnessed the unravelling of his grand plan, he managed to retain his characteristic calm. "It was all my fault;" he would try and assure his men, "get together, and let us do the best we can toward saving that which is left us."[25] It would be several days before his self-blame would be displaced by criticism of his subordinates, specifically Jeb Stuart, for allowing him to fall into this unfavourable situation.

Meanwhile, in perhaps the greatest injustice of the Gettysburg campaign, the victorious General Meade would provoke vilification for his failure to counterattack after Pickett's failure and would spend most of the rest of his career defending his victory. The chorus of condemnation for Meade's timidity began immediately, with his contemporaries such as Pleasonton claiming to have tried in vain to have exhorted their commander forward, while Alexander likened the scale of the lost opportunity to Antietam.[26] Lincoln would eventually add his weight behind the critics: after the joy of learning of Meade's success, he firmly reminded his commander that the job was not finished until Lee's army was destroyed.[27] His dismay would turn to anger as the Army of Northern Virginia eventually manoeuvred their way unmolested back across the Potomac on 14 July.

While Meade would be accused of everything from gross ill-judgement to outright cowardice, a more practical explanation could be found in the spectre of the continuing belief of Lee's superiority in numbers and rooted in his scepticism of Hooker's intelligence machine. Despite the ORBAT information that he had received from

23   Scott, *Battle of Gettysburg*, p.24.
24   *SHSP* Vol. XXXI, p.234.
25   *Battles and Leaders, Vol. III.*, p.347.
26   *Annals*, p.455; Alexander, *Military Memoirs*, p.432.
27   O.R. Series I, Vol. XXVII, Part I, p.83.

The dead litter the battlefield of Gettysburg.

the ceaseless interrogation of deserters and prisoners throughout the fighting, Meade continued to receive reports estimating the Rebel forces to be at least 80,000 men and, in his testimony to the Joint Committee, he would declare that he believed Lee to have 10,000 to 15,000 more men than him.[28] If Meade genuinely believed that the Confederates at least had parity during the campaign, he could not believe it possible that he could have overcome Lee's climactic attack in less than an hour. Even the best intelligence would not have been able to give Meade a comprehensive picture to explain the performance of the Rebel army: Hill had been sick since before the battle had started; Ewell had proven himself well short of Stonewall's legacy; Stuart had been at half strength; and Longstreet had been left literally speechless in opposition to Lee's tactics. Ultimately, the practical effect of Pickett's Charge amounted to just a single action while "seven-ninths of the army in breathless suspense in ardent admiration and fearful anxiety, watched, but moved not."[29]

Meade, who had assumed command only five days earlier and who was nearing exhaustion from the relentless demands of managing the army during three days of battle, could hardly be blamed for expecting more from Lee with his Third and most of his Second Corps still motionless. As he would later confess to Mrs. Meade during the pursuit of Lee:

28   *Report of the Joint Committee*, Part I, p.337.
29   Taylor, *Four Years with General Lee*, p.107.

From the time I took command till to-day, now over ten days, I have not changed my clothes, have not had a regular night's rest, and many nights not a wink of sleep, and for several days did not even wash my face and hands, no regular food, and all the time in a great state of mental anxiety.[30]

Notwithstanding the logistical difficulties of shifting his unprepared forces from defensive to offensive, a military scientist like George Meade simply could not believe that he had won with so little effort.

Once Lee realised that he was beaten, he wasted no time. As a huge summer storm like "a visitation of the wrath of God,"[31] battered his men, the Army of Northern Virginia began its delicate withdrawal from its positions around Seminary Ridge in the late afternoon of 4 July. So began his nerve-jangling march back towards the Potomac. So long was the Rebel train that the final troops did not vacate Meade's front for almost another 24 hours. They were about 75 miles from Virginia with a victorious and larger army on their heels.

In the Federal lines, excellent as his signal officers had performed, the problem of the independent telegraph service immediately manifested itself. The civilian operator of the autonomous Military Telegraph Service attached to the Army of the Potomac, A. H. Caldwell, having decided "to act in an independent manner," was found to have left Gettysburg "without permission" on 3 July with the cipher key.[32] For the next few days, any encrypted messages from Washington would remain unread and Meade would be unable to send his own messages in cipher. Fortunately, not only had the battle already been won by the time Caldwell absconded, but Meade had little need of Washington's input due to the complete tactical intelligence service already at his disposal. Soon Meade would be cursing the restoration of communications with the War Department. Within days of his finest hour, Meade would offer his resignation to Halleck after receiving what he perceived to be sharp criticism from the president.[33] Lincoln could not forgive Meade for stopping short of what he believed was the best opportunity to end the entire War. The total absence of shared strategic vision would again send the commander-in-chief into despair, as Meade sent out his victorious communication exhorting his men to "to drive from our soil every vestige of the presence of the invader."[34] It was clear to Lincoln that Meade completely failed to appreciate that the whole purpose of the fight was to establish that Northern soil did not end at the border of Pennsylvania. With Lee's army seemingly on the run, the president wanted all-out attack. "I left the telegraph office a good deal dissatisfied,"

---

30   Meade, *The Life and Letters*, p.132.
31   Alexander, *Military Memoirs*, p.436.
32   O.R. Series I, Vol. XXVII, Part I, p.78.
33   O.R. Series I, Vol. XXVII, Part I, p.93.
34   O.R. Series I, Vol. XXVII, Part III, p.519.

Lincoln complained to Halleck, while speculating that Meade's operational plans to give chase "appear to me to be connected with a purpose to cover Baltimore and Washington, and to get the enemy across the river again without a further collision, and they do not appear connected with a purpose to prevent his crossing and to destroy him."[35] A little over a week into the job and the new commander of the Army of the Potomac was already feeling the weight of the Lincolnian dichotomy.

The battle of Gettysburg was over, but no one on the Federal side could categorically say that the campaign was over. As he withdrew his army from the field, so Lee had the opportunity to put them back the other side of South Mountain, meaning that it would take a bold pre-emptive move from Meade to get into the Cumberland Valley to stop him reaching the river. Such a move could potentially open up an opportunity for Lee to strike back at him and manoeuvre his way round the Army of the Potomac. The risk that the Army of Northern Virginia might yet get between them and Baltimore was still great. With the stakes so high, George Meade was not prepared to risk his initial victory with a reckless charge into, what he believed to be, a larger foe. "The enemy has withdrawn from his positions occupied for attack. I am not yet sufficiently informed of the nature of his movement," Meade reported to Couch and Halleck. To his wife he was more candid: "The most difficult part of my work is acting without correct information on which to predicate action."[36] The general was still relying on the intelligence system and staff officers of his predecessor. While agreeing to this marriage of convenience had paid off as his troops marched towards the collision with Lee, Meade was never comfortable with Butterfield or the B.M.I. As soon as he had the opportunity, Andrew Humphreys was installed as his chief-of-staff, the first step in the dissolution of Joe Hooker's intelligence apparatus.[37]

For the next ten days, Lee's invasion was reversed as the two armies slowly marched south while the cavalries fenced across the passes of South Mountain. When it became clear that Lee was defeated and moving away from the town, Meade did not dawdle as has occasionally been portrayed. By end of 6 July, the network of telegraphs across the fish hook, which had served him so well, had been dismantled and was ready for transportation. The speed of the Rebel retreat and their course through Maryland, however, all but negated the Federal intelligence effort, save for Pleasonton's reports. Once Lee had retreated beyond the view of the Signal Bureau officers, still stationed on the hills around Gettysburg, their utility would be limited by both the speed of the Federal pursuit and the soggy cloud hanging in the valleys. Instead, their key role transferred from one of intelligence acquisition to pure communications, as they endeavoured to keep the various divisions of the Federal army connected to each other and headquarters. To this end, an additional party of signal officers arrived from Washington to assist communications between South Mountain and the new

35   O.R. Series I, Vol. XXVII, Part III, p.567.
36   Meade, *The Life and Letters*, p.113-4, 125.
37   Sparks, *Inside Lincoln's Army*, p.270.

headquarters in Frederick. Meanwhile, Sharpe and Babcock were still collating information from the battlefield, but their contribution to the pursuit was limited by the reactive information received from the various intelligence sources, indicating where the Army of Northern Virginia had been.[38] Unlike Hooker, who had pushed his intelligence resources to the front of his army to maximise their utility, Meade kept them back. Instead, his corps were pushed ahead on reconnaissance duties to track the Army of Northern Virginia and the Signal Corps was kept one step behind in order to secure communications. George Meade proved himself every bit the traditional Mexican War engineer that Robert Lee was.

This does not mean that Meade was short of sources of information. With his army eventually on the march, reconnaissance parties probed the edges of Lee army from all angles, while Generals Couch and Kelley (from Western Virginia) joined the shepherding of the Army of Northern Virginia southwards out of the valley. All information was consistent: Lee was heading south towards the Potomac and if there was to be a final battle, it would be on the banks of the river. Good planning and good fortune would appear to have presented Meade with the chance to complete the victory that George McClellan had failed to execute less than a year before. In a rare show of initiative from a Federal commander, General William H. French, now in charge of the garrison at Harper's Ferry, moved forward from Frederick to destroy Lee's pontoon bridges at Falling Waters, three miles south of Williamsport.[39] With the summer storms swelling the Potomac to dangerous levels, the Rebel soldiers would not be able to wade across and Lee would need time to build another bridge.

Nine days after Pickett's Charge, Meade finally cornered Lee around the crossing point of Williamsport. While, the engineers of the Army of Northern Virginia desperately constructed a new pontoon bridge now that the storm-engorged waters of the Potomac were receding, General Lee prepared to receive the inevitable Federal onslaught. His defensive line stretched along the road to Hagerstown and was deeply entrenched and heavily armed. Any attack would be met with ferocious defence. The lack of urgency of Meade's chase had infuriated Washington, but now it was time to deliver the *coup de grâce*. "It is my intention to attack them to-morrow," Meade reported to Halleck, but with a caveat "unless something intervenes to prevent it."[40] Sure enough, that something would be another council of war and despite the commanding general being in favour of attacking, only two of his seven corps commanders (Oliver Howard and James Wadsworth), were in agreement.[41] As a result, the attack would be postponed until additional reconnaissance of the enemy position could be undertaken. By the time he pushed his scouts into Lee's entrenchments on 14 July, the Rebels were gone and Lincoln would be left to message Simon Cameron at Meade's

---

38   O.R. Series I, Vol. XXVII, Part III, p.541-2.
39   O.R. Series I, Vol. XXVII, Part III, p.538.
40   O.R. Series I, Vol. XXVII, Part I, p.91.
41   *Report of the Joint Committee*, Part I, p.336.

headquarters impotently to request: "Please tell me, if you know, who was the one Corps Commander who was for fighting, in the council of war on Sunday night."[42]

Meade would be indignant to the criticism that he had let Lee escape and defended his famous victory over the previously invincible Lee. Lincoln, on the other hand, was resigned to pen another message to his general in an effort to translate his strategic misunderstanding: "I do not believe you appreciate the magnitude of the misfortune involved in Lee's escape. He was within your easy grasp, and to have closed upon him would, in connection with our other late successes, have ended the war. As it is, the war will be prolonged indefinitely."[43] Although the president would elect not to send the letter, history would prove him correct. The campaign was over and although Lee had begun a course of retreat that would take him all the way to his fateful meeting with Ulysses Grant at the house of Wilmer McLean in Appomattox Court House, it would take almost two years and several thousand more lives before the Confederacy submitted.

To attempt to blame George Meade for not ending the Rebellion in July 1863, however, was unjustifiably harsh. Undoubtedly weakened from battle, the Army of Northern Virginia was still a formidable fighting force and unlikely to have succumbed to a single additional engagement. It did not take long for the Federal commander to realise the problem he was facing and that "my success at Gettysburg has deluded the people and the Government with the idea that I must always be victorious, that Lee is demoralized and disorganized, etc.",[44] but this would not ease his frustration at the constant badgering he received. The intelligence that Meade was given during the Rebel retreat from the field was not able to establish Lee's final objective until he reached the banks of the Potomac and this time there would be no repeat of Antietam. Lee had won himself the time to dig in and was waiting for the Federal attack, a situation much like Meade had hoped to engineer at Pipe Creek. To compound the problem, despite the bold assertion of men like Simon Cameron that the Army of the Potomac was now supported by a "fine army" from the Department of the Susquehanna, the new additions were the greenest of recruits.[45] Many of these militia fighters had only been called up to service during the previous weeks and to take on Lee's battle-hardened army would have been tantamount to suicide. The Federal commander was under no such allusions and knew that "it [the Army of the Potomac] has been greatly reduced and weakened by recent operations, and no reinforcements of any practical value have been sent."[46]

---

42   Bates, *Lincoln in the Telegraph Office*, p.157; Meade originally telegraphed Halleck to say that "five out of six were unqualifiedly opposed" to attacking on 12 July, (O.R. Series I, Vol. XXVII, Part I, p.91) before correcting this statement in his testimony to the Joint Committee.
43   Macartney, *Lincoln and his Generals*, p.181.
44   Meade, *The Life and Letters*, p.133.
45   O.R. Series I, Vol. XXVII, Part III, p.700.
46   Meade, *The Life and Letters*, p.135.

Instead, it is very possible that Robert Lee had every intention of exploiting the situation to inflict some punishment on Meade before he withdrew back to Virginia. The Federals might have had the numbers, but Lee more than anyone knew that this advantage could be easily negated by good tactics. The more pressing issue for the Army of Northern Virginia was its quickly depleting stores and not the approaching Federal army. "I should be willing to await his attack," Lee explained to Davis the day before beginning his evacuation, "except that in our restricted limits the means of obtaining subsistence is becoming precarious."[47] Ultimately, discretion would be the better part of valour for the Rebels. Lee would order his army across the new bridge and Meade would be left to continue the chase into Virginia.

---

47   Dowdey, *The Wartime Papers*, p.548.

Epilogue

Before the campaign could be called over, there was one final, tragic irony for the Army of Northern Virginia. In the early hours of 14 July, the Confederate rear-guard of Henry Heth's division were guarding the rear of the Rebel army as it marched back across the Potomac, when they were approached by a small brigade of horsemen. Still groggy from the early morning and assuming them to be the last of Jeb Stuart's cavalry, the Confederate soldiers were not too concerned as the troopers galloped towards them. In the confusion of the evacuation, however, Stuart had mistaken the last of Longstreet's men for the tail of the Rebel army and so had already crossed the river.[1] Before they could prepare themselves to receive an attack, Judson Kilpatrick's cavalry were among them, swooping in for one last brazen attack on the Rebel Third Corps. A brief fight ensued as Heth's men overcame their shock and repulsed the Yankees strongly before making it into Virginia. Rebel casualties from the frantic exchange were light in number, but among them was James Johnston Pettigrew, who was shot in the stomach and would die three days later at the Boyd House, near Bunker Hill.[2] Just as they had been in the opening of the battle, the closing act of the Gettysburg campaign would again feature Henry Heth's division as the victim of poor intelligence. Furthermore, it was the very officer who had tried so desperately to warn his hubristic superiors of the dangers awaiting them in the hills around Gettysburg, who would be the campaign's last victim.

The Gettysburg campaign would be cast as the beginning of the end of the Rebellion. The small clump of trees that had been Pickett's target on the last day of the battle would find its place in history as the Confederacy's high water mark. The Rebels were estimated to have lost around 28,000 men either killed, wounded or missing, more than Antietam and Chancellorsville combined. Lee, supposedly all too aware of the premium attached to his soldiers' lives, had lost over 35 per cent of his army and nearly a quarter of his division and brigade commanders. Of his senior officers, Generals Hood, Trimble, Heth, Kemper, Scales, Anderson, Hampton, Jones and Jenkins were

---

1   O.R. Series I, Vol. XXVII, Part II, p.705.
2   O.R. Series I, Vol. XXVII, Part II, p.310.

wounded, while the tragic James Pettigrew would join a list of the fallen including Barksdale, Garnett, Semmes, Armistead and eventually Pender.

No time would be afforded to the Rebels for morbid self-reflection, however, as the Army of the Potomac were still hot on their heels. Instead, the analysis into their loss of the intelligence battle during the campaign would be symptomatic of the Confederate view of intelligence as a whole. For Robert Lee, whose view of information acquisition was limited to basic reconnaissance, spiced with the odd titbit from loyal scouts and spies, it would be Jeb Stuart who was the main culprit. In Richmond, once the double blow of Lee's defeat and the surrender of Vicksburg on 4 July had been absorbed, the loss of strategic information from espionage agents in the capital must be to blame. "That the cause has suffered much, and may be ruined by the toleration of disloyal persons within our lines, who have kept the enemy informed of all our movements, there can be no doubt."[3] Even though Lee did not restrain himself from putting much of the culpability of defeat on to Jeb Stuart, his loyalty to his senior cavalry officer and utter dependence on him as the principal component of his intelligence system remained. Less than a year later, Jeb Stuart would be killed at the Battle of Yellow Tavern and Lee would be left without one of the finest intelligence agents of the War. By this time, the Army of Northern Virginia was locked in a desperate rear-guard action to block the Union Overland Campaign and Ulysses Grant's bludgeoning progress towards Richmond.

As the inexorable retreat gathered pace, Rebel spies would continue their espionage around the Federal capital, but their focus would shift from feeding the Confederate desire for victory to satisfying its thirst for revenge. With Grant's army nearing Richmond, the C.S.S.B. was refocused on operations to save the South through a major act of political sabotage. Frank Stringfellow and Thomas Nelson Conrad were both sent into Washington to prepare for an attempt to kidnap Abraham Lincoln and spirit him into Virginia, via the Secret Line.[4] With the surrender of the Army of Northern Virginia in early April, the value of a kidnap became moot and would instead lead to John Wilkes Booth's visit to Ford's Theatre on 14 April 1865.

From its apex during that summer, the Federal intelligence effort too would be neutered within months of its most famous victory. The U.S. Signal Corps would continue their excellent service for the rest of the War, but never again would they face a situation where they could augment their information transmission utility with such a high level of acquisition. The march of the Army of Northern Virginia up the Shenandoah and then into the Cumberland Valley provided such an ideal environment for sophisticated observation and swift communication that it was unsurprising that they would not be able to replicate this decisive operation around the thickets of Spotsylvania or trenches of Cold Harbor. This is not to say that the Signal Corps would not serve with bravery and distinction during other actions and even William

3   Jones, *A Rebel War Clerk's Diary*, p.374.
4   Conrad, *The Rebel Spy*, p.118.

Sherman, who had "little faith in the signal service by flags and torches" praised their operations around Allatoona during the battle for Atlanta.[5]

The creation of the B.M.I. was a revolutionary step in military intelligence, but its value was never truly appreciated by Meade or many of his compatriots. Within a few months of the replacement of Daniel Butterfield, who had been hit with shrapnel during Pickett's Charge, George Sharpe had been sent back to general duty with the Provost Marshall General's office. John Babcock, John McEntee and Milton Cline would be all but forgotten. Meade was an engineer, like McClellan and Lee; all he wanted was basic tactical information and a good appreciation of the ground on which he was to fight. An interpretive system like the B.M.I. did not fit into his martial vision. For that, he would rather rely on Humphreys and his own staff than the complex apparatus of his predecessor. It was not until the arrival of a new commanding officer to the Eastern Theatre, one who had learned the hard lessons of good intelligence at Shiloh Church two years earlier, that Sharpe and his colleagues were brought back into the fold. As Ulysses Grant bore down on Richmond, the B.M.I. again came to prominence as they monitored Lee's attempts to shift his way out of the Federal vice while also now coordinating the network of espionage agents in the Rebel capital, such as Samuel Ruth and Elizabeth "Crazy Bet" Van Lew, the Union's own Rose Greenhow.

On 9 April 1865, Grant and Lee met in the village of Appomattox Court House to discuss terms for the surrender of the Army of Northern Virginia. Having been stopped from a final desperate bid to link up with Joseph Johnston's army in North Carolina, the great Confederate general was forced to face a fate worse than "a thousand deaths"[6] to spare the complete destruction of his army. The meeting in McLean's house was formal, but friendly, and "it was impossible to say whether he [Lee] felt inwardly glad that the end had finally come, or felt sad over the result." Grant's terms were generous, allowing for all Rebel soldiers who could prove ownership over their horses or mules to keep them, but he insisted that "officers to give their individual paroles not to take up arms against the Government of the United States until properly exchanged, and each company or regimental commander sign a like parole for the men of their commands."[7] Over the course of nearly a week, each of the 28,000 men of the Army of Northern Virginia would be given a printed parole slip to sign before they could head for home. Before the great Rebel general left to return to his audience, he needed to receive his own parole slip. Attending to the details, as he had throughout the latter half of the War, was Brigadier General George Sharpe.

---

5   Getting the Message, p.27-28.
6   Longstreet, *From Manassas to Appomattox*, p.624.
7   Grant, *Memoirs*, p.469-470.

Bibliography

Primary Sources

Official Documents

Report of the Joint Committee on the Conduct of the War, U.S. Congress: Volumes I – III (Washington: Government Printing Office, 1863)

The War of the Rebellion: a Compilation of the Official Records of the Union and Confederate Armies, 128 Volumes (Washington, Government Printing Office, 1880 – 1901)

Private Papers

John C. Babcock Papers (Library of Congress, Washington)

George G. Meade Papers (Library of Congress, Washington)

Secondary Works

Primary Published

—— Alexander, Edward P.: *Military Memoirs of a Confederate* (New York: Charles Scribner's Sons, 1907)

Allan, William: *The Army of Northern Virginia in 1862* (Boston and New York: Houghton, Mufflin and Company, 1892)

—— *The Annals of the War Written by Leading Participants North and South*, McClure, Alexander Kelly eds. (Philadelphia: Times Publishing 1879)

Bascom Smith, Henry: *Between the Lines Secret Service Stories Told Fifty Years After* (New York: Booz Brothers, 1911)

—— *Battles and Leaders of the Civil War Volumes I – IV*, Robert Underwood Johnson and Clarence Clough Buel eds. (New York: Century, 1887 – 1888)

—— *Battles and Leaders of the Civil War Volume V*, Peter Cozzens ed. (University of Illinois Press, 2002)

Bates, David Homer: *Lincoln in the Telegraph Office* (New York: The Century Co., 1907)

Bates, Samuel P.: *The Battle of Gettysburg* (Philadelphia: T.H. Davis & Co, 1875)

von Borcke, Heros: *Memoirs of the Confederate War for Independence* (Philadelphia: J.B. Lippincott & Co, 1867)

Brinton, John H.: *Personal Memories* (New York: The Neale Publishing Company, 1914)

Brooks, Noah: *Washington in Lincoln's Time* (New York: The Century Co, 1896)

Brown, J. Willard: *The Signal Corps, U.S.A. in the War of the Rebellion* (Boston: U.S. Veterans Signal Corps Association, 1896)

Conrad, Thomas Nelson: *The Rebel Scout* (Washington: The National Publishing Company, 1904)

Dodge, Theodore A.: *The Campaign of Chancellorsville* (Boston: James R. Osgood and Company, 1881)

Doubleday, Abner: *Chancellorsville and Gettysburg* (New York: Scribner's, 1882)

Dowdey, Clifford: *The Wartime Papers of R. E. Lee* (Boston: Little, Brown & Company, 1961)

Early, Jubal A.: *The Campaigns of Gen. Robert E. Lee* (Baltimore: John Murphy & Co, 1872)

Fremantle, Arthur: *Three Months in the Southern States* (New York, John Bradburn, 1864)

Gordon, John B.: *Reminiscences of the Civil War* (New York, Charles Scribner's Sons, 1904)

Gibbon, John: *Personal Recollections of the Civil War* (New York: G.P. Putnam's Sons, 1928)

Grant, Ulysses S.: *Personal Memoirs of U. S. Grant, Volume I* (New York: Charles L. Webster & Company, 1885)

Halleck, H. Wager: *Elements of Military Art and Science* (New York: D. Appleton and Company, 1862)

Haskell, Frank: *The Battle of Gettysburg* (Wisconsin History Commission, 1908)

Heysinger, Isaac W.: *Antietam and the Maryland and Virginia campaigns of 1862* (New York: Neale Publishing Company, 1912)

Henty, George A.: *With Lee in Virginia* (New York: Charles Scribner's Sons, 1897)

—— *Histories of the Several Regiments and Battalions from North Carolina in the Great War 1861-'65* Vol 5 (Goldsboro: Nash Brothers, 1901)

Hoke, Jacob: *The Great Invasion of 1863* (Dayton: W.J. Shuey, 1887)

Hood, John B.: *Advance and Retreat: Personal Experiences in the United States and Confederate Armies* (New Orleans: G.T. Beauregard, 1880)

—— *Baron de Jomini: Summary of the Art of War, or a New Analytical Compend of the Principle Combinations of Strategy, of Grand Tactics and of Military Policy*, (translated by Capt. G.H. Mendell and Lieut. W.P. Craighill, 1862)

—— *Inside the Army of the Potomac: The Experiences of Captain Francis Adam Donaldson:* Acken, J. Gregory ed. (Mechanicsburg, Stackpole Books, 1998)

Jones, J.B.: *A Rebel War Clerk's Diary at the Confederal States Capital* (Philadelphia: J.B. Lippincott & Co, 1866)

Kirkley, Joseph W.: *Itinerary of the Army of the Potomac and Co-Operating Forces in the Gettysburg Campaign, June and July 1863* (Washington: Adjutant General's Department, 1886)

Lee's Dispatches: Unpublished Letters of General Robert E. Lee 1862–1865: Douglas Southall Freeman and Grady McWhiney eds. (New York: Putnam's, 1957)

Livermore, Thomas L.: *Numbers and Losses in the Civil War in America* (Boston: Houghton Mufflin & Company, 1900)

Longstreet, James: *From Manassas to Appomattox: Memoirs of the Civil War in America* (Philadelphia: Lippincott, 1896)

Macartney, Clarence Edward: *Lincoln and his Generals* (Philadelphia: Dorrance and Company, 1925)

McClellan, H.B.: *The Life and Campaigns of Major-General J.E.B. Stuart's Cavalry* (Boston: Houghton Mifflin, 1885)

Meade, George G.: *The Life and Letters of George Gordon Meade, Volumes I – II* (New York: Scribner's, 1913)

Mosby, John S.: *Mosby's War Reminiscences* (New York: Dodd, Mead and Company, 1898)

—— *Stuart's Cavalry in the Gettysburg Campaign* (New York: Moffatt, Yard & Co, 1908)

—— *The Memoirs of Colonel John S. Mosby* (Boston: Little, Brown, and Company, 1917)

Page, Thomas N.: *Robert E. Lee: The Southerner* (New York: Scribner's, 1908)

Pennypacker, Isaac R.: *General Meade* (New York: D. Appleton & Co, 1901)

Pinkerton, Allan: *The Spy of the Rebellion Being a True History of the Spy System of the United States Army during the Late Rebellion* (New York: Dillingham 1883)

Pollard, Edward A.: *The Lost Cause; A New Southern History of the War of the Confederates* (New York: E.B. Treat & Co, 1866)

Scott, William A.: *Battle of Gettysburg* (Gettysburg, 1905)

Smith, Gustavus W.: *Company 'A' Corps of Engineers, U.S.A. in the Mexican War* (The Battalion Press, 1896)

Smith, Henry B.: *Between the Lines: Secret Service Stories Told Fifty Years After* (New York: Booz Brothers, 1911)

Sorrell, G. Moxley: *Recollections of a Confederate Staff Officer* (New York: The Neale Publishing Company, 1905)

Stillwell, Leander: *The Story of a Common Soldier of Army Life in the Civil War, 1861-1865* (Franklin Hudson, 1920)

—— *Southern Historical Society Papers, 52 Volumes 1876 – 1959 (Southern Historical Society, Richmond)*

Swinton, William: *Campaigns of the Army of the Potomac* (New York: Charles Scribner's Sons, 1892)

—— *McClellan's Military Career* (Washington: Lemuel Towers, 1864)

Taylor, Walter: *Four Years with General Lee* (New York: D. Appleton and Company 1878)

Taylor, Dr. Charles E.: *The Signal and Secret Service of the Confederate States* (North Carolina Booklet Vol II, Hamlet, North Carolina, March 1903)

Young, Louis: *Histories of the Several Regiments and Battalions from North Carolina in the Great War 1861-1865, Volume 5* (Goldsborough: Nash bros, 1901)

Secondary Published

Articles & Papers

Antonucci, Michael: 'Code Crackers: Cryptanalysis in the Civil War' (*Civil War Times Illustrated*, July – August 1995)

Browne, Edward C. Jr: 'Col. George H. Sharpe's "Soda Water Scouts"' (*The Gettysburg Magazine*, Issue 44)

Canan, H.V.: 'Confederate Military Intelligence' (*Maryland Historical Magazine* Volume 60, Baltimore: Maryland Historical Society 1964)

Cartwright, Terry: 'Who was the War's Premier Cavalry Commander?' (*American Civil War Roundtable of Australia*, February 2008)

Centre for the Study of Intelligence: 'Intelligence in the Civil War' (Central Intelligence Agency, 1999)

Cook, John: 'Military Intelligence during America's Civil War' (*American Civil War Roundtable of Australia*, August 2011)

Cooksey, Paul Clark: 'Around the Flank: Longstreet's July 2 Attack at Gettysburg' (*The Gettysburg Magazine*, Issue 29)

Cullihan, David L.: 'Putting Gettysburg on the Map: How Four Generals Precipitated the Battle' (*The Gettysburg Magazine*, Issue 29)

Either, Eric: 'Intelligence: The Secret War Within America's Civil War' (*Civil War Times*, April/March 2007)

Ethan Allen Hitchcock and the Mexican War Spy Company, Fort Huachuca Museum online, http://huachuca.army.mil/files/History_MHITCH.PDF, (accessed 1 July 2015)

Fishel, Edwin: 'Military Intelligence 1861-63 Part I: From Manassas to Fredericksburg' (*Studies in Intelligence* 10, Number 3: 81 – 96)

—— 'Military Intelligence 1861-63 II: Chancellorsville and Gettysburg' (*Studies in Intelligence* 10, Number 4: 69 – 93)

Freiheit, Laurence: Military Intelligence During the Maryland Campaign (Essay for Antietam on the Web, 2008)

Gaddy, David Winfred: 'William Norris and the Confederate Signal and Secret Service' (*Maryland Historical Magazine* Volume 70, Number 2 Baltimore: Maryland Historical Society 1975)

Glantz, Edwin J.: 'Guide to Civil War Intelligence' (*Journal of U.S. Intelligence Studies* Volume 18, Number 2 Winter/Spring 2011)

Hageman, Mark C.: Espionage in the Civil War (Signal Corp Association)

Haines, Douglas Craig: 'Jeb Stuart's Advance to Gettysburg' (*The Gettysburg Magazine*, Issue 29)

Harper, James H.: 'Intelligence in the Civil War' (*The Vanguard*, July 2013)

Hyde, Bill: 'Did You Get There? Capt. Samuel Johnston's Reconnaissance at Gettysburg' (*The Gettysburg Magazine*, Issue 29)

Kensey, Paul: 'Prelude to War' (*American Civil War Roundtable of Australia*, June 2002)

Lineberry, Cate: 'The Union's Spy Game' (*New York Times*, 15 August 2011)

Luvaas, Jay: 'Lee at Gettysburg: A General Without Intelligence' (*Intelligence and National Security*, 5:2, 116-135)

—— Lee and the Operational Art: The Right Place, The Right Time (U.S. Army War College, 1992)

Peters, Ralph: 'Victor of Gettysburg' (*Armchair General Magazine*, September 2011, Vol. VIII, Issue 4)

Pike, Tom: 'Strategy is a Competition of Ideas: What Gettysburg and Afghanistan Teach Us' (*Small Wars Journal*, September 2012)

Rose, P.K.: 'Black Dispatches: Black American Contributions to Union Intelligence During the Civil War' (Centre for the Study of Intelligence, Central Intelligence Agency, 2007)

Ryan, Thomas: 'A Battle of Wits' (*The Gettysburg Magazine*, Issues 29 – 33)

—— 'The Intelligence Battle' (*The Gettysburg Magazine*, Issues 43 – 44)

Taylor, Michael C.: 'It Begins With A Revolution' (*The Vanguard*, March 2014)

Vermilyea, Peter C.: '"To Prepare for Emergency": Military Operations in the Gettysburg Area Through June 24, 1863' (*The Gettysburg Magazine*, Issue 32)

Books

Adams, Ephraim Douglass: *Great Britain and the American Civil War Volumes I – II* (London, 1925)

Alexander, Bevin: *Sun Tzu at Gettysburg* (New York: W. W. Norton and Company, 2011)

Andrews, J. Cutler: *The North Reports the Civil War* (Pittsburgh: University of Pittsburgh Press, 1955)

Arnold, James R.: *Grant Wins the War* (New York: John Wiley & Sons, Inc, 1997)

Beckett, Ian F. W.: *The War Correspondents: The American Civil War* (Dover: Alan Sutton, 1993)

Bicheno, Hugh: *Gettysburg* (London: Cassell & Co, 2001)

—— *Lincoln's Generals:* Boritt, Gabor, ed. (New York: Oxford University Press, 1994)

—— *The Gettysburg Nobody Knows*: Boritt, Gabor, ed. (New York: Oxford University Press, 1997)

—— *Why the Confederacy Lost:* Boritt, Gabor, ed. (New York: Oxford University Press, 1992)

Brownlee, Richard S.: Gray Ghosts of the Confederacy (Washington: Library of Congress, 1984)

Catton, Bruce: *This Hallowed Ground* (New York: Doubleday & Co, 1956)

Carhart, Tom: *Lost Triumph* (New York: Putnams, 2005)

Coddington, Edwin B.: *The Gettysburg Campaign: A Study in Command* (Dayton: Morningside House, 1979)

—— *Why the North Won the Civil War:* Donald, Herbert D. ed. (New York: Simon & Schuster, 1960)

Crocker, H.W.: *Don't' Tread on Me* (New York: Crown Publishing, 2006)

Drury, Ian & Gibbons, Tony: *The U.S. Civil War Military Machine* (Limpsfield, Dragon's World Ltd, 1993)

Eisenhower, John S.D.: *So Far From God* (New York: Anchor Books, 1989)

Faust, Drew Gilpin: *This Republic of Suffering* (New York, Vintage Civil War Library, 2008)

Fiebeger, G.J.: *The Campaign and Battle of Gettysburg* (New York: United States Military Academy Press, 1915)

Fishel, Edwin C.: *The Secret War for the Union* (Boston: Houghton Mifflin, 1996)

Foote, Shelby: *Stars in their Command* (New York: Modern Library, 1994)

Foreman, Amanda: *A World of Fire: An Epic History of Two Nations Divided* (London: Penguin, 2010)

Freeman, Douglas Southall: *R.E. Lee: A Biography, 4 Volumes* (New York: Scribner's Sons, 1934-35)

Furgurson, Ernest B.: *Not War But Murder* (New York: Vintage Books, 2000)

Gallagher, Gary W.: *Lee and His Generals in War and Memory* (Baton Rouge: Louisiana State University Press, 1998)

—— *Lee the Solider*: Gallagher, Gary W, ed. (Lincoln and London: University of Nebraska, 1996)

—— *The Antietam Campaign*: Gallagher, Gary W, ed. (University of North Carolina Press, 1999)

Greenburg, Amy S.: *A Wicked War* (New York: Alfred A Knopf, 2012)

Griffiths, Paddy: *Battle Tactics of the Civil War* (New Haven: Yale University Press, 1989)

Guelzo, Allen C.: *Gettysburg, The Last Invasion* (New York, Vintage Books, 2013)

Harmon, Troy D.: *Lee's Real Plan at Gettysburg* (Mechanicsburg: Stackpole Books, 2003)

Jenkins, Philip: *The History of the United States* (Basingstoke: Palgrave Macmillan, 1997)

Katcher, Philip: *Gettysburg 1963* (London: Brassey's, 2003)

—— *Great Gambles of the Civil War* (London: Orion Publishing, 1996)

Keegan, John: *The American Civil War* (London: Vintage, 2009)

—— *Intelligence in War* (London: Hutchinson, 2003)

Longacre, Edward G.: *Lee's Cavalrymen* (Mechanicsburg, Stackpole Books, 2002)

Mahon, Michael G.: *The Shenandoah Valley* (Stackpole Books: Mechanicsburg, 1999)

McPherson, James M.: *Battle Cry of Freedom* (New York: Oxford University Press, 1988)

—— *Crossroads of Freedom* (New York: Oxford University Press, 2002)

—— *This Mighty Scourge* (New York: Oxford University Press, 2007)

—— *Drawn with the Sword* (New York: Oxford University Press, 1996)

Miller, David W.: *Second Only to Grant* (Shippensburg: White Mane Books, 2000)

Mitchell, Joseph B.: *Decisive Battles of the Civil War* (New York: Fawcett Premier, 1962)

Nesbitt, Mark: *Sabre and Scapegoat* (Mechanicsburg: Stackpole Books, 1994)

—— *35 Days to Gettysburg* (Harrisburg: Stackpole Books, 1992)

Raines, Rebecca Robbins: *Getting the Message Through, A Branch History of the U.S. Army Signal Corps* (Washington, Centre of Military History, 2011)

Shaara, Michael: *The Killer Angels* (ebook)(Edinburgh: Birlinn Limited, 2013)

Sears, Stephen W.: *Controversies and Commanders* (Boston: Houghton Mifflin, 1999)

—— *Landscape Turned Red* (New York: Houghton Mifflin, 1983)

—— *Chancellorsville* (Boston: Houghton Mifflin, 1996)

—— *Gettysburg* (Boston: Houghton Mifflin, 2004)

—— *George B. McClellan, The Young Napoleon* (New York: Ticknor & Fields, 1988)

—— *To the Gates of Richmond* (New York: Ticknor & Fields, 1992)

Sharpe, Hal F.: *Shenandoah County in the Civil War* (Charleston: The History Press, 2012)

Smith, Derek: *The Gallant Dead* (Mechanicsburg: Stackpole Books, 2005)

Stackpole, Edward J: *They Met at Gettysburg* (New York: Bonanza, 1956)

Stoker, Donald: *The Grand Design: Strategy and the U.S. Civil War* (Oxford, Oxford University Press, 2010)

—— *Inside Lincoln's Army, The Diary of Marsena Rudolph Patrick, Provost Marshal General, Amy of the Potomac*: David S. Sparks ed. (Thomas Yoseloff: New York, 1964)

—— *The Library of Congress Civil War Desk Reference* (New York: Simon & Schuster, 2002)

Thomas, Emory M.: *Robert E. Lee, A Biography* (New York: Norton, 1995)

Tidewell, William A. (with James O. Hall and David Winfred Gaddy): *Come Retribution* (Jackson and London: University Press of Mississippi, 1988)

—— *U.S. Army Military Intelligence History: A Sourcebook*: James P. Finley ed. (U.S. Army Intelligence Center: Arizona, 1995)

Wittenburg, Eric and Petruzzi, J. David: *Plenty of Blame to Go Round* (New York: Savas Beatie, 2006)

Unpublished

Tsouras, Peter G.: A Biography of George Sharpe

Index

INDEX OF PEOPLE

INDEX OF PLACES

INDEX OF MILITARY FORMATIONS & UNITS

INDEXING GENERAL & MISCELLANEOUS TERMS

Wolverhampton Military Studies
www.helion.co.uk/wolverhamptonmilitarystudies

Editorial board

Submissions

The publishers would be pleased to receive submissions for this series. Please contact us via email (info@helion.co.uk), or in writing to Helion & Company Limited, 26 Willow Road, Solihull, West Midlands, B91 1UE.

Titles

No.1 *Stemming the Tide. Officers and Leadership in the British Expeditionary Force 1914* Edited by Spencer Jones (ISBN 978-1-909384-45-3)

No.2 *'Theirs Not To Reason Why'. Horsing the British Army 1875–1925* Graham Winton (ISBN 978-1-909384-48-4)

No.3 *A Military Transformed? Adaptation and Innovation in the British Military, 1792–1945* Edited by Michael LoCicero, Ross Mahoney and Stuart Mitchell (ISBN 978-1-909384-46-0)

No.4 *Get Tough Stay Tough. Shaping the Canadian Corps, 1914–1918* Kenneth Radley (ISBN 978-1-909982-86-4)

No.5 *A Moonlight Massacre: The Night Operation on the Passchendaele Ridge, 2 December 1917. The Forgotten Last Act of the Third Battle of Ypres* Michael LoCicero (ISBN 978-1-909982-92-5)

CPSIA information can be obtained at www.ICGtesting.com
Printed in the USA
BVOW02*2137140916

462156BV00003B/6/P